THINKING WOMAN

Thinking Woman

A PHILOSOPHICAL APPROACH
TO THE QUANDARY OF GENDER

❧

Jennifer Hockenbery Dragseth

CASCADE *Books* · Eugene, Oregon

THINKING WOMAN
A Philosophical Approach to the Quandary of Gender

Copyright © 2015 Jennifer Hockenbery Dragseth. All rights reserved. Except for brief quotations in critical publications or reviews, no part of this book may be reproduced in any manner without prior written permission from the publisher. Write: Permissions, Wipf and Stock Publishers, 199 W. 8th Ave., Suite 3, Eugene, OR 97401.

Cascade Books
An Imprint of Wipf and Stock Publishers
199 W. 8th Ave., Suite 3
Eugene, OR 97401

www.wipfandstock.com

ISBN 13: 978-1-62564-634-7

Cataloging-in-Publication data:

Dragseth, Jennifer

    Thinking woman : a philosophical approach to the quandary of gender / Jennifer Dragseth.

    xviii + 196 p. ; 23 cm. —Includes bibliographical references and indexes.

    ISBN 13: 978-1-62564-634-7

    1. Gender identity—Philosophy. 2. Sex role—Philosophy. I. Title.

HQ1075 D76 2015

Manufactured in the U.S.A.

To my family:
my children, Luke, Phoebe, and Hope;
my husband, David;
my parents, David and Mary

My most honored ladies, may God be praised, for now our City is entirely finished and completed, where all of you who love glory, virtue, and praise may be lodged in great honor, ladies from the past as well as from the present and future, for it has been built and established for every honorable lady.

—CHRISTINE DE PIZAN, *THE CITY OF LADIES*, III.19

Contents

Preface

In the history of Western philosophy much has been written and studied concerning the nature and vocation of man. In contrast, it often appears the question of the nature and vocation of woman has been ignored. Indeed, it is the case that many famous male philosophers wrote little on the topic of women as interestingly distinct from men. Yet with just a little research, one finds that in every era of Western philosophy there were and are female thinkers who intentionally focused on the question of the nature and vocation of woman. Often these thinkers were seeking to understand and explain themselves. Often these women came late in their careers to the question but suddenly found it provocative and significant. Their works form a canon on the subject of woman.

As a philosopher, I myself came late to the recognition of the importance of the question of woman. As an undergraduate philosophy major and as a doctoral student in philosophy I was not introduced to the question or the treatment of that question in any significant way. In fact, as a student of philosophy it seemed to me as if women did not exist. Indeed, in the departments in which I studied, there was very little sexual diversity. Both my undergraduate and graduate institutions had only men teaching in their philosophy departments in the 1990s when I was there. The reading list for doctoral candidates at my university at the time did not include any works by women philosophers. I assumed that the scant number of women in the canon of philosophy was due to a scant number of women doing philosophy. I did not recognize that there was something missing in the canon I studied. There was something missing, however. What was missing was an entire field of inquiry—that of the nature of woman.

Thus, when I found myself in a job interview, at a small Wisconsin Catholic college for women, I was surprised by the first question I was asked: how would I gear my teaching, research, and writing as a woman for women? The question seemed odd to me at the time. It felt as if I had been asked how I might teach as a person with brown eyes to others with brown eyes. That is how little I had thought through the issue at that point in my life. Even though I had always considered myself a feminist, someone who stands up for women, I had never deeply considered the question of what a woman is and what a woman needs in order to be supported. Somehow I blundered through an answer that did not derail the interview. Somehow I was hired. I was told that my first teaching assignment would be a course titled Women Philosophers. The committee assumed I could get a syllabus ready over the summer. I, of course, eager for a job, agreed that I could do so.

I spent that summer in the library reading about women philosophers, about the philosophy of women. I walked into the classroom hoping to teach what I had never been taught. Luckily, my students were up to the task of learning with me rather than from me. My first class on women philosophers changed me in a way that I had not expected. The class was my first experience in a classroom where men did not outnumber women. Indeed, there were only women. The students' comments and insights converted me to the position that the question of woman was exciting and important. They wanted to do their own research, and their work introduced me to a broader canon of thinkers. These were thinkers that my previous education had neglected. I realized that women had been doing philosophy since the dawn of Western intellectual history. I recognized that the discipline of women's studies had been a subcategory of philosophy for millennia.

The class became my most popular course offering. When people outside academia asked me about my work, they became most interested when I talked about my research on these women thinkers and their ideas. I began to be asked by church and civic groups to give talks on Hildegard of Bingen, Teresa of Avila, Christine de Pizan, Mary Wollstonecraft, and others. Inside academic circles I found that many groups were interested in these topics as well. This interest impressed me. This interest led me to take my syllabus, my discussions, and my lectures from the past sixteen years and use them to create a book that would let others share this interest. *Thinking Woman: A Philosophical Approach to the Quandary of Gender* is a book that is both a history of ideas and an invitation to join the philosophical dialogue about women. It is a vibrant dialogue; and I am happy to be part of it.

Acknowledgments

Putting together this book has taken a village of supporters. My acknowledgments begin with those who responded to my urgent pleas for help in 1998 when I was first assigned to teach a course in Women Philosophers. I have deep intellectual gratitude for my dear friend, Eileen Hunt, who sent me my first copy of *The Vindication of the Rights of Women*. She taught me much about liberal feminism, and our conversations continue to shape my learning and thinking on the issue of woman. I am also indebted to my good friend, Gabriela Martinez, who taught me about Edith Stein, opening me to the important movement that is Catholic feminism. Sincere thanks must go also to my colleague, Jim Conlon, who first gave me the task of teaching Women Philosophers, but who did not leave me stranded. He introduced me more fully to many twentieth and twenty-first century thinkers, especially Simone de Beauvoir and Judith Butler. I also owe thanks for all I have learned from the women who form the Milwaukee Area Women in Philosophy group and the Lutheran Women in Theology and Religious Studies group. In the latter group I must thank particularly Mary Lowe and Caryn Riswold for their insights. The encouragement and shared knowledge of all these friends and colleagues has been indispensable.

I am especially grateful to the individuals in the academic institutions where I have learned and taught. Both my undergraduate and graduate programs taught me the process of thinking, reading, and discussing, a process that is applicable to every subject of inquiry including the issue of woman. I am the philosopher I am today because of the education and guidance I learned at Bowdoin College and Boston University. I have, also, been shaped by my students, especially those in my Women Philosophers' classes. They have taught me to recognize the role of being a woman in my identity and in theirs. It was they who asked the hard questions and demanded the critical thinking that led to this book. I especially want to thank Mary Bott, Ariana Everts, Celcy Powers-King, Sharise Hollingsworth, and Jessica Yocherer who, as part of an independent readings course, read and analyzed an early version of this manuscript. A special word of gratitude must go to Mary Bott, who in addition to participating in the independent readings course worked with me for a summer as a research assistant.

Of course I must thank the administration at Mount Mary University for granting me a sabbatical to study Hildegard of Bingen in Germany and for granting me a course release to finish this book. But more importantly, I am grateful to the whole of the community at Mount Mary University. Mount Mary has remained a women's centered institution for over 100 years, holding the nourishing of women as a central piece of its mission and vision. Without being in this place, I would never have begun this field of philosophical inquiry.

Last, and most importantly, I am grateful to my family for whom I am a mother, a wife, and a daughter. My children Luke, Phoebe, and Hope regularly listen to me talk about the philosophers in this book and their ideas. This past year particularly, they have listened agreeably to the discussion, asked questions, and presented challenges. My son read long sections and gave constructive feedback. My daughters offered their insights and questions. I am blessed to be a mother to such philosophically interesting children who continually enrich the whole of my life, including my intellectual life. My husband, David, has offered loving encouragement and thoughtful support enriching my life and work even in the midst of his own busy professional and intellectual life. My parents, Mary and David Hockenbery, have informed my thinking since I was small. Philosophy was always a part of our lives, for this I am truly grateful. For this book, they read through drafts, made helpful suggestions, and served as preliminary editors. More importantly, they have nurtured me to the love of truth and inquiry that I hope to nurture in others.

Introduction

> Sexual difference is one of the major philosophical issues, if not the issue, of our age. According to [the philosopher Martin] Heidegger, each age has one issue to think through, and one only. Sexual difference is probably the issue in our time which could be our "salvation" if we thought it through.
>
> —LUCE IRIGARAY[1]

The French philosopher Luce Irigaray wrote the above quote in 1984, more than three decades ago. Today, the question of sexual difference remains one of critical importance especially to feminists, those who wish to help women thrive and flourish. Nationally, the question of the nature and role of women in society continues to define political battles within the United States. Internationally, debate over the role of women in society and the rights of women influences and forms foreign policy between nations. The debate is rarely framed as a debate concerning the value of women as such. In this sense feminists have won the cultural battle to affirm that women have inherent value equal to that of men. Rather, the reason for the debate is that there is not a clear agreement on what laws and protections are best for women. Today, there is clearly a need for further discussion and thinking through the issues of the nature, destiny, and needs of women. This discussion is necessary especially among feminists.

This book is an attempt to help readers think through the questions of sexual difference. Specifically, this book is a guide for readers as they consider the fundamental question of what it means to be a woman. This

1. Irigaray, *Ethics of Sexual Difference*, 5.

question must be the starting point for conversations about the politics and ethics of sexual difference. However, many people—even those engaged in the political and ethical debates, even those who call themselves feminists—have not had the opportunity to grapple deeply with this foundational question. This book is intended to help the interested reader with this grappling.

The Method and Design of *Thinking Woman*

This is a philosophical book, not a sociological study or a political treatise. This book explores a "What is X?" type of question, namely "What is a woman?" The book's method follows that of the ancient philosopher, Socrates. Socrates's method, which he advocates for both men and women philosophers according to Plato, was to ask a question, hear an answer, discuss the answer, detail the limits or problems of the answer, and then continue with another possible answer. This is the method that is used in each chapter of the book.

As such, this book is an invitation to the reader to a philosophical dialogue on the question: "What is a woman?" The book is by no means comprehensive or exhaustive. I have limited the conversation to four major theories that are active in contemporary Western feminist discourse. These theories are Gender Essentialism, Gender Neutrality, Gender Existentialism, and Gender Fluidity. *Gender Essentialism* is the theory that women have an essential and unique nature that is both biologically and psychologically different from the nature of men. *Gender Neutrality* is the claim that women have the same essential psychological and intellectual nature as men despite biological differences in sex. *Gender Existentialism* is the theory that women, although biologically different from men, have intellectual and psychological habits that differ from men only because of cultural factors. The theory of *Gender Fluidity* claims that both gender and biological sex are constantly changing categories that are culturally defined.

Each chapter presents each system by introducing some of the women thinkers who most famously articulated the theories. Because their views were born in the context of their lives, the lives and historical context of the thinkers are important. Each chapter presents the biographies as well as the ideas of the women who were the main architects of each theory. Included also is a description of the ways the specific theory influenced the feminist struggle to help women thrive. Importantly, each chapter shows an area of contemporary public discourse where the theory remains a dominant voice. This demonstrates that each theory is still very much alive. Each chapter concludes with a discussion of the possible objections to the discussed theory before summarizing the main points of the chapter.

In the conclusion, the book does not advocate for a specific theory of woman as being true or correct. Rather the conclusion acknowledges that the concept of woman is complex. Each of the four theories says something obviously true. Thus, understanding women requires holding all four theories simultaneously while acknowledging their contradictions. However, all four theories also clearly fall short of a comprehensive account of women. Thus, understanding women requires continuing dialogue with women and those who are interested in them.

The Argument for Philosophical Inquiry as Feminist Activism

This book uses a literal definition of the word feminism as a stance for women. Feminist activism is, thus, activism that works to support women as members of society who are equal to all other members of society in dignity and value. The underlying thesis of this work is that such activism requires some philosophical study of the question of woman. Such study nourishes those who participate so that they might grow to greater self-awareness and greater community involvement. In this sense philosophical study about women is a kind of feminist activism. Such activism is important, possible, and empowering.

First, philosophical inquiry about women is important for everybody, not just academics in women studies or in gender studies. The feminist thinker, bell hooks, who herself has written thirty-two books on feminism, has made frequent requests to feminist academics to write books about women for women in language that all people can access and understand. Her view is convincing. Only by understanding oneself and one's culture can one do the work of transforming oneself and one's culture. Feminist inquiry is not an "academic" issue that has no relevance to daily life of ordinary people. It is a central issue to all people who wish to flourish and help others to flourish. Inquiring into the nature of woman is necessary in order to advocate thoughtfully in the areas of women's health care, women's sports, women's political rights, and women's education.

Second, fruitful discussion of this issue is possible. In contemporary times many people feel that dialogue between those who fundamentally disagree is pointless. This is considered especially true if the participants come from widely different perspectives influenced by differing languages, cultures, and religions. Yet, there is much evidence to bolster the claim that thoughtful people can have successful discussions and dialogues. It is not the case that individual thinkers are imprisoned by their worldviews. Those who teach know this to be true. The course that inspired this book is an example. While Mount Mary is a Catholic women's institution, its students come from a wide variety of ethnic, cultural, and religious backgrounds. Moreover, a few male students from a partnering nursing college have chosen to take this class over the years. I have also had students who struggle to place themselves in the gender binary of male or female. Generally, all the students come to the first class with a diverse collection of deeply held opinions about the nature of women. Despite this diversity, the conversation has been fruitful. Indeed, because of this diversity the dialogue has been more productive than it would be if the students had all come from the same background. In the past, each student has shown evidence of marked growth in her understanding of the issue by the end of the course. More importantly, virtually every student has reported that reading, discussing, and thinking about this issue deepened her understanding of her self and her role in her community in significant ways. Fruitful dialogue is possible.

Finally, philosophical inquiry on the definition of woman is empowering. Those who advocate for women's rights, women's health care, women's equality with men, and justice for women require a theory of what a woman is in order to advocate for these things. Thinking deeply about womanhood exposes questions and answers about the real needs and desires for women. Thinking deeply can destroy old structures of thought that imprison bodies and minds in false constructs. Thinking deeply can create new structures that allow more authentic or more autonomous living for individuals in society. This type of deep thought reorients the thinker as she moves and acts in her community. In that sense she becomes an activist.

A Note on the General Purpose of Philosophy

There have been a number of books written in the last century with the title *What is Philosophy?* Thinkers as auspicious as Martin Heidegger,[2]

2. See Heidegger, *What Is Philosophy?*

José Ortega y Gasset,[3] and Gilles Deleuze[4] have sought to both explain the nature of philosophy and argue for its essential importance for human beings. They have made a stand that philosophy is important, possible, and empowering. So, too, argued the poet and philosopher Sappho who ran a school for young women 2600 years ago on the island of Lesbos. She told her fellow Greeks that she who does not cultivate her mind "dying will lie with the undistinguished dead," her life one of perpetual inconsequence.[5] The Greek philosophers, Socrates and Aristotle, agreed. They claimed respectively that "the unexamined life is not worth living"[6] and that "all humans by nature desire to know."[7] In the twentieth century, the controversial thinker Ayn Rand asserted that the choice to be conscious or not is the choice to be alive or not.[8] In the twenty-first century, philosopher Martha Nussbaum frequently reminds her fellow philosophers that their work is essential for the common good.[9] It is in this spirit of philosophy as consequential, as conscious, and as necessary for human flourishing that this book is written. It is written in order to encourage philosophical thinking, questioning, and dialogue for its readers. Whether the readers are thinking on their own or in a community of scholars, whether they are in a library, at home, or in a philosophy or women's studies class, the hope is that they will be encouraged to take the question of "What is woman?" seriously and deeply.

3. See Ortega y Gasset, *What Is Philosophy?*

4. See Deleuze, *Qu'est-ce que la philosophie?*

5. Sappho, "Poem Fragment 65."

6. Plato, *Apology,* 38a.

7. Aristotle, *Metaphysics,* 980a.

8. Rand, *Objectivist Ethics,* 21.

9. See, for example, Nussbaum, *Not for Profit.*

1

Gender Essentialism

According to the intended original order, [woman's] place is by man's side to master the earth and to care for offspring. But her body and soul are fashioned less to fight and to conquer than to cherish, guard, and preserve.

—EDITH STEIN[1]

Many expectant parents eagerly await ultrasound evidence of the sex of their fetus. At birth, the first announcement usually made is the child's sex. This will remain a primary label for the child's life: marked on the birth certificate, checked on the preschool application, written on the kindergarten enrollment papers and summer camp forms. While the label may determine the social and political avenue of the child's life far less than in previous centuries, sex still determines which athletic sports and teams the individual will be able to join, what rate the individual will pay on auto, health, and life insurance, and in many places whom the person can marry. Beyond legal rights and responsibilities the individual's sex will also determine expectations and interactions from the crib to career to nursing home. More primary than citizenship, ethnicity, religion, political affiliation, or any other attribute, sex seems to be considered an essential part of a human person in Western culture. This view that sex matters is the view

1. Stein, "The Ethos of Woman's Professions," *Essays on Woman*, 73.

of gender essentialism, the most common view about sex and gender in contemporary Western society.

This chapter is an exploration of what the theory of gender essentialism says about being a woman. Studies have shown that pre-school age children consider gender a key part of their identity and the identity of their classmates.[2] While adults are less likely than small children to make this claim, the overwhelming majority of adults do claim that their gender is a key part of who they are.[3] Thus the issue of how very young girls and mature women see themselves as female is worthy of deep consideration. Specifically, this chapter will explore how gender essentialism can highlight what is unique and positive about being a girl and woman. The women philosophers discussed in this chapter use arguments that deny the suggestion that women are inferior versions of men. They claim that women are naturally different than men in both body and mind, while making the case that women are equal to men in terms of natural and social value.

What Is Gender Essentialism?

Gender is defined as the classification of male or female that includes social, psychological, emotional, and intellectual characteristics. *Essentialism* is a philosophical position that claims that individuals in a category or class share an essential property. This essential property, this essence, is what makes the individual a member of the category. *Gender essentialism* is the stance that gender is a significant characteristic of a person.

Gender essentialism usually begins with a view that biological sex is connected to gender. This means that most gender essentialists assert that there is a real and essential difference between a male body and a female body in terms of anatomy, chemistry, and DNA. Furthermore, most gender essentialists suggest that the intellectual, social, emotional, and psychological characteristics of a human individual are related to the person's body. Some gender essentialists are materialists. Unwilling to make a split between the mind and brain or the emotions and hormones, many gender essentialists will claim that sex characteristics directly cause gender characteristics. For example, they might argue that the oxytocin in the blood of the nursing mother creates a calming and caring attitude in the mother towards her infant. Many gender essentialists who are not strict materialists

2. See Gelman et al., *Mother-Child Conversations*.
3. See Witt, *Metaphysics of Gender*, xi.

are committed to a philosophical stance concerning the mind and the body known as *hylomorphism*. *Hylomorphism* is a stance that states that the mind or soul is the form of the body. Generally, gender essentialists assert that the difference between the male and the female relates both to the biology and to the psychology of the person. Most gender essentialists claim that being male or female relates to the body and the mind, to chemistry and psychology, to DNA strands and to roles in society.

The reader should note that *most* gender essentialists *usually* hold this stance. There are some contemporary thinkers who have attempted to re-define gender essentialism in other interesting and unique ways that will be explored at the end of this chapter. The key to any theory of gender essen-tialism is the stance that there are real and important differences between a man and a woman that must be considered in order to understand a human individual and in order to help him or her flourish.

Thinking Woman: Hildegard of Bingen

> When God looked upon the human countenance, God was ex-ceedingly pleased. For had not God created humanity according to the divine image and likeness? Human beings were to announce all God's wondrous works by means of their tongues that were en-dowed with reason. . . . God gave the first man a helper in the form of woman, who was man's mirror image, and in her the whole hu-man race was present in a latent way. God did this with manifold creative power, just as God had produced in great power the first man. Man and woman are in this way so involved with each other that one of them is the work of the other. Without woman, man could not be called man; without man, woman could not be called woman. Thus woman is the work of man, while man is a sight full of consolation for woman. Neither of them could henceforth live without the other. . . . And thus the human species sits on the judgment seat of the world. It rules over all creation. Each creature is under our control and in our service. We human beings are of greater value than all other creatures.[4]

---

4. Hildegard of Bingen, *Book of Divine Works*, 122.

Biography

Hildegard of Bingen, a twelfth-century theologian, philosopher, natural scientist, musician, and artist did significant work on the question of the nature and vocation of women. Indeed, she is considered the first Western thinker to articulate a philosophical theory that a woman is not a deficient form of a man but that a woman is a distinct type of human being.[5] Hildegard was born in 1098 in Bockelheim, in Mainz, on the Nahe River in the wine country of Germany, the tenth child of wealthy parents. Even as a young child, she had visionary experiences and unusual intellectual and healing abilities. However, Hildegard was told that she should hide such skills and visions as they could be considered marks of witchcraft.

Around the age of eight, Hildegard was given as an offering to the service of the church and placed with a well-known holy woman, Jutta of Sponheim. Her parents called this offering a tithe, as Hildegard was their tenth child. While later Hildegard argued against the practice of parents tithing their children, evidence shows that her early religious upbringing did cultivate her unique gifts. Jutta lived alone with Hildegard, and possibly a few other girls, near the abbey at Disibodenberg. In this isolation, Jutta taught Hildegard the Psalms, elementary Latin, and a great deal about plants, herbs, and the healing arts. When she turned fifteen, Hildegard joined the Benedictine abbey as a fully habited nun.

Scholars debate the extent of Hildegard's education. While she was certainly literate, she claimed that she struggled to read well. For example, at age forty-nine she wrote a letter to Bernard of Clairvaux in which she asked his opinion of why it was that sometimes she was able to read and understand a text and other times the words bewildered her.[6] In addition, she believed herself to be inadequately educated in philosophy and theology compared to the scholars of her time. Her writings and letters demonstrate knowledge of many of the ideas of Augustine and other fathers of the church; the library of Disibodenberg would have held many of ancient and late-antique texts.[7] But she never referred to specific works and authors in her own writings. Furthermore, while some contemporary commentators suggest that Hildegard's references to herself as an un-lettered woman were

5. See Allen, *Concept of Woman*, 292. "Hildegard of Bingen emerged as the first philosopher to articulate a complete theory of sex complementarity."

6. Hildegard, "Letter 1," in *Letters of Hildegard of Bingen*, 27.

7. See Mews, *Hildegard and the Schools*, 89–110. See, also Mews, *Heloise and Hildegard*, 20–29.

only formulaic expressions of her humility, she herself claimed she could not write like the philosophers do. She admitted her secretary needed to correct her grammar when he copied her original writing from wax tablets onto paper. Even still, many translators note that the texts have particular quirks and are difficult to translate in sections.[8] Interestingly, she wrote many pages in her own hand in a *lingua ignota* (unknown language) using an alphabet that she created herself for reasons scholars still do not understand.

In general, Hildegard's insistence that she was not a typical scholar, not a theologian or a philosopher in the academic sense, must be considered accurate. Unlike her contemporary, Heloise, who was fluent in Greek and Latin and able to quote ancient Greek and Roman texts with ease, Hildegard's writings are those of a woman who had a basic understanding of Latin, no knowledge of Greek, and a self-expressed difficulty with reading and writing grammatically. These deficiencies made Hildegard's genius all the more pronounced both to the community around her and to Hildegard herself.

Hildegard's rise to prominence began when she became the abbess of her community in 1136 after Jutta's death. In 1141, she declared that God was calling her to write a major work called *Scivias (Knowledge)*. The work begins with the call she heard from God.

> Behold, in the forty-third year of my passing journey, when I clung to a heavenly vision with fear and trembling, I saw a very great light from which a heavenly voice spoke and said to me: "O weak person, both ashes of ashes, and decaying of the decaying, speak and write what you see and hear."[9]

Hildegard continued to explain the call in detail.

> In the year 1141 of the Incarnation of Jesus Christ, the Word of God, when I was forty-two years and seven months old, a burning light coming from heaven poured into my mind. Like a flame which does not burn but rather enkindles, it inflamed my heart and my breast, just as the sun warms something with its rays. And I was able to understand books suddenly, the psaltery clearly, the evangelist and the volumes of the Old and New Testament, but I did not have the interpretation of the words of their texts nor the

---

8. See "Introduction" in *Letters of Hildegard of Bingen*, vii. Also see "Editor's note," *Scivias*, vii.

9. Hildegard, *Scivias*, 1.

division of their syllables nor the knowledge of their grammar. . . .
I truly saw those visions; I did not perceive them in dreams, nor
while sleeping, nor in a frenzy, nor with the human eyes or with
the external ears of a person, nor in remote places; but I received
those visions according to the will of God while I was awake and
alert with a clear mind, with the innermost eyes and ears of a person, and in open places.[10]

Hildegard continued in her preface to the *Scivias* to give the words
she received from God. She explained that she was reluctant to begin work
on the book until she was urged by others for the sake of her own health to
answer the call. These others who encouraged her to write and publish her
work included "a noble man and a woman of good wishes,"[11] her confessor
Godfrey, Godfrey's abbot Conon, the archbishop of Mainz, and finally Pope
Eugenius III.

In addition to the *Scivias,* Hildegard wrote two other works of philosophical theology: *Liber Divinorum Operum (The Book of Divine Works)*
and *The Liber Vitae Meritoriam (The Book of Life Merits)*. In all three
philosophical-theological works, Hildegard included a visual picture and
a description of each vision as well as the theological message she believed
the vision proclaimed. In addition to the three works in philosophical
theology, she wrote a treatise on natural science (*Physica*) and a book of
causes and cures that relate to medicine (*Causae et Curae*). She also wrote
two spiritual biographies (one for Saint Disibod and one for Saint Rupert),
several commentaries, many homilies, a large number of liturgies, hymns
and plays, and hundreds of letters to political, academic, and church leaders in Europe. These leaders included bishops, archbishops, popes, and the
Holy Roman Emperor Barbarossa. Besides writing, traveling and preaching throughout the Rhine Valley, Belgium, Switzerland, and France, she
also created the architectural plans for the two convents that she founded.
Throughout Germany and beyond, she was well known as a healer, an artist, a musician, a preacher, and an advisor on spiritual and philosophical
concerns. There are several letters addressed to her from academics at the
University of Sorbonne, from political and church leaders, and from lay
people. These letters asked for her theological and philosophical insight as
well as her prayers.

10. Ibid., 2–3.
11. Ibid., 3.

Despite her popularity, or maybe because of it, she was investigated for impropriety on several occasions. There were concerns that she only allowed women of a certain social class to join her convent. She explained that she believed that the social classes were ordained by God and should not be mixed in community, a view that was held by many medieval thinkers. There were concerns that her nuns should not wear their hair loose nor don elaborate headdresses. Hildegard explained that the beauty of a virgin's hair was not scandalous but pleasing to God. And finally, towards the end of her life, the Church placed her entire community under censure. Her community was denied the right to perform liturgy or participate in the Eucharist, while officials investigated a claim that Hildegard had allowed the burial of a damned man in a sanctified cemetery. Hildegard obeyed the orders of the censure but refused to exhume the man's bones. She was resolute that he had confessed before his death and was right with God. The church, in the end, agreed that the man's body could remain where it lay; the censure was lifted.

On September 17th in 1170 Hildegard died. At her death, many recalled that the sky was filled by two streams of light that crossed over the building in which her body lay. She has been revered as a saint by German Catholics for centuries. In 2012, the Vatican formally named her a saint recognized by the whole of the Roman Catholic Church.

Hildegard's Feminine Epistemology

Like many of the women that will be highlighted in this book, Hildegard's quest to understand the nature and vocation of women began with her recognition of herself as a woman who did not fit the gender stereotypes of her time. Hildegard, in the *Scivias*, claimed that she experienced visions from God from a young age, but that she hid this from others. In addition, as an adult she found herself enlightened by theological insights which she felt compelled to share with others. This was bewildering to Hildegard who believed that the church was right to forbid the preaching and publishing of theology by women, especially unlearned women. In the *Scivias* and in her letters, the reader finds Hildegard struggling to understand herself and her insights. What emerges is an interestingly feminine *epistemology*, a theory of knowledge that explains whence insight comes. Hildegard wanted to explain how women come to know.

Hildegard would have been familiar with the epistemology of Augustine, a fourth-century African theologian and philosopher who was authoritative in the Western Catholic church. Augustine claimed that insight is possible because the divine light of God shines upon the human mind in order to allow it to see clearly. Augustine's *theory of illumination* had become the philosophically accepted epistemological position by the twelfth century in the Western church and academic schools. His own account of his illumination is significant because the reader can see the similarities with Hildegard's account of her illumination. Augustine wrote,

> I entered and I saw such as it was with the eyes of my soul above the eye of my soul, above my mind, an unchangeable light: not this common light seen by all flesh, nor something of the same type but greater. . . . No this light was not that, but another, completely other than all these. Nor was she above my mind, as oil is above water, nor as the sky is above the earth; but superior, because she made me, and I was inferior, because I was made by her. Whoever knows truth, knows her, and whoever knows her, knows eternity. Love knows her. O eternal Truth, and true Love and lovely Eternity! You are my God, to you I sigh day and night. . . . And you cried to me from a long way off: I am that which is. And I heard as one hears in the heart, and there was no use for doubt. . . .[12]

The similarities between this passage from Augustine and the first passage in the *Scivias* Hildegard's are striking. Both Hildegard and Augustine wrote of God as a light that is seen by the soul not the eyes and a voice that speaks not to the ears but to the heart. Hildegard's account of God, like Augustine's, used masculine, neuter, and feminine imagery to explain a deity that is Creator, Sustainer, and Illuminator.

---

12. Augustine, *Confessions*, 7:10. My translation from the Latin which reads:

Et inde admonitus redire ad memet ipsum, intravi in intima mea, duce te, et potui, quoniam factus es adiutor mues. Intravi et vidi qualicumque oculo animae meae supra eundem oculum animae mea , supra mentem meam, ;lucem incommutabile: non hanc vulgarem et conspicuam omni carni, nec quasi exeodem genere grandior erat, tamquam si ista multo multoque clarius claresceret totumque occuparet magnitudine. Non hoc illa erat, sed aliud, aliud valde ab istic omnibus. Nec ita erat supra mentem meam, sicut oleum super aquam, nec sicut caelum super terram; sed superior, quia ipsa fecit me, et ego inferior, quia facus abbe a. qui novit vertiatem, novit eam, et qui novit eam, ,novit aeternitatem. Caritas novit eam. O aeterna veritas et vera caritas et cara aeternitas! Tu es deus meus, tibi suspiro die ac nocte. . . . et clamasti de longinquo: ego sum qui sum. Et audivi, sicut auditor in corde, et non erat prorsus unde dubitarem, faciliusque dubitarem vivere me, quam non esse veritatem, quae per ea, quae facta sunt, intellect conspicitur.

However, in the twelfth century, Hildegard was taught a theory of gender that clearly stated that women were inferior in mind and unsuitable for academics and ministry. Thus, Hildegard was bewildered by her illumination and her ability to understand Scripture deeply. Her initial letter to Bernard de Clairvaux shows that she struggled intellectually to understand how her feminine mind was capable of such great insight. While Bernard and others encouraged her to write and preach about her ideas, Hildegard could not let go of the epistemological question of how she, a relatively uneducated woman, was capable of such knowledge. Her struggle to answer this question in her letters and in her theological works created a new epistemology in Western Christianity that allowed a space for women to understand themselves as thinkers.

Hildegard's feminine epistemology insists that knowledge is a gift of grace from the divine, a gift that can be given to men or to women. While Hildegard's position did not challenge the traditional medieval view that women's minds were inferior to men's, it did challenge the view that women's insights were inferior to men's. In fact, by asserting that a woman with insight was divinely inspired, Hildegard gave power to women's insights and a mandate to women thinkers. Importantly, she used this theory to encourage other women to write and teach their ideas. Most notable is her encouragement of her protégé Elisabeth of Schoneau.[13] Later, her insistence that God can give insight to whomever God chooses was used by other medieval women to explain their own calling to write theology and philosophy.

Further, Hildegard's epistemology makes an important claim that the human mind is often inadequate at discovering profound truths. Rather than claim that women's minds are as rational and capable as men's, Hildegard made the more ancient claim that neither the male nor female mind could enlighten itself. Yet, she explained that the female mind is more aware of its limits than the male. Thus, at times, God chooses to give insight to a woman in order to humble humanity and force the recognition that it is God who has ultimate power and truth.

13. See Hildegard, "Letter to Elisabeth of Schoneau," *Secrets of God*, 163–65. See also Hildegard, "Letter 35," *Book of Divine Works*, 338–49.

Hildegard's Gender Essentialist Theory of Virtue

Hildegard asserted that men and women are essentially different from each other in important ways. These differences are necessary and intended by God, for men and women complement each other. She also asserted that in terms of physical strength, intellectual prowess, and moral self-control, men are superior to women. However, Hildegard's great theological insight for her time was her claim that God does not value one creature over another because of strength, prowess, and control. Indeed, Hildegard in the *Scivias* explained that the fall of Lucifer occurred because of his arrogant trust in his own power.[14] In contrast, Adam, Eve, and humans generally have the ability to be saved, primarily because they are aware of their own weaknesses and thus are open to salvation. One of Hildegard's main objectives in her theological texts was to make the case that value and power are not synonymous. Her message to European Christians and to their emperor Barbarossa was that the belief in the superiority of power, strength, and prowess was a dangerous error.

This is clear in Hildegard's *Scivias* where she wrote in detail about the fall in the Garden of Eden and the salvation that hangs on the cross. Contradicting the mainstream medieval belief that Eve created the first sin because of feminine weakness and evil inclination, Hildegard insisted that both Adam and Eve sinned not because of what was worst in them but because of what was best. Hildegard wrote of Eve's soft and obedient nature as a gift of the divine intended to make her a warm and gentle mother. But these gifts were turned against her and humanity by the Serpent who chose her because her trusting nature was easy to manipulate.[15] Also, Adam's willingness to listen to his wife was not a sign of weakness but a sign of his great love of his wife, a love that had been granted to him to cause peace, harmony, and loving collaborative leadership in Eden. Hildegard insisted that the devil made use of humanity's greatest gifts in order to harm all creation. Human strengths became human weaknesses. God, aware of this, used weakness as strength to conquer Lucifer who was unable to see that value does not come from power. Value comes only from God and love.

14. See Hildegard, "Vision Two," *Scivias*, 32–33.

15. Hildegard, "Vision Two section 10," *Scivias*, 18. "Why did the devil approach Eve? Because the devil knew the tenderness of a woman was more easily conquered than the strength of a man. The devil also saw that Adam's love for Eve was burning so strongly that if the devil was able to conquer Eve, whatever she might say to Adam, Adam would do the same."

God, by taking on the weakness of an infant in the manger and a dying human on the cross, tricked Lucifer. Lucifer falsely believed that he had conquered Christ only to be conquered himself by the triumph of Life over death.[16] Hildegard had no qualms in criticizing her contemporaries when they, like Lucifer, made mistakes of valuing strength rather than recognizing the saving power of humility. She reminded both women and men, "Armed with humility and charity, you do not need to fear the snares of the devil, but you will possess everlasting life."[17]

Thus Hildegard, as a medieval Christian posed an interesting type of feminist spirit. Often she used words that might seem derogatory such as *weakness, tenderness, frailty, and humility* to describe women's attributes only to explain that these are also Christ's attributes that defeated the strength, pride, and power of Lucifer. Women and women's virtues are important and necessary parts of creation that complement men and men's virtues. Yet, ultimately, rather than asserting an equality of men and women in mind or body, she asserted that the equality of men and women is in their value before God. On this equality she was insistent. Because of this foundational theological view that men and women are equal before God, she made claims that natural differences between men and women are not examples of merits and deficiencies but examples of diversity created by God for the good of Creation and for human life.

Hildegard's View of Physiology

Hildegard is still famous today for her explanations and explorations into human physiology and medicine. While these can be taken separately from her theology, it is important to note that Hildegard's theology grounded her studies in these sciences. Hildegard is considered a *hylomorphist*, a philosopher who claims that the soul is not separate from the body but the very essence of the body. The soul gives the body shape, form, and life. The body without a soul is only dust, yet there can be no human soul without the dust it informs. This view had biblical foundations for Hildegard. She read *Genesis* as saying that God created humans by warming and nourishing mud with divine breath. She read *Ezekiel* as proclaiming that God had

16. See Hildegard, "Vision Two: section 32," *Scivias*, 24. "The Word of God snatched humanity from the devil through the shedding of blood, and the Word led humanity back to heavenly glory. How did the Word do this? With humility and love."

17. Hildegard, "Vision Two: 33," *Scivias*, 25.

the power to resurrect the bones of the saved. For Hildegard, the body is an integral part of the human person that is created and redeemed by God.

Indeed, she believed the most dangerous heresy, or unorthodox teaching, of her time was that of the flesh-denying Gnostic cult, the Cathars. The Cathars preached rhetorically seductive sermons about the evils of the body and dangers of the flesh. Their views had gained popularity throughout Germany because of their excellent preaching ability and because of the hypocrisy and moral laxity within the Catholic Church. While Hildegard was concerned about stories of pregnant nuns and lascivious priests, Hildegard's admonishment was that the Church needed to pay more attention to the body, bodily pleasures, bodily needs, and bodily health. This meant that preachers needed training in rhetoric in order to better move the hearts of the believer to faith and works. Her own attention to church music and liturgy was meant to delight the ear of the churchgoer in order that the congregant see that true delight is in faith. In addition, she advocated that the church needed to create better structures and rules within religious communities. Importantly, she did not advocate tightening the rules as a Cathar might advise. Rather she claimed the Church needed to make certain that the rules corresponded accurately to human nature and need. She asserted that not all people were called into the cloister's strict rules of abstinence. She advocated against tithing children who were not of age to discern their own religious calls and firmly denounced putting divorced women into convents against their will. Even in the cloister, she sought changes in rules of fasting so that the health of the religious person could be best attended. She consistently advocated that the health of the body be a primary concern.

Hildegard's gardens, vineyards, and powers as a healer were well known in her own time. Her book of *Causes and Cures* is still read today by readers interested in holistic medicine. In this book, many of Hildegard's views of sexual physiology are presented. Before Hildegard, there were few books in the West discussing the female body and its physical concerns, including menstruation, fertility, sexuality, childbirth, menopause, and migraine. Hildegard explained these uniquely feminine concerns and applicable remedies for feminine disorders. Credited as giving the first scientific account of the female orgasm, Hildegard wrote plainly about female sexuality and how it affects the health and well being of the whole woman. She insisted that for many women and men sexuality is an important part of their well-being. In addition, she more accurately described sexual reproduction and embryology than most scientists and medical practitioners of her era. She rejected the commonly accepted theory of the sperm as a *homunculus*, a tiny but whole human being who needs only a womb in order to grow. Instead, she claimed that the female has reproductive matter, "a weak and sparse foam,"[18] that is essential to the creation of the embryo. Also, essential to the creation of a healthy and strong child, asserted Hildegard, is mutual love and care between the sexual partners.[19]

Hildegard was clear that care of the human person requires care of body and this includes differentiated care that is appropriate for each sex. This is a key part of her gender essentialism. She recognized that the differences in female and male bodies necessarily relate to differences in their personalities and psyches. Hildegard insisted on recognition of these differences while at the same time insisting that these differences are God-given and necessary for the care and sustenance of all creation. Most importantly, while Hildegard did mention the way sex differences allow for reproduction and childrearing, her praise for virginity demonstrates that she believed that sex differences are valuable in themselves. Hildegard praised the virgin woman before God. God's delight in the female nature is not in terms of men's delight, for the female is valuable in herself as a woman. God created gender diversity for its own sake, out of love of differing natures.

Hildegard's Gender Essentialism Beyond the Gender Binary

Hildegard of Bingen has been credited as being the first Western thinker to create a full philosophical account of gender essentialism. Part of what makes her account remarkable is that she strove to explain the phenomena that contradict a simple *gender binary* that claims there are only two genders. She denied that all men share one essence while all women share another. Hildegard, in *Causes and Cures*, wrote as a natural scientist carefully describing four different types of men and four different types of women. For each of the eight types she listed physical and psychological characteristics; and she described the type of care, regulation, and lifestyle that benefits each. For example, she described men who have feminine physical

18. See Hildegard, "Conception, Causes and Cures 78a-b," *On Natural Philosophy and Medicine*, 81. And see "Embryology, Causes and Cures 42a- 44b" *On Natural Philosophy*, 43–44.

19. See Hildegard, "Causes and Cures 24a-25b," *On Natural Philosophy and Medicine*, 51.

characteristics and little facial hair and women who are prone to growing hair upon their chins. She also explained that there are variations in sexual desire caused by these differences in physiology.[20] Most importantly, she was clear that she believed that God can and does enter into human history to give the charisms of one sex type to another. She spoke of women, like herself, who were given the gifts of rhetoric and preaching who had to use male role models for themselves. She also spoke of men who were given the gift of virginity who had to use female role models in order to truly open themselves to God.[21] In her theological works she explained how God uses both male and female characteristics to speak and save human beings. Crucial to her view is that Christ took on the biological male body but used feminine humility for salvation on the Cross.

Feminist Merits of Hildegard's Gender Essentialism

By claiming that male and female human beings are essentially different in body and soul and essentially equal in value before God, Hildegard challenged the dominant medieval idea that women were deficient men. In her theological, philosophical, and scientific texts, she made the rational, scriptural, and scientific cases that women are a kind into themselves. As such she was able to do a number of important things. First, Hildegard wrote frankly and explicitly about women's health care; she made significant contributions to gynecology. Importantly, Herrad of Landesberg (1130–95) later wrote an important and authoritative encyclopedia for women called *The Garden of Delight* using some of Hildegard's insights. Hildegard, herself, became a celebrity in health care in her time. People, especially women, lined the riverbanks hoping to be healed by her words and remedies as she traveled by boat up and down the Rhine. Her remedies for many physiological concerns, particularly her special diets for various female ailments, continue to be studied and used today. Socially and politically, she advocated for new rules governing marriage and religious institutions. She created theological space for women to preach and teach their understanding of Scripture and of the relationship with God. Her understanding of gender as both real and God-given became an important part of Western Christian understanding of woman and woman's value.

20. See Hildegard, "Causes and Cures, 50b-66b," *On Natural Philosophy*, 56–65.
21. See McInerny, "Like a Virgin."

Thinking Woman: Edith Stein

Woman naturally seeks to embrace that which is living, personal, and whole. To cherish, guard, protect, nourish and advance growth is her natural, maternal yearning. . . . This natural endowment enables woman to guard and teach her own children. But this basic attitude is not intended just for them; she should behave in this way . . . to all those in contact with her.[22]

Biography

Edith Stein, one of the most prominent Catholic feminists of the early twentieth century, bolstered the movement for women's political and social equality in Europe by using the perspective of gender essentialism. Born on Yom Kippur, October 12, 1891, in Breslau, Germany, Stein was the seventh child of devoutly Jewish parents. Two years after her birth, Stein's father died. Her mother took over his lumber company and managed it with success. As the youngest child, Stein claimed that she was always eager to join her siblings at school. She recounted that when she was finally old enough to begin kindergarten she put up a tremendous fuss until she was allowed to join the first graders instead. Once she was admitted to first grade, Stein said that she became docile and obedient, while she "swallowed books whole."[23] While money had been too sparse to send the oldest children to university, Stein and her sister Erma were able to attend Friedrich Wilhelm University. Stein, who had been active in the woman's suffrage movement since high school, joined the Woman's Student Union. She called herself "a radical feminist."[24]

Once at University, Stein became deeply interested in philosophy and became a devoted student of Edmund Husserl and his method of *phenomenology*: a way of doing philosophy which focused on the common experiences of human life. Stein became one of Husserl's star students and continued to study with him as a graduate student. When many male students were drafted during the First World War, Stein withdrew from the university to work with the Red Cross. After her service she continued her

22. Stein, "Ethos of Woman's Professions," *Essays on Woman*, 45.
23. Stein, *Life in a Jewish Family*, 75. Quoted in Borden, *Edith Stein*, 3.
24. Stein, *Self-Portrait in Letters*, no. 100. As quoted in Borden, *Edith Stein*, 2.

philosophical studies. Deeply interested in understanding what is common in human experience, she wrote her dissertation on the problem of empathy. The project was difficult, and she suffered severe depression during this period of her life. Yet the text, finished in 1916, was rated *Summa Cum Laude* (with highest honors). For two more years, she continued to work as Husserl's private assistant, preparing his students for his courses and editing his manuscripts for publications. In 1919, one year after women were given the right to vote in Germany, Stein applied for an academic post, with the following recommendation from Husserl himself. "Should the academic profession become open to women I would recommend Dr. Stein immediately and most warmly for qualification as a University lecturer."[25] When she did not receive the post, she wrote a letter to the Ministry for Science, Art and Education protesting discrimination against women in the academy. In 1921, Minister Becker made a public statement that gender should not be an obstacle for a qualified person who wished to teach. Stein noted that she believed this statement to be caused by her act of protest but that she did not think much would really change for women in philosophy. Indeed, thirty years passed before a woman was hired in an academic post in philosophy in a German university.[26]

Throughout the 1920s Stein continued to do philosophical work completing several significant philosophical projects that included the first German translations of Thomas Aquinas's philosophical writings, a major work on philosophy titled *Finite and Eternal Being*, and many lectures and essays written on the nature and vocation of women. In addition she wrote several essays critical of racist and totalitarian trends in Germany. In 1923, unable to secure a university position, Stein began to teach at a girl's high school where she taught Latin, Greek, history, politics, and sexual education. The last two subjects were unusual topics at a girl's high school but Stein insisted on their importance for young women. During this time, Stein continued to research, write, and lecture in philosophy especially on women's issues. She continued to apply for university positions.

She also became more interested in religion. While she claimed in her letters that she had become an atheist at age fifteen, her study of phenomenology required her to consider all human experience including religious experience. While she had continued to practice the rituals of Judaism as a young woman, discussions with both Lutherans and Roman Catholics

25. Neyer, "Letter from Husserl," *Edith Stein*, 30.
26. Borden, *Edith Stein*, 8.

peaked her interest in Christianity. Stein asserted that in 1920 she spent an entire night reading Teresa of Avila's *Life*. The next morning she was compelled to say, "This is true." She was baptized in the Roman Catholic Church on the first of January in 1922. Her baptism greatly distressed her mother. Stein insisted to her mother and the Roman Catholic Church that she remained a Jew even as she became a Christian. She continued to celebrate the Jewish high holidays with her mother and consistently advocated to the church and to society on behalf of Jewish people. In the late 1920s she made private vows of poverty, chastity, obedience, and prayer. She began to consider joining a religious order as she continued her work teaching high school.

In 1932 she was offered a post at the German Institute for Scientific Pedagogy in Münster where she was asked to create a curriculum specifically geared for teaching women. But this position was short lived for in 1933 she was dismissed for being of Jewish descent. Stein had written essays critical of racist and totalitarian trends in Germany in the 1920s; in 1933, she began earnestly to seek support for the Jewish people. She wrote and published her autobiography to demonstrate the normality of Jewish family life; she petitioned Pope Pius XI to make a statement denouncing the Nazi treatment of Jews. She spoke publically and consistently against Nazism and Hitler. Unfortunately while many people, including Pius XI, were sympathetic to Stein, few felt that major acts of protest were necessary concerning the political movement of Nazism. Nazi anti-Semitism continued to grow in power throughout Germany. Despite a previous contract with a publisher, Stein was unable to publish her two treatises *Potency and Act* and *Finite and Eternal Being* because of new laws forbidding non-Aryan publications. In 1935 the Nuremberg Laws labeled any person with at least one Jewish grandparent as being ethnically Jewish; all such persons were stripped of all legal rights.

On April 21, 1938, Stein took her final vows as a Carmelite nun. The destruction of synagogues, shops, and homes during *Kristallnacht* occurred during that same year. The Carmelite community, concerned for Stein's safety, moved her to a convent in the Netherlands. Stein's sister Rosa joined her in Holland. But by September of 1941, the Nazis had taken over the Netherlands and begun to require Jews there to wear a yellow star. In October the deportation of Jews to death camps began. Stein and her sister Rosa attempted to flee to Switzerland, but their exit visas were denied. Previously, the Nazis had been making exceptions for ethnic Jews who had converted to Christianity. But this policy changed shortly after a public protest by Catholic priests and bishops against Nazi ideology on July 26, 1942. In late July and August of 1942 many Catholic Jews and non-Aryan monks and nuns were arrested and deported to death camps. Stein was one of these. She was taken on a train to Auschwitz and executed on August 9, 1942. Many of her philosophical works, denied publication by the Nazis while she was alive, were kept by the Carmelites and published posthumously. Recognized as an important Catholic philosopher, she has been studied and praised by many scholars including Pope John Paul II who declared her a Doctor of the Church. She was beatified in 1987 and canonized on October 11, 1998.

Stein's Phenomenology and Gender Essentialism

Edith Stein's theory of gender grew from her understanding of common human experience. Important to all human experience is that it is embodied experience. Humans experience life in, with, and as bodies. In her doctoral dissertation, *The Problem of Empathy*, she wrote, "The impossibility of being rid of the body indicates its special givenness. This union cannot be shaken; the bonds tying us to our bodies are indissoluble."[27] Of course, she discussed the experience of thinking without sensation, as all humans do this when they experience memories or fantasies. But Stein insisted, "Sensations of feelings or sensual feelings are inseparable from their founding sensations."[28] Stein meant that bodies give rise to the experience of the world, and experiences are thus tied to bodies. This means that even memories and fantasies are tied to bodily experiences.

Because the body is the center of orientation and the center of experience, men and women, having different types of bodies, have different kinds of experiences. For Stein, the sexed body leads to gendered experiences. A woman's physiology leads her to a different experience than a man's experience might be. Learning to have empathy for a person of another sex means recognizing the differences between gendered experiences and appreciating those differences. Stein believes that such empathy is possible. Stein used the example of how those who are not colorblind can learn to recognize that the color blind do not see color. In a similar way, Stein noted that an empathetic teacher recognizes that the child does not have the ability

27. Stein, *Problem of Empathy* [51], 46.
28. Ibid., [53], 48.

to make the same judgments as the adult and treats the child's behavior accordingly.[29] In a similar way that the teacher can come to empathize with the child, a woman can come to empathize with a man, and vice versa. Importantly, because Stein believed that women are different than men but equal before God, she stressed that individuals must strive to see the importance of the opposite gender's experience. For example, a male teacher must learn to appreciate the warmth and openness of the woman teacher towards a child. He must come to see that this is not a failure to be rational but an important way to understand and develop the child. Stein's position is that people must learn to respect and appreciate each gender's attributes of mind. These attributes complement each other. Women should not be expected to be like men but each gender should be exalted.

As noted in the biography section, Stein gave a number of lectures about the nature and vocation of women during her life. The purpose of these talks was to discuss philosophically the role of sex and gender in women's experience and to advocate for the rights of women, including political, economic, and academic rights. Seven of these talks are presented together in the second volume of Stein's collected works under the title *Essays on Woman*. In these essays, Stein used scriptural and empirical evidence to make her assertion that women have an essential nature that pervades both body and soul for a clear purpose that was designed by God.

Stein's foundational claim is that women and men share a basic human nature yet women and men are essentially different. Women have different physical properties from men. Stein asserts that these properties are not accidental differences, but essential differences that result in psychological and spiritual differences between men and women. She wrote,

> Woman naturally seeks to embrace that which is living, personal, and whole. To cherish, guard, protect, nourish and advance growth is her natural, maternal yearning. Lifeless matter, the fact can hold primary interest for her only insofar as it serves the living and the personal, not ordinarily for its own sake. Relevant to this is another matter: abstraction in every sense is alien to the feminine nature. . . . This natural endowment enables woman to guard and teach her own children. But this basic attitude is not intended just for them; she should behave in this way also to her husband and to all those in contact with her.[30]

29. Ibid., [98], 87.
30. Stein, "The Ethos of Woman's Professions," *Essays on Woman*, 45.

Stein asserted that the natural vocation of a woman is motherhood, for her physical characteristics are made for the reproduction and nourishing of children. These physical characteristics result in psychological and spiritual attributes unique to women who, according to Stein, are more prone to gentleness, softness, quiet, openness, and holistic thinking. These assertions Stein backed up with Scripture, at times. But more often she used experiences that she believed the reader would readily recognize. She was adamant that the maternal woman is not inferior to the man whose physical body is made for fatherhood and whose psychological and spiritual attributes tend towards hardness, aggression, and single-mindedness. Rather she asserted that both types of humans are endowed with natural gifts by their Creator in order to best care for each other and the world.

Stein's feminism, thus, had a different ground than that of many other vocal feminists in Europe and America who were also campaigning for women's rights in the 1920s and 1930s. While she did assert women and men have a common human nature, she grounded her argument for women's leadership in the need for diversity. The reason women need to be part of the political process is that they experience the world differently than men. In Stein's view a woman will look beyond numbers and facts to the effects of policies on the lived reality of children, families, and the environment. Women's voices need to be at the political and economic table not because they have similar minds to those of men, but precisely because they have different minds and experiences than men. Their voices complement men's voices. This gender diversity is necessary for sound leadership.

Stein's Vision for Girls' Education:

Stein grounded her theory of gender essentialism in woman's natural biological role as mother. Thus, she, like Hildegard, was a proponent of studying the female body and making these studies known to girls and women. Stein was an especially strong advocate for sex education in girls' high schools claiming that it was dangerous to withhold information about sexuality and physiology from young women. In addition, she believed that teachers must take the bodies of their students into consideration as well as the cultural contexts in which they were raised. She believed it was unwise to expect children to appear in kindergarten as blank slates. Teachers who ignored the physical and cultural properties of the whole child would fail to teach them well.

But Stein, as an academic and a Carmelite nun, did not proclaim that the biological characteristics of the female body or the feminine characteristics of the female psyche were created solely for biological reproduction. Just as men's attributes are necessary for the governance of political society, the growth of the economic market, and the stewardship of the earth, so are women's attributes. Women need an educational system that supports them as women with unique intellectual and psychological gifts. Stein criticized co-education which pretended to treat boys and girls equally when really only treating both sexes as boys. She believed that the education system maximized boy's single-minded interest in facts and figures and minimized girl's desire to contextualize facts and study systems as wholes rather than parts. In order for women to fulfill both their potential roles as biological mothers of children and as mothering participants in economic and political society, girls need their unique talents and experiences to be recognized and developed. She believed this was most likely to occur in single-sex institutions. Her own experiences convinced her that early twentieth-century models of education were not gender neutral but male-centered. Quality female-centered education is necessary if girls are to achieve full equality with men as women. Indeed, according to Stein, female-centered education is necessary if society is to profit from the fully developed diverse views of men and women in public spaces. Stein was adamant that girls were not inferior to boys and equally adamant that girls should be educated according to all their individual talents.

Stein's Gender Essentialism: Beyond the Binary

Edith Stein asserted that every individual is unique. She was one of very few women who held a PhD in philosophy in the 1920s and 1930s. Thus, she recognized that individual women can possess the virtues that are considered male. While she believed that a central openness and warmth surrounded woman's essential nature and inspired the majority of women to prefer studies and occupations that were nurturing and holistically minded, she asserted that women can find many different types of professions fulfilling. In addition, she noted that many individual women have no choice but to take any job that enables them to support their family. After all, Stein's mother had supported her family by running her late husband's lumber business. Furthermore, Stein asserted that many individual women have gifts and talents that especially suit them for more masculine professions in accounting, engineering, and medicine. Such women often brought a maternal spirit to these disciplines widening the perspective within them. Men sometimes had talents for more feminine professions as well. This too should be embraced. Thus, for reasons of economic necessity and of individual preference, Stein argued that no discipline should be closed to either gender based on physical sex, with the possible exception of the priesthood.

Stein's view on the ordination of women is complex. She certainly stopped short of suggesting that women should be ordained in the Roman Catholic Church. However, she proclaimed that women's open nature makes them more readily open to the Spirit. Therefore, she believed, many women are more religious than men. Like Hildegard before her, Stein implied that the religious man must use feminine role models of virtue such as Mary and the holy virgin martyrs. Most importantly, Stein asserted that the Christian vocation is beyond gender. She wrote,

> Whether man or woman, whether consecrated or not, each one is called to the imitation of Christ. The further the individual continues on this path, the more Christlike he will become. Christ embodies the ideal of human perfection: . . . the masculine and feminine virtues are united and their weaknesses redeemed: therefore, His true followers will be progressively exalted over their natural limitations. That is why we see in holy men a womanly tenderness and a truly maternal solicitude for the souls entrusted to them while in holy women there is manly boldness, proficiency, and determination.[31]

This is not to say biology has no influence in religious life. Stein concluded this passage saying, "however, this can never be attained by an arbitrary battle against nature and by denial of natural limitations but only through humble submission to the God-given order."[32]

Feminist Merits of Stein's Gender-Essentialism

In the twentieth century, Stein found the suppression of women's voices to be a great concern. Both as a "radical feminist" student and as a Catholic feminist philosopher she worked to build a philosophically sound framework for gender equality. Her view was a feminism that proposed men

31. Stein, "The Separate Vocations of Man and Woman by Nature and Grace," in Stein, *Essays on Woman*, 84.

32. Ibid., 85.

and women to be essentially the same was actually not a feminism, but a male-centered political view that stated only male experience was valid. She articulated that women's biological differences amounted to essential differences between the feminine experience and the masculine experience of the world. This difference is ordained by God because God wants diversity in human leadership. Men and women in dialogue with each other have better understanding and better frameworks for stewarding creation than either gender on its own. Her view lifts up both the role of biological mother and the role of feminine virtue in society. She explained carefully that women should not be restricted to domestic duties as wife and mother while at the same time declaring that domestic duties should not be dismissed as unimportant by society. While Stein has been criticized for advocating feminine virtue as if she is condoning female submission to the male, her writings are clear that her view of female gentleness, openness, and even obedience is not the same as submission but is a unique kind of leadership. Stein's insistence that women stand against anti-Semitism, Nazism, and political oppression forbids a reading of her texts that would deny women the full power to articulate and act on their individual consciences. Indeed, Stein's gender essentialism, like Hildegard's, is the philosophical framework by which Stein argued that all individuals are valuable in themselves. The individual woman, a co-steward of the earth with the individual man, is not made merely for reproduction. She is made for herself and for her relationship with God.

Hildegard and Stein's Feminist Legacy

Both Stein and Hildegard of Bingen used their theories of gender essentialism to promote a view that women are different than men but not inferior to men. In Hildegard's era, the view that a woman was a deficient male was widely articulated in physiology and philosophy. In contrast, Hildegard claimed that woman is not an inferior kind of man; a woman is a full human being with different but complementary gifts to those of a man. Use of both women and men's gifts is necessary for wise stewardship of creation. Her new way of thinking about gender opened up an interest in women as women. This view led to Hildegard's own studies of women's health, social needs, and ways of knowing. Other medieval women and men followed suit.

In the early modern and Enlightenment eras, many women embraced the idea of modern philosophy that the most essential part of a human person is the rational mind. Enlightenment feminists claimed that the mind had no sex and that men and women had the same nature. Stein rejected this view of the human as neuter. She believed that thinking of women as disembodied rational minds would undermine women's unique gifts. Stein, a twentieth-century feminist who embraced the Enlightenment era's political ideals of democracy and individual rights, advocated for more political and social equality for women than the medieval Hildegard. But Stein argued for this equality from the standpoint of gender essentialism. Precisely because women are different than men, with different physical, psychological and spiritual needs and gifts, women need to have equal access to political and economic power. Women's emotional intelligence, warmth, gentleness, and desire to see the world holistically are not weaknesses compared to men's logical strength and single-mindedness but a complementary way of knowing and leading. Interestingly, a similar standpoint was articulated by Stein's contemporary, the phenomenologist Maria Zambrano, who was writing in Spain and later in Latin America. Stein's work particularly inspired others to study the psychology and pedagogy of girls and women.

Gender Essentialism in Natural Science and Medical Care

> Sometime in the mid-1970s—overnight, as it were—another kind of question took precedence, upsetting my entire intellectual hierarchy: How much of the nature of science is bound up with the idea of masculinity, and what would it mean for science if it were otherwise?
>
> —EVELYN FOX KELLER[33]

> Sex, a biological variable, and gender, a cultural variable, define the individual and affect all aspects of disease prevention, development, diagnosis, progression, and treatment. Sex and gender are essential elements of individualized medicine.
>
> —VIRGINIA MILLER[34]

33. Keller, *Reflections on Gender and Science*, 3.
34. Miller et al., "Embedding Concepts of Sex and Gender," abstract.

In recent decades several feminist scientists have advocated for changes in the study of the natural sciences using the claims of gender essentialism. Evelyn Fox Keller and Virginia Miller are two prominent leaders in this field who have advocated for promoting women's leadership in biology and in medicine in order to overcome a male-bias in these fields.

While many people consider natural science an objective discipline, Keller argues that scientific study is gendered. She asserts that gender colors the way a scientist views her world, including the world she studies scientifically. Therefore, the gender of the scientist affects the scientific experiments and conclusions that are made. In many ways, Keller echoes some of Stein's arguments. For example, Keller explains that modern science is marked by the claim that the scientist can and should examine and report on ultimate reality without bias. However, Keller claims that, first, bias must be recognized. Keller writes that a very firm masculine bias was present in the construction of modern science by foundational thinkers such as Francis Bacon. Science was considered by Bacon to be the discipline that seeks to master, dominate, and control creation.[35]

> For Bacon, knowledge and power are one, and the promise of science is expressed as "leading to you Nature with all her children to bind her to your service and make her your slave."[36]

Keller suggests that in Bacon's view, the scientist is identified as a male who seeks to control and dominate nature, identified as female. Keller claims this view, albeit in a less poetic form, persists today in contemporary science. Scientists seek to study nature in order to control it rather than in order to understand it. Moreover, scientists are expected to relate to their studies as dispassionate subjects who objectively analyze the object of study. Relationships between the observer and the observed are, too often, ignored according to Keller. The result is a poor study of science by scientists who are unaware of the bias they bring to their study. Such scientists also ignore the way they as observers affect the objects of their observation and the way nature acts as a whole rather than as simple reduced parts.

In addition to the ideological bias, in biology there has been an experimental bias towards study of the male rather than the female animal.[37]

---

35. Keller, *Reflections on Gender and Science*, 33.

36. Keller, "Feminism and Science," 285. Bacon's quote is taken from Farrington, "*Temporis Partus Masculus.*"

37. Keller, "Feminism and Science," 280.

While females generally account for fifty percent of animal and human populations, Keller says scientific studies make the assumption that the male subject is the normal subject and use mostly males in experiments. The female is considered "atypical" before the study even begins. Then because there are few females in the study, their results seem to be a minority of results. The typical results apply to the majority of subjects studied, and the majority of subjects studied are male. Results for females are considered, thus, atypical. This is a serious problem for biology if it wishes to understand fully animal and human biology. Keller suggests biologists must study equal numbers of male and female subjects.

Beyond academic understanding, the failure to study the female body leads to poor veterinary and medical care for female animals and women. Concern for women's health care has brought this issue into the national light in recent decades. In 1985 the National Institute of Health's Public Task Force on Women's Health concluded that, apart from reproductive issues, little was known about the unique needs of the female patient. As a result of this report, the NIH Office of Research on Women's Health (ORWH) was created in 1990 "to promote and support research on women's health."[38] The need was clear. In 1990, fifty percent of NIH proposals included only male subjects. Another twenty percent of proposals did not designate the sex of the subjects at all.[39] Only thirty percent of the proposals aimed to study and report clearly their results as they applied to both men and women subjects using sex as a variable. Virginia Miller, an advocate for better NIH study of both men and women claims that the foundational problem was a bias amongst researchers that sex and gender have no influence on experiments.[40] But this bias is false, according to Miller who insists, "Sex, a biological variable, and gender, a cultural variable, define the individual and affect all aspects of disease prevention, development, diagnosis, progression, and treatment. Sex and gender are essential elements of individualized medicine."[41] Miller reports that the XX chromosome is present in every cell of a woman's body. She gives ample empirical evidence that pharmaceuticals affect the cells in women's and men's bodies differently. Yet many drugs are never tested on female animals or female human subjects before going to market. Studies that do include male and female

38. Miller et al., "Embedding Concepts of Sex and Gender," introduction.

39. Ibid.

40. Ibid.

41. Ibid., abstract.

subjects often do not record the efficacy or side effects using sex as a factor. For example, reports often say that some trial subjects experienced certain side effects without noting that the majority of those subjects were female. Thus, the conclusions of the tests do not include the effects on each sex in a way that doctors or patients can use effectively. Even less research and reporting are done on how pharmaceuticals and therapies uniquely affect women who are pregnant, nursing, or post-menopausal. Data is simply reported for the majority of subjects in a study. Information on the effects on women, pregnant women, nursing women, and post-menopausal women is listed as unknown. This is allowed because there is a false assumption that these groups are small minority populations that need not be studied before a drug goes to market.

Another area affected by a male bias in science is the study of sexuality. The Darwinian view of evolution suggests that sexual difference between males and females evolved solely for the purpose of sexual reproduction. Thus sexual health and sexual response has been studied almost only in terms of sexual reproduction. Philosopher Elisabeth A. Lloyd asserts this is a male bias that ignores the possibility of female sexuality for its own sake. Lloyd notes in her article "Pre-theoretical Assumptions in Evolutionary Explanations of Female Sexuality" that for decades biologists interested in evolutionary traits in sexuality studied only male sexual response and the mechanics of sexual reproduction.[42] As a result, false assumptions were drawn and considered authoritative concerning female sexual response. This was because female sexuality was only studied when observed in heterosexual reproductive situations. For example, the assumption was made that female primates are only sexually receptive during *oestrus*. *Oestrus* is defined as the period when the female is fertile. Also, the assumption was made that the female orgasm was an evolutionary trait that improved female fertility.[43] Observations about female sexuality were only recorded for females who were fertile and who were participating in heterosexual reproductive sexual activity.[44] From that data, one scientist hypothesized that the female orgasm relaxed the female so that she would lie still after intercourse allowing more time for fertilization.[45] This hypothesis remained

42. Lloyd, "Pre-theoretical Assumptions," 94.

43. Ibid., 92.

44. Ibid., 94.

45. See Morris, *Naked Ape*, 79. As quoted in Lloyd, "Pre-theoretical Assumptions," 97.

unchallenged in evolutionary biology. Generally, scientists looking only at this narrow collection of data agreed that female orgasm was an evolutionary trait that improved female fertility.

However, research that includes more complex data tells a different story about female sexuality. Challenges arise from new studies in non-human primates and new examinations of data from scientific studies on humans, such as the famous Masters and Johnson study in 1966 and the Kinsey study in 1953. These studies include data about female sexual response in primates who were not in their fertile period and were not participating in heterosexual reproductive sexual activity. First, in studies of monkeys, female homosexual activities were widely observed, and females were much more likely to have an orgasm when they were with a female partner and not in *oestrus* than when having intercourse with a male during their period of fertility.[46] Second, studies of humans demonstrated that the vast majority of women are capable of having orgasms. However, only 20–25 percent of orgasmic women experience orgasm consistently in heterosexual intercourse alone. Indeed, 30 percent of orgasmic women never have an orgasm with heterosexual intercourse alone.[47] In addition, in both monkeys and humans, studies reveal that female orgasm does not produce hormones that relax the female but hormones that usually stimulate movement.[48] These particular studies have falsified assumptions about evolutionary fitness and female sexuality. More radically, they challenge many views about what is considered healthy and natural in female sexuality. Quite simply, women's sexuality and sexual response does not appear to be designed primarily for sexual reproduction.[49] More generally, this claim suggests that sexual diversity may be not only for reproduction either. In other words, there is evidence that the female body has other purposes than the reproductive purpose.

Generally, examples abound of how the failure to study or report data for female subjects has harmed women. But changes are being made. In

---

46. See Chevalier-Skolnikoff, "Male-Female, Female-Female, and Male-Male Sexual Behavior," 95–116; Chevalier-Skolnikoff, "Homosexual Behavior in a Laboratory Group of Stumptail Monkeys," 511–27. Both are referenced in Lloyd, "Pre-theoretical Assumptions," 92–93.

47. See Kinsey et al., *Sexual Behavior in the Human Female*, in Lloyd, "Pre-theoretical Assumptions," 96.

48. See Masters and Johnson, *Human Sexual Response*, in Lloyd, "Pre-theoretical Assumptions," 97.

49. Lloyd, "Pre-theoretical Assumptions," 100–102.

2001 the Institute of Medicine reported, "Sex, that is being male or female, is an important basic human variable that should be considered when designing and analyzing studies in all areas and at all levels of biomedical and health related research."[50] Today, the American Heart Association website warns women not to rely only on information regarding "typical" symptoms of heart disease noting the high statistics of heart disease fatalities in women.[51] The Food and Drug Administration's website highlights a 2011 article titled *Adverse Effects in Women: Implications for Drug Development and Regulatory Policies* which allows searchers to read about issues in drug research, including data on the effects and risks of specific drugs.[52] This article is a tremendous resource for both patients and doctors interested in women's health care.

Such articles show that the work of Keller, Miller, and others is changing how science is done. However, Miller's 2014 essay, "Sex Matters," argues that the changes are still not happening on a broad enough scale. In addition, Miller argues that gender as well as sex matters in medicine. Gender gives rise to unique psychological and cultural factors that need to be a part of medical education so that doctors can best care for their patients and community, according to Miller.[53] Both Keller and Miller believe that science and medicine will be improved if both sex and gender are considered essential characteristics of the human biological subject.

Contemporary Feminist Gender Essentialism

Today, many feminist activists use gender essentialism to ground their arguments for better equality for girls and women as gendered beings. For example, many feminist educators advocate that girls' high schools, women's colleges, and women's leadership institutes are uniquely capable of nourishing girls and women in women's ways of knowing, problem solving, and leading in order to produce educated women that can take powerful leadership roles in society. By exposing girls and women to female

50. Institute of Medicine, *Exploring the Biological Contributions to Human Health*, 173, in Miller, *Embedding*, introduction.

51. http://www.heart.org/HEARTORG/Conditions/HeartAttack/HeartAttackTool-sResources/Heart-Attack-Risk-Assessment_UCM_303944_Article.jsp.

52. Parekh et al., "Adverse Effects in Women: Implications for Drug Development and Regulatory Policies."

53. Miller, *Embedding Sex*, 5.

teachers, administrators, and political leaders, such institutions offer role models to girls that share their physical attributes and often their social gender roles as mothers, caretakers, wives, and partners. In addition, many of these institutions strive to help women with issues that specifically relate to their gendered roles by providing women's health clinics, child care, and women-centered counseling services. Similarly many advocates of women's rights use a gender essentialist argument to ground their fight for political changes, social programs, and protective laws that impact women specifically. For example, there are supporters of programs like Women, Infants, and Children (WIC), a program aimed at improving the nutritional well-being of women, infants, and children. In addition, many support policies that offer protections against sexual harassment and gender discrimination in the work place. Some supporters of the Family Medical Leave Act advocated that this policy would most positively affect women who otherwise might lose a job based on their gendered social role as mother or caretaker. Legislation that protects victims of domestic violence and policies that ensure access to contraception and abortion are often pursued under the banner of women's rights. Indeed, groups that advocate for "women's rights" and "justice for women" often have a gender essentialist foundation. They assume that women are a unique group of human beings with specific needs, interests, and talents that differ from those of men.

Indeed, one of the major foci of the feminist movement in the last few decades has been the celebration of a woman-centered perspective. This is seen in some contemporary feminists who argue that women, whether by nurture or nature, have a unique and valuable perspective. For example, Nel Noddings and Carol Gilligan both made the argument that women have a different way of thinking and discussing ethics than men. Noddings's *Ethics of Care* emphasized that women find care, rather than reason, to be the foundation for ethics. Gilligan's *In a Different Voice* presented case studies of the relational and empathetic way women make ethical decisions. Gilligan coined the term *difference feminism* to advocate for a feminist stance that women have a different but equally important voice that complements the male voice. These groundbreaking authors encouraged readers to consider women's ways of thinking as uniquely important.

In a similar vein of thought, Patricia Hill Collins writes in her essay *The Social Construction of Black Feminist Thought*, whether the essence of woman is given by nature or created by society, women ought "to value their own subjective knowledge base" and celebrate what is distinctive about their viewpoint.[54] Collins's point is that all thought is biased. The problem with those who seek to free women from their cultural construct is that they often force women into a male construct. The standpoint of much of the history of Western political and philosophical thought has been the standpoint of the white male. To call this standpoint objective is to deny the white male bias is a bias. Moreover, this silences other valid voices. Collins explains, "Black female scholars may know that something is true but be unwilling or unable to legitimate their claim using Eurocentric masculine criteria."[55] In contrast to the Euro-centric male model that views individuals as distinct and that privileges mathematical reason and devalues emotion, the Afro-centric feminist model is holistic, seeing relationships rather than individuals. Afro-centric feminism privileges experience and emotion over mathematical reason. Collins acknowledges that this position is not shared by all women, or even by all African American women. She claims that differing segments of society have constructed gender roles differently. In this way Collins is not a strict gender essentialist in the same manner as Stein or Hildegard. However, her point agrees with Stein's and Hildegard's idea that there is more than one essential way of thinking that is valid.

In addition, many other African American *womanists* also advocate an appreciation of the unique way of thinking that characterizes African American women. Thinkers, like Zora Neale Hurston and Alice Walker, believe that accepting and appreciating the unique essence of women of color is essential for teaching self-love and authentic living for these women. *Chicana feminists*, likewise, advocate appreciating the uniqueness of Hispanic women. Both groups suggest that the combination of nature and nurture has given rise to the unique and valuable ways of being human that is the African American female way and the Chicana way.

Further, this type of cultured gender essentialism has also been used in to promote men and women's equality in the church. Many twentieth- and twenty-first-century theologians such as Mary Daly are examples of this type of gender essentialism. For example, in *Beyond God the Father*, Daly stressed the need for girls and women to reject masculine imagery, symbols, and icons. Daly's position is both socio-political and theological. On one hand, she argued that images of a male God powerfully reinforce the idea that male humans should assume positions of leadership. Daly's position is both socio-political and theological. She argued that images of

54. Collins, "Social Construction," 225.
55. Ibid., 226.

a male God powerfully reinforce the idea that male humans should assume positions of leadership. Her critique of these images is meant to broaden society's vision to include women leaders and feminine power. Yet, as a theologian she stressed that images of a male God undermine the goal of understanding God's ultimate reality as a being beyond gender. She wrote, "As marginal beings who have no stake in a sexist world, women—if we have the courage to keep our eyes open—have access to the knowledge that neither the Father, nor the Son, nor the Mother is God, the Verb who transcends anthropomorphic symbolization."[56] Daly's earnest exploration of a theology "beyond God the father" seeks to inspire women to see beyond cultural gender stereotypes. However Daly's theology is founded on the belief that culture, and to some degree nature, has led to real gender differences between men and women that must be considered when doing theology and pastoral care. Similarly, works of other feminist theologians, including Rosemary Ruether and Elizabeth Johnson, have the same foundation. They urge readers to explore feminine attributes of the divine, because they assume that there are distinctly feminine and masculine traits in the Divine. Moreover, there is value in both the feminine and masculine way of being.

Generally many feminists today take arguments from gender essentialism in order to lift up what they believe to be feminine virtues and values that have been undermined by society. Such arguments can be seen in a wide variety of contemporary writers who might not call themselves gender essentialists or even difference feminists but do use these arguments at times especially in order to unite women to a common cause. Such writers include Luce Irigaray, Naomi Wolf, Catherine MacKinnon, and many others.

Problems with Gender Essentialism

While gender essentialism is the most common view of gender in contemporary Western society, there are major philosophical problems with this theory. Gender essentialists often claim that gender and sex is a natural division. But often times what seems "natural," "innate," or "obvious" is actually a cultural habit. Hildegard and Stein were very aware of this as each challenged the views of gender that were considered natural in their times. Hildegard criticized the cultural view of women as more sinful than the male and deficient to him. Her explanation of *Genesis* in the *Scivias* claims

56. Daly, *Beyond God the Father*, 97.

that women's softness, gentleness, and warmth are gifts from God meant to complement the gifts of men. Stein was even more pointed in her attempts to differentiate cultural habits from natural structures of reality. Her philosophical project from her dissertation to her final works in philosophy centered on the method by which one can know real essences from cultural constructs. She specifically targeted racist and sexist stereotypes, reminding people of the need to look beyond their emotional reactions. She urged readers and listeners to attempt to uncover their own background experiences and cultural attitudes that might have predisposed them to see people and types incorrectly.[57]

With this in mind, the reader must consider how Western culture has affected the view that there is an essential feminine or masculine nature at all. Perhaps the experience of a definite female or male nature is due to the way observers are cultured to expect that the female and male are essentially different. In the next chapters, thinkers such as Mary Wollstonecraft, Sojourner Truth, Simone de Beauvoir, and many others will claim these gender differences fall away under deeper analysis. Indeed, Stein and Hildegard recognized experience shows all men do not share all the same gendered characteristics, nor do all women. Both Stein and Hildegard found themselves in vocations that were culturally considered male. Hildegard found enough diversity among the people she knew to describe four different types of women and four different types of men, each with unique needs and talents. Stein asserted that many women have a masculine approach to looking at problems as well as masculine talents and many men have feminine approaches and talents. In addition, both stressed that true virtue requires striving towards the virtues of one's own gender and those of the opposite gender, thus asserting that holy people often seem beyond gender. Further, both stressed that God's grace allows one to transcend one's gendered role.

57. To avoid this deception the person must not only consider her experience but what Stein called "the Secondary Motivations" behind her hatred. Stein wrote, " We cannot bring these other motives clearly to givenness to ourselves because they are not actual, but "background," experiences. . . . People are generally inclined to ascribe to themselves better motives than they actually have and are not conscious of many of their emotional impulses at all because these feelings already seem to have a disvalue in the mode of non-actuality, and people do not allow them to become actual at all. But this does not cause the feelings to cease enduring or functioning. . . . Thus, an actual valuing can be based on a non-actual memory or expectation." Stein, *Problem of Empathy* [37], 33.

Science, too, gives us a more complex story than simple gender essentialism will allow. While Keller and Miller give ample evidence for the necessity to consider sex characteristics when studying biology and medicine, many biologists and doctors assert the need to consider the many people whose sex characteristics do not fit the biological definitions of male and female. Studies indicate that at least 1 in 2000 children born do not fit the anatomical definition of male or female, and many more than that number find in adulthood that their hormonal, genetic, and post-puberty anatomical attributes do not fit into either sex category neatly.[58] Gender essentialism is not helpful in providing a framework for science and politics for intersex people.

Finally, while the women thinkers highlighted in this chapter claim men and women are equal and complimentary, many other gender essentialists have highlighted differences between men and women in order to ground discrimination against women. Hildegard's and Stein's own words have been used to argue against women's equality in certain avenues. Indeed, the idea that men and women are essentially different often has been linked politically to the idea that men are inherently more valuable than women and that their attributes are more virtuous than those of women. In the same way that ethnic differences were often emphasized in order to devalue and even deface specific ethnic groups, gender differences have also been used. While some such thinkers have been obviously motivated to oppress women's leadership, others' motivations have been more subtle. There were anti-suffragists, for example, who seemed to have a genuine concern for the soft and maternal nature of women when they advocated letting women forego the political process. There were opponents of the equal rights amendment that were afraid women would lose necessary protections. And there are good-hearted educators today who claim that differences in girls' and boys' learning styles mean that boys need more recess and hands-on learning than girls who excel at doing quiet seat work and obeying their teachers. In contrast to these claims, feminists working within the ideals of gender essentialism assert that gentle natures will create a more gentle political process, that all people should have protections as unique individuals, and that all children need recess and lab work for holistic learning. But these examples show that while the theory of gender essentialism takes a common sense approach to acknowledging very obvious differences between men and women, the danger of common sense

58. See Dreger, *Hermaphrodites and the Medical Invention of Sex,* 42–44.

is that it too often forgets to examine experience wholly and to treat each individual with dignity. Common sense too often promotes the *status quo* and fails to create the social systems that develop the whole person.

Conclusions

There are thinkers who have used gender essentialism to degrade the nature and vocation of women and to legitimate social and political practices that diminish the rights of women and exclude them from certain spheres of society. But there are also thinkers, like those highlighted in this chapter, that use gender essentialism to lift up the unique nature and vocation of women. A general difference between the two types is how gender essence is defined. Those who degrade the role of woman often concentrate on the reproductive role of women as critical to their difference from men. An example is the French philosopher Jean Jacques Rousseau who argued that women were created as objects of delight for men and as mothers of children.[59] Rousseau, thus, thought that a woman's duty is to her husband and children; she does not require liberal education or economic or political rights for these roles.[60] However, the women thinkers named in this chapter do not center their gender essentialism on the reproductive role of women. The medieval Hildegard and the twentieth-century Stein both looked to a Christian concept of women and men as made in God's image for the purpose of guiding, leading, and caring for creation. More importantly, they made the claim that women are created for their own selves in relationship with their Creator. Their theology insists that women and men are differentiated not simply for the purpose of procreation, but because their different natures are needed to steward all of Creation. Just as importantly, both Stein and Hildegard advocated for women's unique way of enjoying health, pleasure, enlightenment, and relationship with the divine. Their interest in women's medicine, education, and spirituality went beyond interest in reproductive medicine and sexual education in order to help women in

59. See Rousseau, *Emile*, 357–405. For example, "[E]verything man and woman have in common belongs to the species, and that everything which distinguishes them belongs to the sex. . . . Once this principle is established, it follows that woman is made specially to please man" (ibid., 358).

60. See ibid., 361. "The strictness of the relative duties of the two sexes is not and cannot be the same. When women complains on this score about unjust man-made inequality, she is wrong. This inequality is not a human institution—or, at least, it is the work not of prejudice but of reason."

the entirety of their lives. This same interest is also seen in the theological writings of Daly, Ruether, and Johnson who write to help women recognize themselves more clearly in relationship to the divine Creator. This same interest is seen in the writings and research of Keller, Miller, and Lloyd who advocate for continued research on how the sexed bodies of women and gendered psyches of women need further research so that women can live longer, healthier, more pleasurable lives for their own sakes. This type of gender essentialism can be extremely powerful for women who desire to exalt feminine bodies and nurturing natures in a society that often promotes a single-minded focus on power and strength rather than cooperation and gentleness.

2

Gender Neutrality

But there is a class of objectors who say they do not claim superiority, they merely assert a difference. But you will find by following them closely, that they soon run this difference into the old grove of superiority.

—ELIZABETH CADY STANTON[1]

The Mind is common to both sexes.

—SUSAN B. ANTHONY[2]

When expecting parents are asked if they are hoping for a boy or girl, many will say that they do not have a preference. In today's society many parents do not expect that their child's sex will radically determine the child's intelligence, drive, future occupation, or even lifestyle. Most parents also expect that society will afford their child equal rights and opportunities regardless of the child's sex. The argument that all children are equal and should have equal access to education, the work force, economic power,

1. Stanton, "Address Delivered at Seneca Falls, July 19, 1848," *Stanton/Anthony: Correspondence*, 31.

2. Anthony, "Speech 1856," in Sherr, *Failure Is Impossible*, 23.

and political power is the argument of *Liberal Enlightenment Feminism*, sometimes simply called *liberal feminism*. Such feminism is founded on a theory of *gender neutrality*.

This chapter is an exploration of what a theory of gender neutrality says about being a woman. The vast majority of early feminist activists, later named *first wave feminists*, held a theory of gender neutrality. In contrast to gender essentialists, these women claimed that their sex was not a key part of their identity. Rather they believed that the essence of one's identity is one's human nature. These women stressed what men and women have in common in order to argue for equal rights and opportunities for all people. This view is still the most common view used by those who advocate for gender equality in education, economics, and politics.

What Is the Theory of Gender Neutrality? What Is Liberal Enlightenment Feminism?

Gender is defined as the classification of male or female that includes social, psychological, and intellectual characteristics. The theory of *gender neutrality* is a theory that claims that biological sex does not inevitably determine social, psychological, and intellectual characteristics. Feminists who argue for gender neutrality do not emphasize gender or sex as a major characteristic of a human person.

The term *feminism* was coined in 1890 to denote the movement and the ideology that argued for women's rights. Literally *feminism* means a stance for women. Since 1890 the term *feminism* has been most often used to discuss the *liberal feminism* born in the Enlightenment era (1770–1900). This is the stance that claims women and men are essentially the same in regard to their value and duty before God, in regard to their mental faculties, and in regard to their rights and responsibilities in society. This type of feminism was born from revolutions in theology, philosophy, and political theory.

Theologically, the Reformation in the sixteenth century challenged medieval Roman Catholic views that human individuals are placed in a hierarchy of class and vocation before God. While many medieval thinkers certainly asserted that humans were all valuable in the eyes of God, these thinkers, also, claimed that each person's stance before God was differentiated based on class, occupation, and gender. For example, Hildegard of Bingen asserted that the hierarchy of the feudal classes, like the arrangements of the angels, was ordained by God. She refused her convents to be integrated with nuns from lower socio-economic classes. She also upheld the medieval view that members of the clergy were more sacred in their vocations than those chosen by God to work in the secular world. Moreover, she believed that men and women had separate vocations in the world. In contrast, the reforming doctrines of Martin Luther radically challenged these medieval views causing changes both inside and outside of the Roman Catholic Church. On one hand, Luther was certainly a medieval feudalist and a gender essentialist. On the other hand, he proclaimed that every Christian is both a lord of all and a servant of all as well as a member of the priesthood of all believers. This proclamation of the equality of all Christians became an important piece of Enlightenment liberalism and liberal feminism. In addition, Luther claimed that all people had one duty as Christians: to obey the commandment to love their God and serve their neighbor. In order to fulfill this commandment all children needed to be able to read Scripture for themselves, according to Luther. He urged the Christian nobility of his time to immediately increase the number of schools, particularly the number of schools for girls. This new understanding of the importance of female literacy spread far beyond Lutheran provinces, influencing Anglicans like Mary Astell and Mary Wollstonecraft. By the 1800s many philosophers and political theorists agreed on the importance of at least rudimentary education for all classes and both genders. The new understanding of the individual standing alone before God began to undermine old views about the importance of hierarchy and occupation. A newly literate middle and working class began to advocate for political changes.

Philosophically, in the early modern era, many European philosophers adopted a philosophical position that claimed the most essential part of a person is the mind, the thinking thing. As scientific discovery, geographic exploration, religious reformation, and political revolution accelerated in Europe, philosophers sought a method to find universal truths that would transcend cultural fads and personal opinions. With math and logic as his guide, the French philosopher, René Descartes, the father of modern European algebra, ushered in a new way of thinking termed *modern philosophy*. *Modern philosophy* reigned from the middle of the seventeenth century until 1800. This way of thought advocated for the supremacy of reason over emotion, of mind over body, and of individual discovery over adherence to ancient authorities. Many women who were able to obtain an education embraced this modern view of philosophy. They found it liberating to see themselves primarily as rational minds and only secondarily as sexed human bodies. An interest in developing the rational talents of their sisters urged these women to begin to campaign for more opportunities for girls' and women's education. This new understanding of the human person as mind began to undermine old views about sex and gender's influence on the whole person.

Politically, in the era of the Enlightenment, liberal political theory reigned. Feudalist structures based on class distinctions were challenged by new *liberal* views about the relationship of the citizen to the state. *Liberals,* as the name suggests, believed that all men are created equal with a natural right to liberty. The writings of John Locke, Adam Smith, Jean Jacques Rousseau and other liberal thinkers advocated that every individual has an inalienable right to *autonomy* or self-rule. Rather than argue for the collapse of all government and social order, most liberal thinkers advocated for all men to have representation in their government. They supported democracy over aristocracy. The idea of natural class distinctions was denounced by liberals as an out dated cultural opinion that denied what reason and experience proved: every human being has an equal natural right to his own body, possessions, and liberty. While most of the prominent political philosophers spoke of this natural right only as it applied to males, more and more women began to argue that these rights were human rights not men's rights.

Liberal Enlightenment feminism, sometimes called *first wave feminism*, was the movement influenced by protestant theology, modern philosophy, and liberal political theory that came into prominence in the late eighteenth century through the early twentieth century. Liberal Enlightenment feminists argued that sex and gender are real attributes of a person but that they are not attributes of significant importance. Thus, they claimed men and women should have equal legal, political, and economic rights. While gender essentialism remains the most typical way of thinking about gender in the West, Liberal Enlightenment feminism's claim of gender neutrality has been the most common foundation for the pursuit of equal rights in the West.

Ante-Enlightenment Feminists

> Who are women? Who are they? . . . And by God, it is so that these are your mothers, your sisters, your daughters, your wives, and your friends: they are you yourselves and you yourselves are they.
>
> —Christine de Pizan[3]

3. "Letter from October 2, 1402," as quoted in Birk, *Christine de Pizan,* 24.

Even before the era of the liberal Enlightenment, there were women who asserted the equality of mind between men and women. These late medieval and early modern women differed from the Enlightenment and post-Enlightenment feminists because their ideals were not liberal or democratic. Content with a feudal structure that concentrated political and economic power in the hands of an elite, the views of these women concentrated purely on equalizing the roles of women and men. The reason they are considered forerunners to modern feminism is due to their theory of gender neutrality. Unlike gender essentialists they maintained that women and men are essentially the same and should strive towards similar virtues. Their view was that a woman is essentially a human being; her greatest asset is her mind. Her physical characteristics are secondary and inessential. They believed that sex did not affect the universal ability to reason that men and women share. These women's arguments concentrated on giving women and men similar educational opportunities and giving women and men of similar social classes equal economic opportunities and rights within marriage.

Christine de Pizan

What can be more beautiful than learning? And what uglier than ignorance, so ill befitting human nature? One day, a man criticized my desire for knowledge, saying that it was inappropriate for a woman to be learned, as it was so rare, to which I replied that it was even less fitting for man to be ignorant, as it was so common.[4]

Christine de Pizan was born in 1364 in Italy. Her family moved to Paris when her father became a physician and astrologer at the court of Charles V. Married at age fifteen to Etienne du Castral, Christine claimed her ten years of married life were happy. She rejoiced in the daughter and two sons it produced. However, by 1389, Charles V had died and so had Christine's father and her husband. At the age of twenty-five, she found herself alone with her mother and children under a new regime. Moreover, she had no money to pay her husband's outstanding debts. In an age when most women in her circumstances were forced into prostitution or abject poverty, Christine found an occupation as a copyist and later as a court poet. She was able to support her family with this work. In a short time, she

---

4. Christine, "The Vision of Christine," *Writings of Christine*, 16.

became well known as an author on virtue who wrote books for young men on how to be chivalrous knights, lovers, and husbands. Importantly, however, rather than simply poetizing the mores of her time, she used her position to denounce the treatment she saw of many women by their lovers and husbands. Particularly she denounced the then popular *Romance of the Rose* as a text that simply romanticized rape. She advocated strongly that marriage should be a meeting of two equals with both partners educated and respected. Having earned a reputation as an excellent moral writer, she was able to publish a large number of works, including three treatises for women: *The City of Ladies*, *The Vision of Christine*, and *The Treasury of the City of Ladies*.

The City of Ladies, her most well known work today, is a description of a fictional city where women lived to study, write, and create. The book begins with Christine's description of her own despair at being a woman. "And I finally decided that God formed a vile creature when He made a woman, and I wondered how such a worthy artisan could have deigned to make such an abominable work which, from what they say, is the vessel as well as the refuge and abode of every evil and vice."[5] As she despairs that she is a "female body in this world," three Ladies appear to her: Reason, Rectitude, and Justice. Lady Reason contradicts Christine's claim that women are of less value than men and lists biblical heroines, mythical goddesses, and historical examples of brilliant and heroic women. The three ladies urge her to build a city for women with towers and palaces to protect them as they read, write, paint, think, and pray. Specifically, Lady Rectitude speaks of the needs of women to be educated in order to support themselves when they are abandoned or widowed by husbands, fathers, and brothers. The three ladies also advocate that all women for the sake of justice and their own happiness must see their role in the great literary and philosophical tradition that has included women throughout the ages. The book is, thus, itself the citadel whose reader can find comfort and refuge in its pages. Indeed, by reading this book a woman can put on the armor of the city of ladies and the helmet of reason in order to go back into society with secure confidence. As a thoughtful, articulate, able human being, the reader can recognize herself as part of an armed battalion of thoughtful women working to protect themselves and other women.

The City of Ladies and other writings were well received by Christine's audience. However, in 1418, when a new political regime came to power,

5. Christine, "Book of the City of Ladies 1.1," *Writings of Christine*, 172.

Christine was no longer protected and adored. She fled Paris to retire and to live with her daughter. She discontinued most of her writing. But in 1429, she came out of this retirement in order to write one last work, a poem for Joan of Arc, a woman "more brave than every man at Rome!"[6] Christine saw in Joan a living physical example of what she had mythically proposed in *A City of Ladies.* Joan, the female knight, proved that women are capable of all the virtues of men. Christine wrote,

> What honor for the female sex!
> God's love for it appears quite clear,
> Because the kingdom laid to waste
> By all those wretched people now
> Stands safe, a woman rescued it
> (A hundred thousand men could not
> Do that) and killed the hostile foe!
> A thing beyond belief before![7]

Christine died the year she published the poem and did not witness Joan's capture and death. Her poem was widely read as Christine's last words for all those, male or female, who wished to be chivalrous warriors of virtue.[8]

For centuries, Christine's *City of Ladies, Treasury of the City of Ladies, Vision,* and *Poem of Joan of Arc* inspired women. Christine's work to inspire women towards the full development of their minds and virtues makes her a fine example of an ante-Enlightenment feminist.

Mary Astell

> For since God has given Women as well as Men intelligent Souls, why should they be forbidden to improve them?[9]

Born in 1666, Mary Astell was a child of modernity. The daughter of a wealthy coal merchant in New Castle, she grew up in upper class society as part of the landed gentry in North Umberland. She was well educated

---

6. Christine, "The Poem of Joan of Ark," *Writings of Christine de Pizan,* 356.

7. Ibid., 358.

8. Ibid., 362.

9. Astell, "A Serious Proposal to the Ladies 1694," as quoted in Perry, *Celebrated Mary Astell,* 79.

in the philosophies and science of Descartes, Galileo, and others who had begun a revolution in method that put the center of human inquiry in the individual human mind. In Astell's lifetime Isaac Newton was developing calculus, John Locke was composing the *Inquiry on Human Understanding*, and Francis Bacon was writing the rules of the modern scientific method. It was the beginning of an era of optimism in human reason. Many philosophers and scientists were asserting that the mind was the most important part of the human being, capable of solving complex scientific, ethical, and political problems. Astell believed that this was true of women as well as men. Because the most important part of a human being, whether male or female, is the rational mind, Astell believed that women deserve and require an education to develop their minds just as men do. Her own knowledge of modern mathematics, theology, science, and philosophy was outstanding.

Although Astell is considered a modern thinker, she was not a liberal Enlightenment thinker. Indeed, Astell was a royalist at a time when many thinkers in England were considering the idea of radically changing the political class system to a more democratic system. Astell wrote in favor of absolute monarchy against John Locke's treatises on democracy. She believed democracy was a dangerous idea that would unravel important elements of society. Yet, she did believe a change was necessary in the cultural structures around gender. Particularly, she did not favor the hierarchy of husband over wife. She claimed marriage was too often an institution that victimized women. In order to change the institution of marriage and to change society generally she advocated for women's education. Such education, she believed, would be the best antidote to the prevalent victimization of women. Furthermore, she believed women's education was a key part of religious devotion. She announced that women and men have the same responsibilities and duties before God. Thus their salvation depends on their development of mind and spirit.

Astell published several treatises on the necessity of educating girls. *A Serious Proposal to the Ladies*, published in 1694, advocated that wealthy women create colleges so that their daughters could earn the highest possible education in the liberal arts. She believed that education would cure the vices that were considered natural feminine deficiencies. She maintained that these vices were a result of ignorance not sex. In 1697 she published *A Serious Proposal to the Ladies: Part II*, which gave advice for women who wished to educate themselves. *Some Reflections on Marriage* was published in 1700. In addition, some of her most important arguments for the full equality of women with men were based on Scripture. These can be found in *The Christian Religion as Profess'd by a Daughter of the Church.*

Not content to merely write about the need for girls' schools, Astell founded her own charity school in 1709, The Chelsea School was founded specifically and solely for girls. Astell died in 1731 of breast cancer. But her writings about the necessity of education for girls continued to inspire English women until the age of the Enlightenment and beyond.

The Merits of Ante-Enlightenment Feminist Thinkers

There were many other medieval and early modern proto-feminists in addition to Mary Astell and Christine de Pizan who articulated the same definition of woman as later Enlightenment feminists. They proclaimed that the mind is the essence of the person. The mind, they argued, has no sex or gender. These women believed themselves to have been liberated by philosophy to be able to recognize themselves as rational beings first, and women second. They sought educational opportunities for women and spoke of women's ability to do virtuous tasks. Their efforts have given broad encouragement to women to pursue philosophy, math, literature, and science for centuries. These women also sought legal rights for women to be the equal of men within their social classes. In this way these women lay the foundations for later arguments for equal rights made by later liberal feminists.

Thinking Woman: Mary Wollstonecraft

> My own sex, I hope, will excuse me, if I treat them like rational creatures, instead of flattering their fascinating graces, and viewing them as if they were in a state of perpetual childhood, unable to stand alone.[10]

Biography

While the term *feminism* was not coined until 1890, there is widespread consensus that liberal Enlightenment feminism, or first wave feminism, finds its first major philosophical proponent in the person of Mary

---

10. Wollstonecraft, *Vindication of the Rights of Women*, 31.

Wollstonecraft. Wollstonecraft was born in April of 1759 in London, England. She was the second child of Edward John and Elizabeth Wollstonecraft. Her grandfather, a successful weaver and capitalist, had left his trade and wealth to her father. But her father was more fond of amusement than business. Throughout his life he slowly lost most of his inherited wealth through bad business deals, drink, and gambling. Wollstonecraft described her childhood bitterly. Her father was prone to both drinking and violence. From a young age, Wollstonecraft found herself in the position of protecting her mother and siblings from her father's abuse. While she was forced into the role of second mother to her younger siblings, her older brother was the one who gained the rights of *primogeniture*, the legal benefits of being the first-born son. Wollstonecraft claimed that her brother Edward also had the majority of his parents' affection. He was the only child given an education for a formal career—law. Wollstonecraft herself attended a day school only until second grade. Then money became too scarce for her parents to be able to justify spending it on the education of a girl.

Wollstonecraft said that after leaving school she continued to read. Also, she was able to spend copious time playing outdoors with animals. She later recommended such play as an important part of quality education for all children. However, especially as a young adolescent she longed for a room or space where she could be alone, quietly reading and thinking. At age fifteen, her own private reading was supplemented by the friendship of an elderly neighbor couple, the Reverend and Mrs. Clare. This clergyman and his wife, who had no children of their own, invited Wollstonecraft to spend time with them. They gave her books to read and to discuss. Through them she met another bright young woman, Fanny Blood, whom Wollstonecraft saw as her model of perfection. This small community of readers formed the totality of her formal education as a young adult.

At age eighteen, Wollstonecraft took a paid position as a companion to a rich widow in Bath. The two did not get along well; and after two years Wollstonecraft gratefully accepted an invitation to move in with Fanny Blood's family. While Mr. Blood, like her father, was prone to drink and extravagant spending, he was not physically or verbally abusive. Wollstonecraft became deeply involved with the younger children in the Blood's family and recognized the family's dependence upon her. However, her own family's demands changed Wollstonecraft's situation again.

In 1782, her sister Eliza, who had joyfully married, called her to help nurse her back to health after childbirth. After a bout of depression, Eliza begged not to return to her husband. Out of concern for Eliza, Wollstone-craft helped her leave her marriage. Due to patriarchal custody laws, this required leaving Eliza's newborn baby with the father. This was a departure that Eliza mourned deeply, especially after the daughter died while still in infancy.

Needing to support herself and Eliza, Wollstonecraft conceived a plan to start a school for girls. She, Eliza, their younger sister Everina, and Fanny Blood decided to set up a school for girls in Newington Green. It might seem incredible that three young women with little formal education of their own would propose to teach and administrate their own school. But at the time teaching required no qualifications. The Clares, who had first introduced Wollstonecraft to the world of learning, helped the young women find housing and start their academy. In Newington Green, the women found a large house and a few pupils. They began their routines of daily lessons. They used ideas from Rousseau and other contemporary philosophers of education to provide one-on-one instruction in reading, writing, and nature. While teaching, Wollstonecraft's circle widened. She began reading and discussing political issues with a wide variety of liberal thinkers who asserted the universal nature of human rights for all men.

The school was successful and Wollstonecraft was able to take on the emotional and financial burdens of her two younger brothers for a time. But the success was short-lived. Fanny left in order to marry and move to Portugal with her new husband. Wollstonecraft hoped that the warmer climate and stability of marriage would aid Fanny's health, which had been compromised by consumption. However, Fanny's immediate pregnancy caused her tuberculosis to advance faster. A concerned Wollstonecraft sailed to Lisbon to nurse her back to health, but despite her aid both Fanny and the newborn baby died within days of childbirth. In her absence, Wollstonecraft's two sisters quarreled and managed the school so badly that the families of the students pulled their daughters from the academy. The school was closed. But Wollstonecraft used her experiences to write *Thoughts on the Education of Daughters*. This book served to introduce her to the London literary scene.

Homeless again and ignored by her older brother Edward, the only well-established member of her family, Wollstonecraft took a position in Ireland as a governess. There, her experiences of wealthy family life led her to a derogatory view of traditional marriage and motherhood in the upper classes. Wollstonecraft was shocked by those wealthy women who spent the majority of their time tending to fashion and beauty rituals and who had more affection for their dogs than their own children. Wollstonecraft was well loved by the oldest daughter and seemed to have a special intellectual friendship with the father. But the mother found Wollstonecraft haughty and difficult, eventually calling for her dismissal.

During her time as a governess, Wollstonecraft had a room of her own where she completed her first novel, *Mary*, and a collection of children's stories called *Original Stories from Real Life*. These she took with her when she left Ireland to return to London. Her publisher Joseph Johnson, immediately published both works, hiring William Blake to illustrate *Original Stories for Children*. Johnson set up a house for Wollstonecraft urging her to write full time. From 1788 to 1792 she entered a period of thriving intellectual life among the most notable of London political theorists and philosophers. In 1790, having been inspired by the French Revolution, she wrote an important rebuttal of Edmund Burke's *Reflections on the Revolution in France* which she titled *Vindication of the Rights of Men*. Impressed by the work, her publisher Johnson asked her immediately to write a *Vindication of the Rights of Women*. She agreed to the topic and the deadline, writing in only six weeks the work that would make her most famous. While she worried that it was a mere ragbag of ideas, the book was immediately positively reviewed. However, Wollstonecraft, herself, was deemed by the press to be a hyena in petticoats.

Wollstonecraft, inspired by the liberal political ideals of French women, moved to Paris in 1792, where French women radicals hoped to expand women's economic and political rights in the new French constitution. In Paris, she met Gilbert Imlay, an American businessman with an undisclosed history of outstanding debts. Despite Wollstonecraft's initial dislike, she came to feel passionately towards Imlay. The pair did not marry, but she did take his name for a time when French legislation threatened to imprison English nationals. In May 1794, Wollstonecraft gave birth to her first daughter, Fanny Imlay. Almost immediately, Imlay pulled away from the relationship moving back to London. Wollstonecraft followed Imlay to London where she found that he had taken up with another woman.

At this time, Wollstonecraft's biography reveals the human tension of reason and philosophy with sentiment and passion. Rationally and lovingly committed to Fanny, Wollstonecraft modeled the type of mothering she had advocated in her written works. She was committed to breastfeeding and forming a close knit relationship between mother and child. She advocated that reason rather than simply sentiment ought regulate the bond. In addition to mothering, she continued her own intellectual work, publishing *An Historical and Moral View of the Origin and Progress of the French Revolution*. Yet in the same time period, Wollstonecraft found herself mired in such deep emotional distress over Imlay that she attempted suicide. After this episode, Imlay, hinting that their relationship might be salvageable, asked Wollstonecraft to help him close a few business deals in Scandinavia. Wollstonecraft gathered her wits and her baby daughter and nanny to travel to Sweden on Imlay's behalf. Her writings during this time reveal the complexity of her thought. The main thesis of her work insists on the necessity of the supremacy of reason to regulate the emotions. Yet her romantic descriptions of Norway, Sweden, and Denmark inspired the Romantic poets after her. While arguing for the necessity of rational mothering, her descriptions of her infant and her emotional ties to Fanny are self-consciously sentimental. Any working mother will understand her agony at being away from Fanny when a short weekend trip to Norway was extended for three weeks because of bad weather. Yet Wollstonecraft derided herself in her writings for wasting her tears. She reminded herself to use reason, trusting in the knowledge that her nanny would protect Fanny well. Both the strength of her emotions and her insistence on the necessity for women, particularly mothers, to use reason to guide them is clear in the published *Letters from Sweden, Norway, and Denmark.*[11]

Returning to London, Wollstonecraft found Imlay happy to have had his business troubles solved but clearly uninterested in renewing a romantic relationship. In suicidal despair, Wollstonecraft threw herself off Putney Bridge. Her dress was too buoyant to allow her to drown; a man who had watched her jump easily rescued her. Deciding that dying took more effort than living, Wollstonecraft committed herself to life once more. But she was more pessimistic about the possibility of creating real change for women in her time. Her writing began to expose this pessimism. This is evident in her unfinished novel, *Maria*, which takes the perspective of a hopeless poor woman. Yet at this same time Wollstonecraft's books were gaining popularity in London.

Within months of the attempted suicide, she began a new romantic relationship with an old friend, William Godwin. In less than a year she found she was pregnant. Godwin proposed marriage, and Wollstonecraft agreed. The marriage was happy. Both Godwin and Wollstonecraft were

---

11. See, for example, "Letter VI," in Wollstonecraft, *Letters*.

content to parent three-year-old Fanny and wait for the new baby in domestic delight. In addition, Wollstonecraft felt confident she would be able to continue to be an independent thinker. On August 30, 1797, Mary Wollstonecraft Godwin was born to her delighted parents.

Wollstonecraft had expected an easy birth, like Fanny's. She had hoped to model to other women healthy motherhood rather than complaining of weakness after labor. But Mary's birth was complicated because the placenta was not immediately expelled. A doctor was called to remove the placenta with his bare, and likely unwashed, hands. The next day Wollstonecraft was jubilant and all seemed well. But a few days later she spiked a high fever. Wollstonecraft claimed that she would will herself to live. She did manage to continue hopefully for several days. But she did not recover. The irony that this great proponent of women's equality, "died a death that strongly marked the distinction of the sexes" was marked immediately.[12] Many mourned her death. Her grave was marked with a stone that read "Mary Wollstonecraft Godwin: Author of A Vindication of the rights of Woman"[13]

Her husband, William Godwin, in grief and devotion, attended immediately to publishing her unabridged memoirs, her unfinished novel *Maria, or the Wrongs of Women,* and many of her letters. The memoirs, appeared in print in January of 1798. They recounted Wollstonecraft's considerable accomplishments, but also her difficulties as a governess, Fanny's out-of-wedlock birth, and the two suicide attempts. To Godwin's grief the memoirs became a source of scandal. Worse, they became fodder for those that argued that education harms women. Some of her former supporters began to distance themselves from her arguments. That said, Wollstonecraft's remarkable books, especially *Thoughts on the Education of Daughters* and *The Vindication of the Rights of Women* did become major philosophical inspiration for women, especially the suffragists in America. Wollstonecraft has been named by historians as the mother of feminism.

12. This comment was made the Reverend Richard Polwhele as quoted in *Life and Death of Mary Wollstonecraft*, 226.

13. Tomalin, *Life and Death*, 228.

Wollstonecraft's Gender Neutrality
and the Vindication of the Rights of Women

> I wish, sir, to set some investigations of this kind afloat in France;
> and should they lead to confirmation of my principles when your
> constitution is revised, the Rights of Woman may be respected,
> if it be fully proved that reason calls for this respect, and loudly
> demands JUSTICE for one-half of the human race.[14]

Wollstonecraft was an articulate proponent of a theory of gender neutrality. Importantly, her theory did not deny that there are physical differences between the sexes. She wrote,

> In the government of the physical world it is observable that the
> female in point of strength, is in general, inferior to the male. This
> is the law of Nature; and it does not appear to be suspended or
> abrogated in favor of women. A degree of physical superiority cannot,
> therefore, be denied, and it is a noble prerogative![15]

However, she articulated that corsets, high heels, and a lack of physical training exaggerate the physical inferiority of women. Ironically, this physical inferiority is exaggerated by such fashions because it is considered beautiful. "But not content with this natural preeminence, men endeavor to sink us still lower, merely to render us alluring objects for a moment," wrote Wollstonecraft.[16] Wollstonecraft imagined that a society with different fashion sensibilities and rigorous physical training for girls would develop far less physical differences between the sexes. More importantly, Wollstonecraft made the liberal claim that legitimate power does not come from brute strength but from reason. Thus her theory of gender neutrality focused not on the body but on the mind. Importantly, Wollstonecraft's view of the mind included not only reason and critical thought, but also the faculties of imagination and feeling. A rightly ordered mind ordered all of these functions appropriately.

Wollstonecraft was a liberal Enlightenment thinker in the same tradition as John Locke, Thomas Paine, and Thomas Jefferson. This is clear in *A Vindication of the Rights of Men* where she explained,

---

14. Wollstonecraft, *Vindication of the Rights of Women*, 24.

15. Ibid., 30.

16. Ibid.

> It is necessary emphatically to repeat that there are rights which men inherit at their birth, as rational creatures, who were raised above the brute creation by their improvable faculties; and that, in receiving these, not from their forefathers, but from God, prescription can never undermine natural rights.[17]

Wollstonecraft's position is clear: human beings are primarily, preeminently, essentially, rational creatures with natural, inalienable, and God-given rights to self-determination. However, unlike many liberal male philosophers, Wollstonecraft expanded this argument to insist that these natural rights are not only men's but women's as well.

Wollstonecraft's theory of woman focused on the universal aspects of human nature. She minimized differences between men and women in order to stress the similarities between the sexes. Ultimately, the most essential part of a woman, as of a man, is her human ability to reason. And the key to a woman's virtue is her ability to reason well. In contrast to most of the philosophers of her time, she rejected the view that women are naturally more emotional, more nurturing, and more frail and refuted the view that the virtues of women include beauty, sentimentality, and obedience. Her fundamental position is that all human beings are born with the potential to be rational, a potential that must be educated and nourished in order to allow the male or female to flourish as a full human person.

In the *Vindication of the Rights of Women*, Wollstonecraft, as Astell had done, indicated that she found a clear scriptural mandate for her theory of the nature and vocation of women. Political conservatives as well as anti-feminist gender essentialists in Wollstonecraft's day used Scripture routinely to argue that the hierarchy of king over citizen and man over woman is ordained by God. In contrast, Wollstonecraft maintained that Scripture read correctly not only refutes monarchy but also gender hierarchy. John Locke had used passages from the Old and New Testament to refute the position of conservatives that the law of primogeniture was ordained by God. Wollstonecraft did likewise to refute primogeniture and patriarchy. Moreover, using Anglican values, Wollstonecraft argued that a woman's salvation depends on her ability to use reason to define her faith and her behavior. She explained that each individual stands before God who seeks evidence of virtue rather than ignorant obedience to a ruler. She insisted that God expects a return on the investment made in each human being at the judgment day. She demanded that a woman be able to say upon

---

17. Wollstonecraft, *Vindication of the Rights of Men*, 13.

rising from the grave, "Behold, Thou gavest me a talent, and here are five talents."[18] In addition she insisted that the duties of women before God and to the world are the same as those of men. "I throw down my gauntlet, and deny the existence of sexual virtues, not excepting modesty,"[19] wrote Wollstonecraft.

Modesty and sexual virtue were important to Wollstonecraft. Her insistence that virtue is the same for both sexes did not advocate libertinism for women, but modesty and chastity for men. Wollstonecraft argued that cultivating women to strive towards the virtues of beauty and chastity was oxymoronic. A woman needed to understand that her virtue did not lie in her physical beauty but in her mind. This view of virtue would increase her modesty. Moreover, men must be taught that chastity is as much a male virtue as a female virtue. Wollstonecraft decried the double standard that advocated women's role be placed in the sexual realm while simultaneously demanding chastity for women and celebrating libertinism in men. She proclaimed that men and women with cultivated minds who were fully educated about their bodies would use reason to order their emotions. They would be chaste, modest, and generally virtuous.

Wollstonecraft on Gender Neutral Education

As vehemently as Wollstonecraft insisted that all human beings are equal in their rational potential, Wollstonecraft admitted and decried the apparent distinction of the sexes. Indeed, Wollstonecraft denounced the women of her age as pale, weak, and sentimental creatures striving for beauty, obedience, and other childish virtues. This shocking degradation of human beings was due, not to women's lack of rational potential, but to women's lack of nourishment by society. As an *empiricist*, Wollstonecraft believed that humans learn by experience. Thus, a human child who was raised to be the appealing object of a lover and the obedient servant of a master would develop these attributes and no more. The potential to reason and master one's sentimentality can be only be realized through education.

Most modern liberal thinkers were strong advocates of education for all citizens. Wollstonecraft, well read in Enlightenment education theory, argued that the foundation of equal rights for women lay in public co-education. Like other liberals, she maintained that the cost of private education

18. Wollstonecraft, *Vindication of the Rights of Women*, 77.
19. Ibid.

created class divisions that were unnatural. Because human beings, by nature, require education to foster their natural rational abilities, differences
in education result in differences in abilities and virtues. Wollstonecraft
insisted that this is the key to the apparent differences between the sexes.
She knew how common was her own experience as a girl pulled out of
grade school in order that her parents might save money for her brothers'
education. In addition, she was well aware from her experience as a governess that the education given to wealthy girls was usually quite different than
that given to wealthy boys. Worse, the French philosopher, Jean Jacques
Rousseau, whose popular *Emile* had impressed Wollstonecraft and many
others as an enlightened model of education, had advocated a radically different approach to girls' education than that for boys. Rousseau had insisted
that "man and woman are not and ought not to be constituted in the same
way in either character or temperament, . . . they ought not to have the
same education."[20] The girl was to be educated to be an object of delight
for the boy. She was to be taught how to dress, how to enamor, and how to
please her future husband, while the boy was to be taught to value his own
enriched intellect as the source of his autonomy. Wollstonecraft knew how
culturally accurate Rousseau's description of gendered education was and
believed the only antidote was co-education of the sexes.

In response, Wollstonecraft proposed a model for quality public co-
educational day schools that would nourish the minds of both girls and
boys for democracy. Her arguments for the necessity of public education
copied that of other liberals. Education needed to be equally accessible
for both rich and poor; and citizens of a democracy needed to experience
friendships with children from all social-economic classes. In addition,
Wollstonecraft argued against both boarding schools and private tutors in
order to recommend day schools which would allow children to enjoy the
natural platoon of family life while still being exposed to the diversity of
ideas in society.

Wollstonecraft's arguments for co-education were rooted in her
philosophical belief that the mind has no sex. In her opinion, boys and
girls needed the same type of education, including physical education and
sexual education, in order to become rational masters of their emotions
and sentiments. This would enable girls to grow into able mothers who
would be less likely to abuse their children and who would be more likely to
raise healthy children with good character. Moreover, boys educated beside

20. Rousseau, *Emile*, 363.

girls would learn to see girls as fellow human beings rather than as a different species. This would encourage modesty and chastity in both sexes as well as promote healthy and respectful friendships between the sexes. The healthier friendships and mutual respect would lead to the flourishing of happy marriages and a lower divorce rate.

Further, Wollstonecraft, in *A Vindication of the Rights of Women*, advocated career preparation for adolescents in secondary school who were from the middle and lower classes. She believed upper class children should experience a co-educational liberal arts education to prepare them for their lives amongst the educated elite. Lower and middle class children would be exposed to this same education in the morning, but practicality demanded they be prepared in vocational training in the afternoon. This was as important for girls as for boys. Those girls who were unable to marry or who were widowed would then be able to be self-reliant. This would reduce prostitution and poverty.

Feminist Merits of Wollstonecraft's Theory of Woman

Wollstonecraft was not a political idealist but very much a realist and a utilitarian in her *Vindication*. Thus, her arguments for education of girls were founded on the ways this education would improve women as wives and mothers. The greatest benefits of education women for society, according to Wollstonecraft, would be their abilities to be rational partners to their husbands and intelligent teachers of their children. However, Wollstonecraft claimed that society might receive more benefits to society if it created more roles for women. Moreover, the last page of her *Vindication* announces "Let woman share the rights, and she will emulate the virtues of a man."[21]

While *A Vindication of the Rights of Women* stops short of advocating full economic and political equality for women, Wollstonecraft was clear that this was her ultimate goal. She recognized that this short book had to lay the foundations for this goal by first making a philosophical argument for the equality of men and women and second creating a framework of education that would make this natural equality into an apparent equality. Wollstonecraft claimed in her introduction that this work's goal was "to render my sex more respectable members of society."[22] But in her prefatory

21. Wollstonecraft, *Vindication of the Rights of Women*, 226.

22. Ibid., 31.

letter to M. Tallyrand-Perigord she clearly indicated that it is "inconsistent and unjust to subjugate women" and that men who continue to do so show themselves to be tyrants who "will ever undermine morality."[23]

While the governments of France, the United States of America, and England did not grant political emancipation to women for another 130 years after the publication of *A Vindication of The Rights of Women,* Wollstonecraft's arguments for the equality of men and women were foundational for the feminist movements in all three of these nations. In addition, her views on education for all children, especially her views on physical education for girls, continue to be influential in educational theory today.

Women of the American Suffrage Movement

> If particuliar care and attention is not paid to the Ladies we are determined to foment a Rebelion, and will not hold ourselves bound by any Laws in which we have no voice or Representation.
>
> —ABIGAIL ADAMS[24]

> It matters not whether the solitary voyager is man or woman; nature, having endowed them equally leaves them to their own skill and judgment in the hour of danger, and if not equal to the occasion alike they perish.
>
> —ELIZABETH CADY STANTON[25]

The American woman's suffrage movement is often characterized as a movement beginning in the mid-nineteenth century. However, it is important to note that from the very origin of the United States women were arguing that they be included in the new constitution. Abigail Adams's famous request that those men declaring independence ought to "remember the ladies"[26]

23. Ibid., 23.

24. "Letter from Abigail to John Adams on March 31, 1776," in Rossi, *Feminist Papers,* 11.

25. Stanton, "The Solitude of Self,: *Stanton/Anthony: Correspondence,* 248.

26. See Adams, "Letter from Abigail to John Adams on March 31 1776," in Rossi, *Feminist Papers,* 10–11. ". . . by the way in the new Code of Laws which I suppose it will be necessary for you to make I desire you would Remember the Ladies, and be more generous and favourable to them than your ancestors. Do not put such unlimited power into the hands of the Husbands. Remember all Men would be tyrants if they could. If particular care and attention is not paid to the Ladies we are determined to foment a

was not a singular demand. Excluding women from full citizenship was a decision not an oversight. Even at the time of its ratification, many Americans noted that the disenfranchisement of women, like the institution of slavery, was a logically and morally incoherent part of the otherwise liberal democratic document that was the United States Constitution. For the first 144 years of the United States history, women fought for their inclusion in the constitutional promise of the protection of the inalienable rights of mankind.

Like Wollstonecraft, many of these women stressed the importance for equal education for girls. These American women put a special emphasis on the necessity of education for the American ideal of self-reliance. Elizabeth Cady Stanton wrote in *The Solitude of Self,* "The strongest reason for giving women all the opportunities for higher education, for the full development of her faculties, her forces of mind . . . is the solitude and personal responsibility of her own individual life."[27] Like Wollstonecraft, they argued for more co-educational opportunities. As Susan B. Anthony said in a speech in 1856, "Everything which relates to the operations of the mind is common to both sexes. . . . It certainly will not injure them to use chalk at the same blackboard."[28] But importantly, even with the lack of educational opportunities available to women at the time, many American women believed women were already ready for full legal, political, and economic equality with men.

This equality was necessary to right the wrongs in society in eighteenth and nineteenth century America, particularly as they affected women and children. At this time husbands alone had the right to divorce, and fathers had sole ownership of children. Dying men could give guardianship to anyone they chose. No legal prerogative was given to the living mother. Men could consign their wives to mental institutions against their will. Women who earned a wage had to entrust their money to their husbands, even if their husbands were known alcoholics or gamblers. This legal duty to absolute obedience to the husband was a key complaint amongst eighteenth and nineteenth century supporters of women's rights. Many suffragists wanted married women to have the right to own property separately from their

---

Rebelion, and will not hold ourselves bound by any Laws in which we have no voice or Representation."

27. Stanton, "The Solitude of Self," *Stanton/Anthony: Correspondence,* 247.

28. Sherr, *Failure Is Impossible,* 23.

husbands, to divorce abusive husbands, and to legally sue for custody of their own children.

In the mid-nineteenth century, many Northern women were drawn to protest slavery and the wars of aggression that expanded slavery. These issues in addition to the matters of public drunkenness and legalized domestic abuse drew women in large numbers to abolition, pacifism, and the temperance movement. But abolitionists, pacifists, and supporters of temperance found that their inability to vote greatly hampered them in their moral duty to stand up for what they believed was right.

Thus, in 1848 the fight for women's suffrage became an official movement rising from the First Convention for Women's Rights, which was held in Seneca Falls, New York. Key to the argument of those in the movement was the understanding of woman as human being first, woman second. The theory of gender neutrality claims that a woman's role as human supersedes any gendered role. Most of the women argued for suffrage from the point of view that women and men are similar in all qualities of mind and thus have equal moral rights and responsibilities. Further, while most of the suffragists were married and had children, many advocated that womanhood did not require motherhood.

Of course, there were also women who thought that their role as mothers specifically gave them a better perspective to bring to the ballot. These women argued that voting women would bring a moral compass to the country. Julia Ward Howe and Susan B. Anthony both spoke of the cruelty of expecting mothers to bring up gentle and moral sons in a political society of violence and greed, a society that they were legally unable to temper. Importantly, Susan B. Anthony argued that women's moral gentleness was cultural rather than natural. Thus, given political equality, women could teach this virtue to men. Once men and women were in regular political conversation, Anthony believed, the best ideals would emerge in both sexes equally. She explained, "From the cradle the children of the manly woman and the womanly man of the twentieth century will be trained in the principles of good government. They will be taught that might is not right . . . that arbitration rather than human slaughter should settle all international difficulties."[29]

The American women who fought for suffrage were convinced of the rightness of the liberal political philosophy that had founded the United States. The suffragists used the American Constitution and the ideals

29. Ibid., 300.

that produced it as their foundational philosophy even as they sought to amend the document. To the New York legislature Elisabeth Cady Stanton explained,

> [W]e, who have guided great movements of charity, established missions, edited journals, published works on history, economy, and statistics, who have governed nations, led armies, filled the professor's chair, taught philosophy and mathematics to the savants of our age, discovered planets, piloted ships across the sea, are denied the most sacred rights of citizens because for 'sooth we came not into this republic crowned with the dignity of manhood! ... You who have declared that all men were created equal—that governments derive their just powers from the consent of the government, would willingly build up an aristocracy that places the ignorant and vulgar above the educated and refined ... an Aristocracy that would raise the sons above the mothers that bore them.[30]

Importantly, while many of the nineteenth century suffragists were abolitionists, pacifists, and temperance supporters, the women who campaigned for women's right to vote were numerous and diverse. Elizabeth Cady Stanton, Susan B. Anthony, Lucretia Mott, Sarah Grimké, Maria Stewart, Ida Wells, Anna Julia Cooper, Margaret Fuller, Charlotte Gilman, Lucy Stone, Julia Ward Howe, and Sojourner Truth are just a few of those remembered for their activism for the cause of women's suffrage in the nineteenth century.

At the end of the civil war, slavery was abolished and black men were given full citizenship. Yet, the women's suffrage movement failed to make significant progress. Although a handful of States gave women the vote in local school elections and a few Western States gave women the vote in all elections, the vast majority of women in the United States continued without any representation in government. Many of the women who had stood to speak in Seneca Falls in 1848 lived long lives and died without ever legally casting a ballot.

In the early twentieth century a new set of tactics and a new philosophy about suffrage arose—that of the *new suffragists*. These women were fueled not by a specific issue, such as temperance, abolition, or pacifism, but by the issue of suffrage itself. Whether to concentrate on specific issues or simply suffrage was a fracturing debate in the movement separating the old and

---

30. Stanton, "From the Address to the Legislature of New York on February 14, 1854," *Stanton/Anthony: Correspondence*, 45.

the new suffragists. Many of the younger women who led this movement were more highly educated than their foremothers. For example, Crystal Eastman was a Vassar graduate with a Masters in sociology from Columbia and a degree from New York Law School. Alice Paul had a Masters degree in economics and political science as well as a law degree. Her doctoral dissertation was titled *Towards Equality*. In addition, the new suffragists were more willing to engage in civil disobedience. Certainly, Susan B. Anthony had been arrested for casting a ballot in 1872, and other nineteenth-century women had done likewise. But the new suffragists found civil disobedience to be a more fundamental and necessary part of the movement. Indeed Lucy Burns first met Alice Paul in a police station in London where they had both been brought after demonstrating for women's rights with British Women.

In 1913, the new suffragists hosted a suffrage parade in Washington DC on the same day as Woodrow Wilson's inauguration. Many of the older suffragists marched with the younger women. Of particular note, Ida Wells, who had been actively working for suffrage and for African American rights for decades, used her own body to integrate the parade despite a desire by some suffragists to segregate black women to the back of the march. Almost half a million spectators watched 8000 marchers, twenty-six floats, and ten bands. Wilson found his entrance to the city marked by empty streets. Next, boycotts and demonstrations marked the new suffragists push for equal rights after the National Woman's Party began in 1916. In 1917, many of the women, including Paul and Burns, were arrested for protesting in front of the White House. Stories of their abuse by interrogations, beatings, and force feedings were published in the media. As information about the treatment of the women spread, support for suffrage increased. By 1920, the amendment was fully ratified and women were given the right to vote across the United States.

After the passing of the 19th amendment that recognized women's right to vote, many of the suffragists, including Alice Paul, began to work for an Equal Rights Amendment assuring that women would receive full economic, legal, and political equality with men. Almost a century later, American women still have not seen the ratification of such an amendment. One of the major reasons cited for the failure of the Equal Rights Amendment has been the disagreement amongst American citizens concerning whether men and women are complementary or similar in natures. Those who argue the similarity of men and women continue to advocate for equal legal rights, responsibilities, and protections for all citizens regardless of sex.

Thinking Woman: Sojourner Truth

S'pose a man's mind holds a quart, an a woman's do n't hold but a pint; ef her pint is full, it's as good as his quart.[31]

Ef women want any rights more'n dey's got, why don't dey jes' *take 'em*, an' not be talkin' about it.[32]

Biography

Sojourner Truth, considered in her own day to be one of the most powerful voices in the abolition and suffrage movements, is an especially important thinker in defining the American feminist understanding of a woman. Susan B. Anthony once said, "Sojourner combined in herself the two most hated elements of humanity. She was black and she was a woman. And all the insults that could be cast upon color and sex were hurled at her."[33] But despite this hatred and the lack of resources and education that it caused, Sojourner Truth had a remarkable ability to logically and forcefully make an argument and a self-confident poise in public speaking that enthralled audiences. More importantly, her understanding of the nature and natural rights of women was distinctive among the American suffragists. She had not read the liberal philosophers but had come to her philosophy of women from her own life experiences and her own reasoning. Moreover, her experiences as a slave demonstrated that the idea of femininity as an essential part of womanhood was a cultural myth. She believed that rights for blacks and women were endowed by the Creator. Thus, women's rights were not gifts to be begged from men. Women's rights were given by God. She was publically praised by Susan B. Anthony, Harriet Beecher Stowe, and Abraham Lincoln. Sojourner Truth, who never learned to read or write, dictated the *Narrative* of her life to Olive Gilbert. Gilbert, who edited and editorialized the *Narrative*, first published the text in 1850. Truth narrated

---

31. Truth, *Narrative of Sojourner Truth*, 112.

32. Ibid., 112.

33. Quoted in Sherr, *Failure Is Impossible*, 31.

other incidents in the *Book of Life*, which was later added to that *Narrative* and published in full in 1884, the year after her death. Earlier, obviously less complete, versions had been published in 1853, 1855, 1875, 1878, and 1881. The life and words of Sojourner Truth were understood to be important while she was still alive and continue to be an important voice in feminism today.

Truth was born a slave in New York and suffered the effects of slavery and racism her whole life. As a slave, Sojourner Truth was never told her birthday. Her parents did not have a calendar that would have allowed them to mark the year. Historians believe she was born around 1797. She was born in Ultster County, New York and named Isabella. She later changed her name to Sojourner. Her mother, whom she called Mau Mau Bett, and her Father, whom she called Bomefree, told her that they had born many other children before her. These were taken from them and sold by their Dutch master, Colonel Hardenbergh. Truth recounts that her parents would repeat often the tearful story of her brother and sister, ages five and three, being sold and taken away while she was still in the cradle. Truth often found her mother in tears thinking of her children and not knowing how or where they were.

A slave child was considered an item of property. Hardenbergh died while Truth was still an infant; and she and her parents and ten to twelve other slaves were inherited by his son Charles Hardenbergh. A few years later this son decided to sell much of his property including his slaves. Truth's father was considered too old and infirm to sell; so it was determined that the cheapest course of action was to free Mau Mau Bett on the condition that she take care of her husband. Relieved to remain together in their old age in a state of freedom, Truth's parents mourned as their last two children were sold on the auction block. Truth and a flock of sheep were sold together for one hundred dollars to John Nealy, an English speaking man who had never previously owned a slave but was eager to fit in with the Dutch slave owners of New York. Truth, who spoke only Dutch was beaten by Nealy for not knowing English. Generally, she recounted the time with Nealy as being one of trial and abuse. Truth explains in her *Narrative* that she refrained from giving explicit information on the treatment of slaves because she did not think people would believe the degree of horror. But, she did show the deep and ugly scars from Nealy's beatings at anti-slavery conventions in order to give the audience some understanding of the torture slaves endured. After a few years as Nealy's slave, in 1810 she was sold to John Dumont. In Dumont's custody, she grew into adulthood and remained until 1828 when she escaped.

In her time serving Dumont, Truth fell in love with a slave named Robert. But Robert's master forbade the union claiming it would not increase his property but unfairly increase Dumont's. Later, Dumont had her marry a slave of his choosing, Thomas. Thomas had been married to two other wives who had both been sold away from him. Together Truth and Thomas had a number of children who "were laid on the altar of slavery."[34] Truth spoke of the pain of letting her children go hungry while she nursed the white infants of her master and the sad irony of teaching her children to be honest and obedient to a master who stole from them their rights, liberty, and very selves. Worst she recounted the horror of having her children sold as slaves away from her. She hated not knowing where or how they were as they grew to adulthood. Extremely painful was the event when her five-year old son was sold. Dumont had sold him to a Northern man who had subsequently sold him to his brother, Solomon Gedney. Gedney then sold the child to his son-in-law who was moving to the South. Truth understood what this meant. Changes in New York law meant that the boy was legally free under New York law. Under a grandfather clause, he was obliged to serve his master until ago twenty-five. But the master was not legally allowed to sell him to a state where slavery remained legal. The boy could not be sold to a Southerner legally. Truth was outraged at this breach of law by Dumont, both Gedney brothers, and the son-in-law, Mr. Fowler.

Another breach of law came soon after. The State of New York had passed many resolutions outlawing slavery since Truth's birth, but there were always grandfather clauses that allowed owners to keep their slaves a little longer. These conditions were often used illegally against slaves who were supposed to be freed. Abolitionists became vocal about these clauses. Truth, even as a slave, was able to learn of the laws. In 1827, Truth knew the law claimed her legally free. Yet, her master refused to grant her freedom despite a previous promise he had made to free her. She claimed that the pain of another promise being broken in regard to freedom was too terrible to bear. She decided to try to escape. However, she remained and did the hardest part of the fall work for Dumont before taking her freedom into her own hands. One morning under the cover of the darkness before dawn, she walked away from Dumont's property to a home of Levi Rowe, a known abolitionist whom she thought likely to befriend her. Rowe did help her. He

34. Truth, *Narrative of Sojourner Truth*, 25.

sent her to the home of two abolitionists, Isaac Van Wagener and his wife who agreed to house her. When her former owner came to reclaim her, the couple paid Dumont a fee to buy Truth and then immediately emancipated her.

Once her own freedom was secured, Truth began to search for her son who had been illegally sold to a Southerner. She found and approached the wife of Solomon Gedney in order to condemn the selling of her legally free son to a Southerner. Mrs. Gedney mocked Truth for her interest in a mere child especially a black child. Gedney said that her own daughter had been married off to this same Southerner, but she had been forbidden to cry about that. Truth found the analogy of marriage and slavery to be utterly offensive at the time. Truth was not deterred. She hired a lawyer, borrowing money from Quaker friends for the fees he charged. The lawyer won the case. Truth was able to have her son returned to her. The child was scarred terribly from physical and emotional abuse at the hands of Fowler. Sadly, Truth noted, Fowler later violently killed his wife in a drunken rage. Truth recounted how she held Mrs. Gedney in her arms for hours while the woman wept for her own child.

At about the time her son was returned to her, she decided that her name Isabella was a mark of captivity. She explained,

> My name was Isabella; but when I left the house of bondage, I left everything behind. I wa'n't goin' to keep nothin' of Egypt on me, an' so I went to the Lord an' asked him to give me a new name. And the Lord gave me Sojourner, because I was to travel up an' down the land, showin' the people their sins, an' bein' a sign unto them. Afterward I told the Lord I wanted another name, 'cause everybody else had two names; and the Lord gave me Truth, because I was to declare the truth to the people.[35]

Truth's faith that she was named and given value by God was an anchor in her life. She proclaimed that no human had ever told her as a child that she had any worth or deserved any rights. Instead she recounted visions of Jesus coming to her and telling her of her worth and the absolute wrongness of slavery. She recounted a particular vision at a field empty of corn where the Lord showed her that a weasel had eaten all the corn. Then in the same vision she saw the Constitution empty of rights for her. When she asked where her rights were, the Lord replied that a weasel had eaten them. She was convinced that God gave rights, not the Constitution. She

35. Ibid., 111.

began giving speeches against slavery at camp meetings, church meetings, and conventions throughout New York at a time when few women spoke at these sessions. Over six feet tall, with a loud and powerful voice, Truth was a favorite speaker amongst both abolitionists and suffragists.

In 1849 her former master Dumont called to her to visit him. At that visit he confessed that he now knew "slavery was the wickedest thing in the world, the greatest curse the earth had ever felt. . ."[36] She saw it as a confession although not an apology. Although she insisted that the evil of slavery was obvious to anyone, she, also, recognized that reason and exposure could change the hearts and minds of men and women who did not see the obvious truth. This must have helped fuel her lectures for the next thirty years.

As she continued to speak, knowledge of Truth spread. In 1863 Harriet Beecher Stowe published an article about her titled "The Libyan Sibyl" in the *Atlantic Monthly*. In 1864 she had an interview with Abraham Lincoln at which he apologized for moving so slowly to end slavery. She responded, "Oh wait, chile! Have patience! It takes a great while to turn about this great ship of state."[37] She also called him "the best president who has ever taken the seat."[38] But he acknowledged that it was merely luck and the hand of God, which gave him an opportunity other president's simply did not have. He also claimed to have been inspired by Truth long before he was president.

After the civil war and the final abolition of slavery, Truth continued to work for equal rights for blacks and for women. Always knowing the exact nature of the law, she strove to use it to her advantage whenever possible. In her *Book of Life,* she spoke of her rule in desegregating streetcars in Maryland. At the time streetcar drivers in Maryland were legally obligated to take black and white passengers without discrimination, but most drivers would not allow black passengers aboard. To change this practice, Truth just began to climb aboard stopped cars and take a seat. While verbal abuse often followed, she would rise to her full height and repeat the letter of the law. When one driver physically shoved her injuring her arm and shoulder, she immediately went to the hospital and to a lawyer. The driver lost his job, and after just a few weeks the streetcars looked like "pepper and salt."[39]

36. Ibid., 96.
37. Ibid., 118.
38. Ibid., 120.
39. Ibid., 126.

She advocated for women's rights at many conventions well into her 80s. She insisted that the protection of women could not be used to justify anti-suffrage legislation since the nation did not have a history of seeking protection for women. After all, slave owners had not protected women slaves. She also worked to find land in the West to create an independent place for freed slaves to make their own living. Until the last three months of her life, she was active and involved politically and intellectually in the movement for equal rights for all people. She died on November 26, 1883 in Battle Creek, Michigan.

Sojourner Truth's Theory of Woman

Truth proclaimed that women and men were not different in nature. In a speech given at the Woman's Rights Convention in Akron Ohio in 1851, Truth proclaimed that intellectually, physically, and emotionally, she was the equal of every man she has known. Her famous "Ain't I a Woman" speech commanded the audience,

> Look at me! Look at my arm! I have plowed, and planted, and gathered into barns, and no man could head me—and aren't I a woman? I could work as much and eat as much as a man, . . . and bear de lash as well—and arn't I a woman?[40]

She reminded the crowd that black women did not get any protection for being female. Indeed, slaves proved women and men can do the same work. This includes intellectual work as well. Like Wollstonecraft, Truth claimed that there is not a difference between men's virtue and women's virtue. There is only human virtue. Even if some women fall short of intellectual ability (as certainly some men do), they should still be allowed to exercise their intellect as much as anyone else.

Rather than acknowledge that Truth had proved the equality of men and women, at one convention a group of men made the claim that Truth was so strong and so clever that she could not be a real woman. They claimed her height, her manner of speaking, and her intellect demonstrated that she was not really female. They demanded that Truth bare her breasts to prove them real. They asked a group of women to be her witnesses. The group of women, horrified by the suggestion, refused to be witnesses to her disrobing. Truth took the accusing men aside and showed her breasts saying she

---

40. Ibid., 92.

would show them to the whole congregation if they desired. Then, she used this opportunity to explain again the unity of male and female natures. Baring her breasts she reminded men that their flesh and strength as infants came from a woman and that most men, white and black, gained their flesh and strength from black women who suckled them. If women and blacks were inferior, those they suckled, whose flesh they had formed, would be inferior too. If men and whites were superior, than those who nourished their bodies must be of a superior nature too.

Using her experiences as a slave often in her speeches, Truth refuted those who suggested women needed special protection as mothers. She pointed out the hypocrisy of those people who said they were interested in protecting women but had never shown interest in protecting slave women. Particularly she refuted the idea that political power would weaken a woman's maternal instincts and love for her children. She argued that nothing can be done to dampen the affection of a mother for a child. If slavery had not destroyed the maternal love in women, certainly the right to vote would not do so. "We has heard a great deal about love at home in de family. Now children, I was a slave and my husband and my children was sold from me . . . .What has 'come of de affection I had for dem?"[41] She denounced those whose real interest was only in protecting the power of wealthy white men. "I tink dat 'twixt de niggers of de Souf and de women at de Norf all a talking' about rights, de white men will be in a fix pretty soon."[42] Truth was fully convinced that both God and reason were on the side of abolition and women's rights.

Indeed, an important part of Truth's argument, like Wollstonecraft's, was her understanding of Scripture. While Truth was illiterate and unable to read the Bible herself, she used scriptural stories she had heard. Arguing against male clergy who claimed Jesus showed preeminence for men by being a man she proclaimed that the story of the Incarnation gives women preeminence. "Den dat little man in black dar, he say women can't have as much rights as man, cause Christ wasn't a woman. Whar did your Christ come from? Whar did your Christ come from? From God and a woman. Man had nothing to do with him."[43] Truth's biographer wrote that the crowd responded in absolute stillness. "Rolling thunder could not have stilled that crowd as did those deep, wonderful tones, as she stood there

41. Ibid., 102.
42. Ibid., 93.
43. Ibid., 92.

with outstretched arms and eyes of fire."[44] Truth, also, used the theological argument against Eve as a rational argument for giving women rights, for if Eve was powerful enough to change the world then women today must be just as powerful. "If de fust woman God ever made was strong enough to turn the world upside down, all 'lone, dese togedder, ought to be able to turn it back and get it right side up again, and now dey is asking to do it, de men better let em."[45]

While Truth used Scripture and claimed to have visions from Christ, her arguments were always rationally based. She cleverly found the logical holes in the arguments of her opponents and made these holes obvious to the audience. Then she would give a more coherent case for the equality of all people regardless of race and sex.

Feminist Merits of Truth's Work

Clearly Truth's speeches and the published book of her *Narrative* and *Book of Life* were a powerful force in the abolition and women's suffrage movements. Standing outside the educated white upper and middle classes she was able to use her experiences to expose the damage of slavery and the hypocrisy of the protection of the feminine. In this way she broadened feminism to include what would later be called *womanism. Womanism* acknowledges the role of race and class in promoting inequality and thus works to end all oppression not just gender oppression. While she died thirty-seven years before women were given the right to vote, her understanding of herself as a full human being regardless of race, sex, or circumstance has been an inspiration. Her words still are used to fight for equal rights for women.

Liberal Feminism and Gender Neutrality in Contemporary Feminism

Amongst some academic feminists, liberal Enlightenment feminism or *first wave feminism*, is often considered outdated and simplistic. However, in contemporary culture, feminism is usually equated with a theory of gender neutrality. A great deal of legal advocacy has been waged and won with this

44. Ibid.
45. Ibid., 93.

view in mind. For example, twentieth- and twenty-first-century divorce laws, inheritance laws, custody laws, and suffrage laws are written in such a way as to avoid discriminating against women as women. In addition, the opportunity for women to attend institutions of higher education has greatly expanded. Currently more women are studying in undergraduate and graduate programs than men. There are policies in place, such as Title IX, that require schools to offer equal opportunities for extra-curricular activities, including sports, for girls as boys. Recent changes in structure in the U.S. military have been made in order to increase equality of opportunity and pay for female and male soldiers. Many Christian, Jewish, and Muslim sects and denominations have changed their rules and structures to allow women as well as men to serve as clergy. In other denominations and sects, women continue to use the theory gender neutrality to advocate for changes of gendered structures.[46] First wave feminism and its theory of gender neutrality radically changed the Western view of woman's nature. This change in the philosophical view of woman changed policy. New policies and increases in opportunity reinforced the asserted view that the differences between women and men are minimal.

Today, while many academic feminists may debate against first wave feminism, many women politicians claim a theory of gender neutrality. This includes some of the major political women of the late twentieth and early twenty-first centuries, including Geraldine Ferraro, Margaret Thatcher, Sandra Day O'Conner, Angela Merkel, Hilary Clinton, and Condoleezza Rice.

Contemporary Liberal Feminism and Women's Leadership:

Recently, Sheryl Sandberg, the COO of Facebook, wrote a popular and controversial book titled *Lean In: Women, Work, and the Will to Lead*. The

---

46. For example, see the argument for ordaining women into the priesthood made by Elisabeth Behr-Sigel, a woman with Lutheran, Jewish, and Orthodox roots. She explained, "Jesus notes sex differences but points to what in each of us is beyond sex, beyond it but raising it up to a higher order" (*Ministry of Women in the Church*, 158). Contemporary theologian Sarah Hinlicky Wilson expands: "In truth, women are persons and men are persons because the Father, the Son, and the Holy Spirit are Persons too." Hinlicky Wilson, *Woman, Women, and the Priesthood*, 165. As Astell and Wollstonecraft did, Hinlicky Wilson believes that it is as a person not as a woman or a man that the individual stands before God.

book is largely a work of a contemporary feminist with a theory of gender neutrality. She writes,

> A truly equal world would be one where women ran half our countries and companies and men ran half our homes. I believe this would be a better world. . . . When more people get in the race, more records will be broken. And the achievements will extend beyond those individuals to benefit us all.[47]

Sandberg's position is that humans are essentially equal in mind. Of course, like the liberal Enlightenment feminists, she acknowledges that women's experiences and bodies do affect their lives and choice. But ultimately Sandberg claims that they should have all the same rights and responsibilities as men. The benefit to society is in increasing the pool of qualified applicants, not necessarily in providing a different gendered framework. On one hand, she fully expects women in power will take women's bodies into consideration in a way men have not. She wrote that she herself has advocated for special parking for pregnant women, flexibility for nursing mothers, and more women's bathrooms. Sandberg clearly assumes most women will want to marry and many will want to have children. She believes equality for women will have to include changes that allow women to lead as mothers. On the other hand, as a liberal feminist, she does not think that there is a great deal that separates the roles of father and mother other than cultural ideals that can be changed. Indeed, she suggests that women are capable of full economic and political equality if they are educated properly. And she insists that men are capable of full domestic equality if they are educated by experience and child-rearing literature. She urges women not to see motherhood and career as contradictory vocations. Particularly, she urges women not to "lean back" from leadership positions because they worry that they might not later be able to handle it if they have children. Her point is that it is not actual motherhood that keeps women from leadership roles, but simply the idea of motherhood as a woman's sole vocation that keeps women from taking on leadership positions.

Sandberg's most prominent argument is that women need to see virtue similarly defined for them as well as men. As Wollstonecraft did, Sandberg decries the teaching of the virtues of beauty and obedience for girls and intelligence and leadership for boys. This is a twenty-first-century problem as well as an eighteenth-century problem, according to Sandberg, who

47. Sandberg, *Lean In*, 7.

names several studies that suggest that teachers and parents demand more obedience from girls than boys while expecting more physical dexterity and critical thinking from boys than girls.[48] In addition she notes items in popular culture like "Smart like Daddy" onesies marketed to parents of boy babies and "Pretty like Mommy" onesies marketed for girls.[49] The result is a dominant culture does not expect women in leadership roles and women who are cultivated not to expect leadership in themselves. Adult women doubt their own abilities, constantly fear they are not really as smart as the men beside them, and too often take a step back from leadership roles out of their own internalized insecurity. Even when women are able to master their own insecurity the cultural expectation of two separate virtues for the genders causes problems in their ability to lead. While men who are successful in business are considered likable and generally successful, women who are successful in business are considered selfish and unappealing. This is not a casual observance on Sandberg's part but the published results of a carefully crafted study in which a Columbia Business School professor and a New York University professor tested perceptions of men and women in the workplace by asking students to evaluate the biography and resume of a real-life entrepreneur named Heidi Roizen. Some students were told the name of the entrepreneur was Heidi, but the others were told the name was Howard. While both students rated the resume as competent, those that thought they were rating "Howard" found him appealing, and those that thought they were rating "Heidi" found her "selfish" and not "the type of person you would want to hire."[50] The studies Sandberg quotes suggest that contemporary media would call Wollstonecraft a hyena in petticoats just as the eighteenth-century journalists did. They would also doubt the real femininity of Truth just as the nineteenth-century commentators did.

As long as women have to choose between being a successful person and a successful woman, there is not true equality according to Sandberg and any who hold a theory of gender neutrality. Sandberg explains,

> If a woman is competent, she does not seem nice enough. If a woman seems really nice, she is considered more nice than competent. Since people want to hire and promote those who are

48. See the examples cited in Sandberg, *Lean In*, 19, one of which is Halim and Ruble, "Gender Identity and Stereotyping in Early and Middle Childhood."

49. See Gray "Gymboree Onesies," as cited in Sandberg, *Lean In*, 19.

50. See McGinnand and Tempest, "Heidi Roizen Harvard Business School Case Study #9–800–228," as cited in Sandberg, *Lean In*, 39–40.

both competent and nice, this creates a huge stumbling block for women. Acting in stereotypically feminine ways makes it difficult to reach for the same opportunities as men, but defying expectations and reaching for those opportunities leads to being judged as undeserving and selfish.[51]

Sandberg, as Wollstonecraft and Truth did, believes that reason is the foundation for all arguments, whether made by men or women. But Sandberg does not expect culture to change just because the rational argument says it should. Thus, she gives specific negotiating tactics for women so that they can appear as gentle leaders. Unlike gender essentialists, the liberal feminists do not believe that women are, by nature, more gentle leaders. But Sandberg suggests women can and must use the cultural stereotype to achieve power and then, when in power, change the stereotypes. She suggests once there is a quorum of women in power the stereotypes will change and women can finally be themselves as leaders rather than trying to straddle two opposing virtues of obedience and leadership. Until then her main line is "Gender-specific expectations remain self-fulfilling."[52] Her goal is to eradicate these gender-specific expectations from her readers' minds in order that they gain gender-neutral expectations.

Problems with Liberal Feminism and Gender Neutrality

The response to Sandberg's *Lean In* by contemporary academic feminists has been often negative. These responses generally correspond to twenty-first century feminism's refutation of what has been termed "first wave feminism" as being "simplistic" and "long ago challenged by visionary feminist thinkers."[53] The critiques of liberal Enlightenment feminism have two major foci. The first is a critique of the liberal Enlightenment itself. The second is a critique of the theory of gender neutrality.

Liberal Enlightenment feminism, like liberal Enlightenment political theory generally, advocates for democracy and a truly free market as the best protection of the inalienable rights of persons. But critics suggest that the very structures of the liberal Enlightenment are male-biased and part of "imperialist white supremacist capitalist patriarchy."[54] Further, some femi-

51. Sandberg, *Lean In,* 43.
52. Ibid., 114.
53. hooks, "Dig Deep: Beyond *Lean In.*"
54. Ibid.

nists have decried the absence of the categories of race and socio-economic class in first wave feminist thought. They suggest that twentieth- and twenty-first-century liberal advocates of gender neutrality, like the ante-Enlightenment thinkers, only advocate for gender equality within their current socio-economic class structure without rethinking that structure.

The reader might consider Christine de Pizan and Mary Astell as well as possibly Alice Paul and certainly Sheryl Sandberg. These women wanted women to have the same rights as men in their social classes. They were advocates of gender equality, but not advocates of further social movement as feminists. Alice Paul and the new suffragists made a conscious decision not to work for social reform, pacifism, or any other social movement until women had the vote. Paul's position was to advocate for political equality so that women could make changes to the system as part of the system. However, after 1920, Paul spent the rest of her life advocating for social causes that applied specifically to women.

Moreover, the reader might also consider Mary Wollstonecraft, Sojourner Truth, Susan B. Anthony, or Elisabeth Cady Stanton. These women were revolutionaries advocating for liberal democracy as a structural change. They did not just want the same rights as men in their class, they wanted the men in their classes and the classes beneath them to have equal rights with others. Wollstonecraft advocated for the French Revolution and for revolutionary policies in England in terms of political and economic restructuring, beginning with public education for all classes. Truth, Anthony, Stanton, and the majority of the nineteenth-century suffragists began their crusade for women's rights with their crusade to abolish slavery. Truth did not want to be treated like a male slave. She wanted to be treated like a male citizen. And Anthony, Stanton, Howe, and others wanted the vote, in part, in order to end slavery and unjust wars.

Yet, these women did believe in the ideals of the liberal Enlightenment. They believed that the American Constitution had a solid foundation, and they wanted the United States to live up to its ideals. While many European and American feminists in the nineteenth and twentieth centuries did advocate for socialism, and even communism, as a more just economic system than laissez-faire capitalism, most did so on the basis of reason and liberal political ideals rather than on the basis of being feminist. Also, while many of the nineteenth-century suffragists were abolitionists, many of them did not understand the full implications of racism for women of color. Those who call themselves second and third wave feminists often claim that this is a flaw in first wave feminism. These next wave feminists believe that capitalism is predatory on women and women's bodies and that feminism should fight to end all oppression.

The second critique of liberal enlightenment feminism is a critique of the theory of gender neutrality. This critique suggests that feminism must not underestimate the role of the gendered body and the gendered mind. Twentieth- and twenty-first-century thinkers highlighted in the first chapter such as Edith Stein, Virginia Miller, and Evelyn Fox Keller assert that gender neutrality often leads to an under-evaluation of women's specific natural differences. In the previous chapter, their arguments for the necessity of gender essentialism in science and health care were presented. Another place this argument is waged is in athletics. Many first wave feminists argued for physical education and an increase in women's athletic opportunities as part of gender equality. And while no one could deny the great strides women athletes have made in the last one hundred years,[55] very few feminists are asking that gender neutrality be the rule in the Olympics. Clearly women and men need separate but equal opportunities in sports, say gender essentialists. This is true in many other realms, according to the critics of gender neutrality. Giving both men and women the same rights and obligations does not actually give them equality because what often looks like gender neutrality is actually male biased. For example, giving unwed fathers and unwed mothers equal rights towards custody ignores both the role of pregnancy for the mother's body and the way societal and economic structures give the female a disadvantage in court in terms of income and independence. Also, failure to take the female body's needs into consideration leads to inequality in education and in the work place, according to this critique.

Other critics claim that the first wave thinkers' main mistake was to ignore how gendered experience affects the minds of women and men. These critics claim that liberal feminists were naïve to expect that political and even economic equality would create real equality without a radical change in the way culture genders persons. Of course, Wollstonecraft, particularly, was interested in changing culture by changing the nature of education. But many feminists today believe that she radically underestimated how much

55. For example, the women's mile record holder in 1954 barely broke the five-minute mile. Today the women's mile record is 4:16. Compare this to the men's record. In 1954 the first man broke the four-minute mile. Since then only sixteen seconds have been shaved off, compared to forty-four seconds by women. See Rosenbaum, "Fastest Mile Times."

women are formed by the way culture treats them as women. Some critics believe, thus, culture must be changed in order to be more truly gender neutral. Others believe that women's way of thinking must be embraced. For example, Carol Gilligan and Nel Noddings say that women's experience as caretakers must be taken into account when women make moral judgments. These feminists argue that the ethics of justice is very different from an ethics of care. They believe that culture needs to be reformed to consider the feminine perspective.

An additional critique of liberal feminism's gender theory is that it misunderstands gender in seeking gender neutrality. The argument is made by Judith Butler, Donna Haraway, Angela Davis, and bell hooks among others. They claim that most first wave feminists saw the world as divided between heterosexual women and men. In general, the expectations for women to be wives and mothers are still intact in their arguments. There is not room for those who find themselves outside the gender binary, according to this critique.

The critiques against liberal Enlightenment feminist are many and varied. While some argue against modern liberalism as such, many argue against the theory of gender neutrality and the concept of the mind having no sex, race, or class.

Conclusions

While first wave feminism has fallen out of favor for some feminists in the contemporary academy, it is still the type of feminism most easily recognized in common culture. Founded on the idea that every individual stands as an individual with rights and responsibilities, liberal Enlightenment feminism promoted education and equal opportunity for all. Most women in the movement believed that the natural light of human reason would reveal and fight injustice when it was nourished in all humans not just in men. By promoting education, individual thought, and the protections to act on this thought, women believed that society would progress. But more importantly, they believed that whether society progressed or regressed women should be an equal part of that society.

While many of the critiques of the theory of gender neutrality criticize the lack of specific political or social goals beyond equality before the law, this may indeed be a benefit. Certainly, the critique is apt that gender neutrality without full gender equality will harm women. For example, in the absence of an equal pay for equal work law expecting men and women to have the same opportunity for economic well-being is simply unfair. Using economic factors to rate the success of a person, or the fitness of a parent, will be biased against women as successful or fit. But it is just such inequalities that first wave feminism sought to neutralize. Other political and social views concerning capitalism, socialism, universal health care, reproductive women's rights, and even racism differ among women.

Feminists who hold a theory of gender neutrality advocate for reason, not gender, as the ground for all arguments. While reason, itself, has been criticized as too narrow and too parochial a ground, thinkers like Wollstonecraft advocated that the use of mind includes the use of feeling and sentiment. Moral education requires not only logic, but broad experience with nature and society in order to foster the growth of moral sentiments. Thus, Wollstonecraft might be said to argue that there is no real shift between an ethics of justice and an ethics of care, for true justice must include care. Most importantly, this is true for both men and women. If one divides these two between the genders, one will have a care-less male ruler class, and an overly emotional, unordered female servant class. Neither genders nor their society will be served by such a structure. For Wollstonecraft, and those that followed in her tradition, the key was reason as the ordering principal of the mind. Despite her own gendered experience as a daughter, sister, governess, caretaker, lover, mother, and wife, she believed that the ordering powers of reason are not gendered. Indeed, it is because the mind has no sex that there is a common foundation for all members of society to discuss issues that affect them.

In contrast, those who believe that women, because they are women, must argue for one side or the other risk dividing feminism so deeply that the word no longer has meaning. Alice Paul famously once said, "I never doubted that equal rights was the right direction. Most reforms, most problems are complicated. But to me there is nothing complicated about ordinary equality."[56]

---

56. Alice Paul, "Interview, 1972" in Carol et al., *Alice Paul Biography*.

3

Gender Existentialism

One is not born a woman, but rather becomes a woman.

—SIMONE DE BEAUVOIR[1]

When parents first bring a new baby into their home, the clothes, the toys, and the nursery décor often announce the infant's gender. This is often true even when the parents themselves claim to have a theory of gender neutrality. The surrounding culture and market proclaim to the parent that gender should dictate the possessions and surroundings of the tiny person. Some parents, of course, might take a stand on gender neutrality in the nursery and strive to find gender neutral toys, clothing, and decorations. Often these parents will realize that what they defined as gender neutral has been labeled as masculine by the dominant culture. These parents will discover that culture in the West defines non-gendered experience as masculine and gendered experience as feminine. This realization leads some thinkers to consider that all humans, despite the hopes of Enlightenment feminists, are still forced into a culturally constructed gender binary. Fairy tales, religion, marketing, and the media influence children to become their gendered roles. The theory that gender is a cultural construct that radically affects the way a human person acts, thinks, and sees himself or herself is called *gender existentialism*.

1. Beauvoir, *Second Sex,* 267.

This chapter is an exploration of what a theory of gender existentialism says about being a woman. This view of gender is held in what is often called *second wave feminism*.[2] In contrast to first wave feminists who held a theory of gender neutrality, second wave feminists, or gender existentialists, proclaim that their gender affects their relationships, their roles in society, and their identities. But unlike gender essentialists, gender existentialists believe that gender is not innate, natural, or essential. Rather they claim that gender is a cultural construct created by social (and often market driven) values. Thus, gender can be deconstructed and analyzed by women who wish to find their authentic selves beneath the mask of gender.

What Is Gender Existentialism?

Gender is defined as the classification of male or female that includes social, psychological, and intellectual characteristics. *Existentialism* is a philosophical position that claims individuals are always in a process of becoming who they are. The *theory of gender existentialism* is a theory that claims that one becomes one's gender in accord with one's experiences and choices. While most gender existentialists believe that biological sex is innate, they believe that gender is formed and adopted by living in a society that creates gender constructs. For example, girls learn that being a girl means being pretty, polite, and nurturing. Girls then adapt in order to fit the existing cultural categories. Thus, gender existentialists claim that there is a unique way of being a woman. Yet gender is not linked to sex by biology but by culture. Moreover, gender existentialists believe that this cultured way of being a woman masks the woman's true or authentic way of being human.

Second wave feminism with its theory of gender existentialism has roots in nineteenth and twentieth century critiques of the Enlightenment's liberal view of freedom. These critiques are found in works by the philosopher and economist Karl Marx and in the pioneering work of psychology. Both Marxism and the advent of psychology called into question the nature of freedom by suggesting that freedom can be limited by economic policy or by socially constructed mental forces.

2. The term second wave feminism was coined by Martha Weinman Lear in 1968 as a term that explained twentieth-century feminists' push for social change beyond political equality. See Weinman Lear, "Second Feminist Wave," 24–25, 50–60. Reprinted in Sochen, *New Feminism*, 161–72.

First, *Marxism*, in particular, influenced many gender existentialists. Karl Marx was a nineteenth-century German philosopher and economist who critiqued the liberal ideal that true equality could occur when paired with the economic system of capitalism. Liberal advocates of capitalism, like the Scottish economist and philosopher Adam Smith, argued that a free market system would free individuals previously caught in a rigid class system. Yet, Marx asserted that capitalism ushered in a new class system, which it rigidly preserved. Marx argued that capitalism rewards the *bourgeois*, those who own the means of production: the plantations, factories, or corporations. Yet, capitalism enslaves the *proletariat*, those who work to do the producing as farm hands, factory workers, or middle managers. This slavery consists of economic chains, as those in power create systems that prevent workers from living with self-reliance. And this slavery consists of psychological chains, as individuals measure their own value only in terms of economic worth. Marx did not believe there could be authentic freedom for individuals to develop fully their talents and live autonomously without a new framework for economic power. Moreover, Marx's philosophy claims that economic power corresponds to political power. Thus Marx asserted that the class structure of capitalism prevented democracy from flourishing as a government by and for all people. Real freedom for all individuals, according to Marx, would require a social, economic, and political revolution that would create a truly egalitarian economic system. To truly be free to flourish human beings had to see themselves as more than units of production for those who owned the means of production. Many gender existentialists decided that Marx's critique of capitalism was especially important to consider for women who were often defined in terms of their ability to work, reproduce, and consume rather than as authentic human beings. Indeed, the first woman philosopher to consider this was Karl Marx's daughter Eleanor, who worked for woman's suffrage. She wrote, "The position of women rests, as everything in our complex society, on an economic base."[3] Eleanor Marx believed that all humans need a fair economic system in order to be truly free.

At the same time that Marx and like-minded communists, such as Friedrich Engels, were exposing the economic limits of freedom in liberal democracies, other European philosophers were considering the psychological limits of freedom. The advent of psychology exposed the possibilities

---

3. Eleanor Marx as quoted by Benston, "Political Economy," 13–25. Reprinted in Sochen, *New Feminism,* 192.

of hidden forces in the psyche that limit an individual's conscious freedom. These ideas are seen both in the writing of proto-existentialist philosophers Søren Kierkegaard and Friedrich Nietzsche and in the studies of the psychoanalysts Josef Breuer, Sigmund Freud, and Carl Jung. Kierkegaard's understanding of anxiety, Nietzsche's view of the herd mentality, and Freud's concept of the super-ego explained how unconscious forces radically determine the way individuals think and behave. The discovery that sub-conscious ideas and hidden memories can determine a person's beliefs or actions without his or her awareness led thinkers to consider other unconscious influences such as collective myths, corporate advertisements, and historical memories. While later feminists criticized Freud's own unconscious biases and blatant sexism, his work heavily influenced second wave feminism. Most gender existentialists adopt both the view that hidden influences constrict individual freedom, and the view that individuals can be freed of such unconscious influences through thoughtful analysis.

The goals of most gender existentialists include psychological health and authentic freedom. Achieving these goals requires analyzing the structures of thought that determine an individual's sense of self. Studies of history, literature, and pervading cultural myths are an important part of gender existentialist work. Such studies uncover how gender identity is formed in order to make the unconscious conscious. This will free the individual from the unconscious influences allowing her to be who she wants to be. While most gender existentialists consider biological sex to be a fixed part of their identity, they believe the *concept* of woman is a construction that tyrannizes the woman who lives in *bad faith*. The term *bad faith* is used by existentialists to denote an intellectual misunderstanding that prevents a person from recognizing her freedom to be. The majority of *gender existentialists*, including Simone de Beauvoir, Betty Friedan, and Angela Davis, see capitalism and corporate marketing as instrumental to this bad faith. These women fought and fight against the economic structure of capitalism as well as the psychology of sexism in order to liberate women for authentic psychological health. Most of these women also discuss the ways the constructs of race and class can hinder authentic living.

Gender existentialists consider the biography of a person to be key to understanding the ideas of the person. Indeed, some of these philosophers have written their own autobiographies in order to explain themselves to their readers and to themselves as well. Others have embedded autobiographical details into their philosophical works. Each of these women poignantly note how their race, class, gender, nationality, education, and general lived experiences affect their thought.

Proto-gender Existentialist: Veronica Franco

While the theory of gender existentialism is first fully developed by Simone de Beauvoir, there are aspects of this theory in earlier thinkers. One interesting example is found in the poetry and letters of the sixteenth century Venetian courtesan Veronica Franco. Franco, born in 1546, shared private tutors with her brothers thus gaining an unusual level of education for a woman of her time. Her profession as a courtesan, a woman who makes a living by selling sexual services, was one that she inherited from her mother. With this profession, she was able to support herself, her children, and a large household of servants. Franco lived at times with great wealth and at other times in poverty. She died at the age of forty-five.

In her poems she wrote highly of her worth as a courtesan. However, in her letters and in her will, another story emerges. In her letters, she urged women not to encourage or allow their daughters to become courtesans. In addition, she proposed to the Venetian council in 1577 that the government ought to create shelters for women with children. At the end of her life, she left money in her will to be set aside to help prostitutes who wished to leave their profession.[4]

In many of the poems, Franco suggests a view of woman that is similar to that of the gender existentialists who wrote nearly five hundred years later. While her poetry was clearly part of her advertised mystique as a courtesan, she also used this medium to explain women to the men who read her work. She suggested that women are "weak in body, and not only quite unfit / to injure others, but also far distant,/ through their timid hearts, from self-defense."[5] However, she claimed this is due to training rather than to nature. She, as a woman trained differently than many women, wrote, "blade in hand, I learned warrior's skills,/ so that by handling weapons, I learned/ that women by nature are no less agile then men."[6] She continued, "When we women, too, have weapons and training,/ we will be able to prove to all men/ that we have hands and feet and hearts like yours;" although she

4. For more information about Franco see "Introduction," in *Poems and Selected Letters,* 1–22.

5. Franco, "Capitolo 16," *Poems and Selected Letters,* 161.

6. Ibid., 163.

admitted "[w]omen so far have not seen this is true."[7] The weapons and training that Franco advocated are pens and education. She clearly believed that education and intellectual achievement change the way a woman is seen and sees herself. However, she also acknowledged that the prevailing culture of her time defined women as weak flesh that must submit to male desire. Even education could not free a woman from the sexual and social role this construct enforced. Franco, for all her education and talent, was still not free. Franco uniquely and clearly demonstrated to the reader that the essence of woman is nothing but a cultural construct. Moreover she also explained that the construct differs for women of different classes and occupations. Courtesans, common prostitutes, married noblewomen, and nuns were considered to embody femininity in very different ways. Yet, in Franco's opinion, all of these were imprisoned by the concept of woman as one who is weak and forced to submit to the rule and the sexual desire of men. None of them were free. She subtly advocated for the deconstruction of that general construct of women as passive objectified body in order to allow women to become more fully who they are.

Thinking Woman: Simone De Beauvoir

> A man would never get the notion of writing a book on the peculiar situation of the human male. But if I wish to define myself, I must first of all say: "I am a woman"; on this truth must be based all further discussion.[8]

Biography

As an existentialist Simone de Beauvoir considered the facts of her biography important to understanding her philosophical thought. She wrote several volumes of autobiography and participated actively in the writing of a major biography by Deirdre Bair. Although Bair suggests that Beauvoir, like all people, saw her life through a particular bias, Bair also insists that Beauvoir was committed to understanding herself and presenting that self to the public that wanted to know about her.

7. Ibid., 163–65.

8. Beauvoir, *Second Sex*, xxi.

Beauvoir was born January 9, 1908. She was the much-adored first-born child of Françoise Brasseur de Beauvoir and George Bertrand de Beauvoir. As a young child, Beauvoir loved being beautiful and adored, although she was also known for her wild temper tantrums. Her sister Hé-lène, nicknamed Poupette, was born two years after Simone. She recounts that Poupette was the prettier and more feminine child. The sisters were very close friends throughout their lives.

Beauvoir was particularly influenced by what she saw as the gendered differences of her parents. She noticed the faith and femininity of her bright, devoutly Catholic mother, and the political life and intelligence of her secular father. These differences were shown in the way each parent interacted with their daughters. Her mother insisted on a traditional Catholic education for the girls. She strictly censored their reading, took them to daily mass, and taught them daily prayers. In contrast, her father mocked both her mother's devotion and the church services that he did not attend. Her father gave Beauvoir the secular adventure books her mother tried to ban. Beauvoir felt that he expected her to advance her mind as if she were a boy. As a result, Beauvoir decided from a young age that there were two different kinds of life, the devout, domestic, and feminine life and the secular, political, and masculine life. As a young girl she wanted to be a nun; as a teenager she decided to become an atheist.

Fluctuations in the economy and her family's own resources meant that Beauvoir experienced a young childhood of wealth and privilege and an adolescence of frugality. The difference in economic status taught her at a young age the ways that economics defined an individual's choices. Moving from a grand home to a small apartment in Paris where food was rationed, Beauvoir came to realize that she would have to find a career that would support her. Indeed, her father advocated for a higher education for his daughters when he realized that their lack of dowry would make them unfit for marriage. He believed such an education would allow them to be independent, a trait necessary and desirable only for women if they were middle and lower class.

At her mother's request Beauvoir's education remained in Roman Catholic schools. There, she was first attracted to philosophy by learning the systematic thought of Thomas Aquinas. Educated at the Institute Adeline Désire, Beauvoir was awarded the Baccalaureat in 1924–25. She studied mathematics at Institut Catholique, Paris, in 1925. While her father hoped she would make a career in public policy, she decided to pursue philosophy and teaching as a career. In 1928, she was awarded certificates in literature, Latin, Greek, and philosophy at the Institut Sante-Marie, Neuilly. She graduated second in her class, behind Simone Weil and ahead of Maurice Merleau-Ponty. The three of them all became famous in the field of philosophy. In 1928–29 she was awarded Agrégée de Philosophie at the Sorbonne, where she had written her dissertation on the philosophy of the seventeenth-century German rationalist Gottfried Leibniz. In the history of the Sorbonne, Beauvoir was the youngest person to graduate with this degree in philosophy and only the ninth woman to graduate in philosophy. In her studies she claimed to be influenced most by Plato, Leibniz, Kant, Schopenhauer, Nietzsche, and Bergson. Interestingly, not until the 1930s did she study Hegel, Marx, Husserl, or Heidegger. With her degree she began to lecture at secular lycées rather than the private Roman Catholic schools in which she had studied.

While at the Sorbonne, Beauvoir met Jean-Paul Sartre and began their fifty years of intimate friendship. Their relationship involved mutual sharing of ideas, editing of work, and romance. Sartre's respect for Beauvoir's mind and philosophical talent was obvious. He nicknamed her *Castor*, the Beaver, when they were students because of her earnest work and study ethic. The name stuck. From the beginning Beauvoir and Sartre paraded their relationship in public, refusing to participate in what they considered the bourgeois institution of marriage. This scandalized her parents, but Beauvoir claimed that Sartre had convinced her that they deserved every opportunity for happiness. Throughout their academic lives both partners insisted that the other had taught them the main portion of their ideas. Indeed, their philosophical systems were created in the community of each other.

Beauvoir's own records of their relationship are at times disconcerting. At Sartre's urging they both had multiple affairs, sometimes with the same young woman. In some of their descriptions, the affairs seemed simply attempts to hurt each other or each other's lovers. At times Beauvoir noted that her resulting depression and anger became debilitating. However, Beauvoir insisted in her writings about their relationship that while each had flaws of character, both strove to be honest and free with each other. They remained deeply involved until Sartre's death. The French philosopher, Julia Kristeva, wrote,

> I like to see Sartre and Beauvoir as the most irreligious beings in our modernity, who managed to shatter the glorification of love

... all the while keeping the couple alive; not the couple as ecstasy but the couple as debate. . . . The couple as a space for thinking, or thinking as dialogue between the two sexes, is that not utopia indeed?[9]

Together, Sartre and Beauvoir, in the 1930s and early 1940s, began to read a new philosophical canon. Reading Virginia Woolf, Karl Marx, Friedrich Engels, Edmund Husserl, Martin Heidegger, G. W. F. Hegel, and Søren Kierkegaard, they were fully introduced to phenomenology as well as the thought of the early existentialists. Suddenly Beauvoir began to see her place in the history of philosophy. She wanted to publish her philosophical work. But at the same moment in which she found her philosophical voice, she discovered misogynism in the world of publishing. She was told when her work was rejected for publication that

the house of Gallimard did not understand books written by women which were about the lives of women of my generation and background; that modern France and French publishing were not yet ready to deal with what women thought and felt and wanted; that to publish such a book would brand them a subversive publishing house and they couldn't risk offending all sorts of patrons and critics.[10]

Devastated at first, she was encouraged by Sartre to continue to seek publication and to continue writing. She did so and burst into both the philosophical and literary scenes with the publication of her philosophical novel, *She Came to Stay*, in 1943. This novel introduced several new ideas concerning the nature of the self as well the nature of consciousness and social interaction. Many of these ideas were developed in Sartre's *Being and Nothingness*, a book of philosophy published shortly after *She Came to Stay*. Beauvoir's novel was reviewed by Merleau Ponty who praised both the idea and the structure of the work, hailing the breakdown of the barriers between literature and philosophy.[11]

In 1940, Beauvoir first read American author Richard Wright's *Native Son*. The book struck her as immediately important. Beauvoir was moved by Wright's expression of himself as a black man seen by white men as "the other." She agreed with Wright's claim that the concept of the black race

9. Kristeva, "Reinvention of the Couple," 44–45.

10. Bair, *Simone de Beauvoir*, 207–8.

11. For an excellent analysis of the importance of *She Came to Stay*, see chapters 3–5 in Fullbrook and Fullbrook, *Simone de Beavuoir*.

was created only in contradistinction to a white race which was considered the norm.[12] In 1946, she met Richard Wright who was visiting Paris. Wright and Beauvoir continued to correspond as Beauvoir performed an extended lecture tour in the United States after the publication of *The Ethics of Ambiguity* in 1947. This correspondence led Beauvoir to consider how the concept of woman was created to distinguish women from men who considered themselves the norm. She began to reflect upon her own understanding of herself as a human subject who considered herself an object, particularly an object of the male gaze. In 1949, she published *The Second Sex* in which her understanding of phenomenology, existentialism, and racism unified with her desire to understand herself as a woman. *The Second Sex* became one of the most important and influential works of philosophy of the twentieth century.

Throughout her life, Beauvoir wrote many works of fiction, philosophy, and autobiography. She was active in campaigning for political policies that she believed best liberated citizens. Particularly she was involved during World War II in the French Resistance, later she was active in the movement to liberate Algeria from French rule. She was interested in the civil rights movement in the United States and participated in the fight for the legalization of birth control and abortion in both the United States and in France. She and Sartre both joined protests against nuclear proliferation. In 1975, she was awarded the Jerusalem prize for writers who have promoted the concept of individual liberty. Until the end of her life, she was active in the feminist movement in France and a willing correspondent with American feminists. Her relationship with Sartre continued both intellectually and romantically until his death in 1980. She died six years later on April 14, 1986.

Simone de Beauvoir's Theory of Gender Existentialism.

Beauvoir's *Second Sex* is one of the most profoundly influential books of philosophy of the twentieth century. In this book Beauvoir explains her central thesis that women are constructed by culture to be seen and to see themselves as the *second* sex. This work reveals Beauvoir to be a philosopher

12. For more detailed information on the relationship between Richard Wright and Beauvoir see Beauvoir, *America Day by Day*. Also, see Simons, *Beauvoir and The Second Sex*.

who was a significant figure in the development of both existentialism and gender theory.

However, the roots of Beauvoir's existentialist theory were first presented in *She Came to Stay*, a philosophical novel in which the young protagonist, Françoise, narrates her experience of coming to understanding herself as a human being. In the first pages of the novel Françoise is depicted analyzing her surroundings in a small theater, she gazes at the ashtray, the lamp, the bottle of whiskey, and the tired face of a friend. Françoise has the perception that things only exist insofar as she looks at them. She describes the world as if she is the only conscious mind, a mind that creates value by its gaze. When she turns her back on a gleaming rose-colored window, she thinks that now the window must "gleam in vain; it would no longer shine for anyone."[13] "Only her own life was real,"[14] according to Françoise. She has a marked experience of herself as a conscious being, different than all inanimate beings. Yet, the novel is about Françoise's experience of reckoning with the reality of other conscious minds. While in the beginning she looks with surprise in a mirror, "[f]or most of the time she was not aware that she had a face,"[15] she comes to recognize that others are looking at her. She realizes that her friend judges her face and that her lover looks at other women's faces with rapture. She notices other human minds observing her, naming her, and limiting her. Suddenly she finds that she is in competition with these other minds in determining how the world will be for her.

Analyzing the tension between minds became an important part of Sartre's work; there are many links between his work in *Being and Nothingness* and Beauvoir's philosophy in *She Came to Stay*. But Beauvoir's novel is uniquely feminine in perspective. Beauvoir came to realize this only later when she began to explore feminine consciousness as that which considers itself secondary to the male conscious mind. *The Second Sex* is Beauvoir's exploration of the female as the second sex. The most interesting aspect of this to Beauvoir was that women consider themselves secondary. This uniquely feminine psychology is revealed in the consideration of the woman as the Other, the Womb, and the Eternal Feminine.

13. Beauvoir, *She Came To Stay*, 13
14. Ibid.
15. Ibid., 22.

Beauvoir's View of Woman as Other

Beauvoir claimed in her introduction to the *Second Sex* that she had disregarded thinking about her gender as a younger woman. She claimed that she had been more interested in being a human than a woman. Indeed, she had considered the idea of essential femininity to be merely a myth to be disregarded. However, she explains she had come to the recognition that to "decline to accept such notions as the eternal feminine, the black soul, the Jewish character, is not to deny that Jews, Negroes, women exist today—this denial does not represent a liberation for those concerned, but rather a flight from reality."[16] Rather she believed she must consider what it means to experience the world as a woman. Her central claim is that to be a woman is to be not a man. Thus a woman is the negation of man. Men are considered the normal human observer, the typical subject. In contrast, women are taught from a young age they are divergent, atypical. They are not human; they are women. Women are, thus, used to considering themselves as that which is *Other* than the man.

In some ways it is natural that men would consider themselves the normal standard and characterize that which is different from them as the *Other*. "The category of the *Other* is as primordial as consciousness itself,"[17] Beauvoir notes. Indeed, in the nineteenth century the German philosopher G. W. F. Hegel, had written in *The Phenomenology of Spirit* about a significant conflict that was given the name *The Master-Slave Dialectic*. Beauvoir had interpreted this passage in Hegel to be about the fundamental hostility of a conscious being towards other conscious beings. Each conscious being wants to be the only Subject, the one who determines the values of the world. There are, of course, according to Beauvoir, many instances of this conflict in society, between individuals, between races, and between nations. But Beauvoir insists there was something quite unusual about the way the conflict was waged between men and women.

Beauvoir notes there is something unique about sexism. She explains that racism and anti-Semitism arose when a local majority attempted to dehumanize and objectify individuals in a minority. But, Beauvoir reminds the reader that this was not the case with the birth of sexism, for men have always encountered women as equal in number to themselves. She explains, "But women are not a minority, like the American Negroes or the

16. Beauvoir, *Second Sex,* xx.
17. Ibid., xxii.

Jews; there are as many women as men on earth."[18] Beauvoir continues to explain the difference between sexism and other forms of prejudice.

> Again, the two groups concerned have often been originally independent; they may have been formerly unaware of each other's existence, or perhaps they recognized each other's autonomy. But a historical event has resulted in the subjugation of the weaker by the stronger. . . . In these cases the oppressed retained at least the memory of the former days; they possessed in common a past, a tradition, sometimes a religion or a culture.[19]

To explain Beauvoir's point, the typical understanding of Hegel's Master-Slave dialectic is that one group of people assign a label and value to another group in order to devalue and objectify that group. But even as the dominant group does so, the oppressed group has a memory of doing likewise to the dominant group. There is a mutuality of objectification, at least in the beginning. But for men and women, there does not seem ever to have been any such mutuality. The odd thing, according to Beauvoir, is not that men objectify women as the *Others*, but that women objectify themselves as the *Others*. Women, as well as men, see men as the norm and themselves as the *Other*.

Unfortunately, simply recognizing the problem does not solve it. In fact, Beauvoir believed many woman prefer to remain in the role of the *Other*. This is because a woman who sees herself as the *Other*, the object of the male gaze, does not have to confront the radical freedom she really has herself. Beauvoir claims it is terrifying and even nauseating to throw off the bad faith that one is predetermined to be a certain type of person who has a certain value in the world. Rather than being contented to be petted as a housewife and valued for her sexual and reproductive role, a woman who wishes to see herself as the value making subject of her own life will have to take responsibility for the person she chooses to be. On one hand, constant socialization to consider herself as the object who exists for the pleasure and comfort of the man makes it difficult for a woman to see herself as the true Subject she is. On the other hand, fear of responsibility and desire for ease too often allows a woman to continue to be objectified and to objectify herself.

In *The Second Sex*, Beauvoir analyzes the cultivation of young girls. She writes pointedly about how girls are cultivated to see their value as

18. Ibid., xxiv.
19. Ibid.

objects. They are praised for being small, pretty, polite, and obedient; while they are criticized for being large, strong, assertive, and willful. Mythology, fairy tales, art, and religion reinforce these values. Indeed, Beauvoir noted, as Wollstonecraft did 170 years earlier, that girls are taught lifelong feminine virtues that correspond to what is adorable in young children and attractive for dolls or potted plants. In contrast, boys are praised for the very same attributes that are seen as vices in girls, learning they ought to control their environment and to persuade the will of others to their own in order to be heroic. When romantic relationships develop the differences are clear. The man sees his romance as a small part of his life, his lover as a particularly fine object in his collection. The woman sees her relationship as the goal of her existence, for her lover is the one who gives (or denies) her value. The woman comes to passively accept her role as an object of the male gaze. She is nothing if not a sexual object. Such a mode of being is not innate in women but is cultivated by society. Yet, the result is that both men and women come to accept this as an immutable reality.

Beauvoir's View of Woman as Womb

While Beauvoir claims that gender is a cultural construct that is adopted as an act of bad faith, she does discuss the facts of biological sex. She presents the physical features of the female human being as *facticity,* the fixed background that limits human freedom. Examples of such fixed facts include the ovaries of a woman, her womb, her menstrual cycle, and the process of menopause. She discusses how these biological facts affect the way a woman interacts with the world about her, acknowledging that human consciousness is always rooted in a body. However, Beauvoir claims that the degree to which sexual difference affects the human individual is greatly exaggerated. Using examples from natural science, Beauvoir explains how much variance there is in the gender roles of various animal species. If the mere presence of a womb changes the human woman into a subservient creature, this ought to be true of the tigress, but it is not. Beauvoir turns, also, to the data of anthropology. The role of women is different in different societies. In some tribes, women have leadership roles. Thus, science demonstrates that the female reproductive system is not the natural cause of the female's place as secondary in Western human society.

Indeed, Beauvoir decries the very search for a biological cause of woman's role. Such a search reveals the primary bias that females are determined by biology. Scientists and philosophers are trained to expect biological factors to be the cause of women's ways of being. Yet, says Beauvoir, they do not look for similar correspondence in male subjects. This is because Western society has labeled the female as a creature of the flesh, while it has labeled the male as an autonomous mind. Beauvoir details the work of male philosophers who praised the transcendence of the human mind and human spirit over the mortal limits of the body. Beauvoir notes that most of these same philosophers implied that such transcendence is part of men's nature rather than universal human nature. Beauvoir writes that women, in contrast, are imagined to be confined to their bodies, their biology, their flesh. Women are considered immanent, completely in their bodies and unable to transcend them. Feminine virtue is synonymous with physical beauty. A woman's virtues are attributes of the flesh, particularly attributes of passive flesh. Defining the assets of a woman based on her large bust, her small waist, her long neck, and her plump rear end leads to a view of feminine beauty as passive. In contrast, male virtue is not synonymous with physical beauty, and even male beauty is defined by power: his muscularity, the broadness of his back, the might of his thighs. In contrast, even the moral and intellectual virtues of women are passive. Heroines of fairy tales are hailed for their chastity, their patience, their gentleness, and their obedience. Quietly waiting for the hero to act, the virtuous woman is drawn as a still life object.

Beauvoir never denies that women and men are embodied creatures, with specific bodily requirements. She does note that the biology of women required specific tools for women's liberation. Such tools include access to female centered sexual education, birth control, and abortion. But, she insists that the constraints of a female body are small compared to those of the feminine mind. She was adamant that "the varieties of behavior reported are not dictates to woman by her hormones nor predetermined in the structure of the female brain: they are shaped as in a mold by her situation."[20] Freeing the woman to be all that she is able to be requires recognizing that both men and women are transcendent in mind and immanent in flesh.

Beauvoir's View of Woman as Eternal Feminine

According to Beauvoir, the strongest psychological constraint for women is the cultural impression of the *Eternal Feminine*, which suggests that there

20. Ibid., 597.

is an essence of femininity all women naturally and spiritually share. This notion is self-fulfilling as children are introduced in the cradle to myths, fairy tales, and marketing that teach them there is an essential nature to women. Girls strive to embody these eternally feminine characteristics. The fact that many women try to embody the feminine ideals reinforces the opinion that the feminine essence is innate and eternal.

The myth is complex, however. Little girls learn from culture that not all women do develop true feminine characteristics. They are taught that there are two types of women in the world: small, pretty, fragile, obedient, good women, and large, ugly, strong, willful, evil women. The good woman is often portrayed in literature and advertising as childlike and helpless in the clutches of the evil woman who is willing to destroy anyone, including her lover and her child. Fairy tales and romance novels posit the goal of the good girl's life is to be loved by a man who will protect her from the evil woman. Even religious stories value the martyrs of the church who choose to show their power only by suffering with the poor and dying at the hands of the oppressor. Everywhere the girl encounters virtue in terms of weakness and submission and vice in terms of power and strength of will. The concept of the eternal feminine shapes the girl's understanding of herself, her sexuality, and her relationships.

Yet, Beauvoir insists that women can choose to recognize the myth of the eternal feminine as a myth and reject it. In order to do so, however, the woman must be willing to uncover the social roots of her values and beliefs. Then, free of myths and *bad faith*, the woman can choose to be the woman she will become. She can choose her lovers and her relationships free of the chains of cultural ideas about heterosexuality and submission. She can become herself.

Feminist Merits of Simone de Beauvoir's Gender Existentialism

One of the main criticisms of *The Second Sex* is that the majority of the book simply exposes the myths that subjugate women. There is very little in the text that informs the woman how she ought to proceed once free. However, Beauvoir argues that the liberation of the woman is its own goal, not a means to another end. Beauvoir's end-goal was individual freedom. While she certainly offered her political views on what type of society best promotes free citizens, her goal was freedom itself. The woman who has done the philosophical and psychological work necessary to grasp the radical nature of her freedom to determine her own life must do so on her own. Beauvoir's hope was her book would begin that process for the reader. Indeed, her book did just that for many readers. When the feminist activist Martha Weinman Lear first coined the term *Second Wave Feminism* she gave credit to the beginning of the movement to Beauvoir. She quoted feminist activist Ti-Grace Atkinson as a way to explain, "Then friends recommended that I read de Beauvoir's *The Second Sex*. Whammo. It changed everything for me. It changed my life."[21] Indeed, Beauvoir's in-depth analysis of the ways Western culture has constructed gender began the work of second wave feminism's advocacy for a social revolution to promote true equality of women with men.

American Second Wave Feminism: Betty Friedan, The Feminine Mystique, and NOW

I've tried everything women are supposed to do—hobbies, gardening, pickling, canning, being very social with my neighbors, joining committees, running PTA teas. . . . But who am I?

—AN AMERICAN HOUSEWIFE QUOTED IN
THE FEMININE MYSTIQUE[22]

Feminist activist Betty Friedan brought to American housewives many of the concepts in Simone de Beauvoir's *Second Sex* when she published *The Feminine Mystique* in 1963. Friedan's focus specifically targeted the way post-World War II America had adopted a new construct of the eternal feminine in naming the ideal woman as housewife and mother. This new construct Friedan named *the feminine mystique,* a construct created in the 1940s and 1950s for white middle and upper class American women. This new construct of the ideal feminine woman was in marked contrast to that advocated in the 1920s and 1930s. Culture had, indeed, shifted. While white wealthy girls in the 1920s had been urged to study at top universities, girls in the late 1940s and 50s were told that education would make them anxious and discontent in their natural role as mothers. As a result while 47 percent of college students were women in 1920, only 35 percent were women in 1958. Moreover, 60 percent of those women who did start college dropped out in order to get married. Marriage and motherhood were

21. Ti-Grace Atkinson quoted in Weinman Lear, "Second Feminist Wave," 169.
22. Friedan, *Feminine Mystique,* 21.

suddenly considered the ideal. Even *birth control* was renamed *planned parenthood*. The new image of the ideal woman was as a stay-at-home mother. This was in contrast to the role of the working woman that was promoted as patriotic during the Depression and the war. Policies had shifted, too. The government closed the federally funded child-care centers that had allowed women to work during the war era. The birth rate increased at a rapid rate, as the average college educated woman in the 1950s had twice as many children as the average college educated woman in the 1920s. Marketing and advertising had shifted. Gone were the images of the working woman with the strong arms who would help the country win the war. Instead, corporations showed femininely dressed women happily cleaning and caring for children. Their goal was to market new products created for the sole purpose of exploiting the economic power that housewives newly had.[23]

The result of the new and pervasive feminine mystique was a large majority of middle class and upper class women who believed that they should be most happy in a domestic role. Unfortunately, as Friedan demonstrated with anecdotes and statistics, the majority of women were unhappy and unfulfilled. Their unhappiness was labeled "the problem that has no name."[24]

> What were the words women used when they tried to express it? Sometimes a woman would say, "I feel empty somehow... incomplete." Or she would say, "I feel as if I don't exist." Sometimes she blotted out the feeling with a tranquilizer.... A number of women told me about great bleeding blisters that break out on their hands and arms. "I call it the housewife's blight," said a family doctor in Pennsylvania. "I see it so often lately in these young women with four, five, and six children who bury themselves in their dishpans. But it isn't caused by detergent and it isn't cured by cortisone."[25]

Friedan interviewed 200 women and came to the conclusion that these women faced one basic psychological problem that had physical symptoms. The problem was trying to adjust to an inauthentic feminine role.

Like Beauvoir, Friedan argued that the authentic human life was one in which the person chooses her vocation for herself. Friedan's work exposed how specific corporations and agencies had worked to redefine women's role. Friedan hoped that this would allow women to see through

23. For these and more statistics see ibid., 16–17.
24. Ibid., 20.
25. Ibid., 21.

the propaganda's real agenda of selling products that women neither needed nor authentically desired. Friedan's book also critiqued Freudian analysis of women's problems by suggesting that what he named "penis envy" was not really an envy of male biology, but an envy of male privilege. She wanted women to see that they were entitled to live the lives they chose to live, pursuing their own interests that lay beyond motherhood. In order to free girls to pursue all that they had finally won the right legally to pursue, Friedan advocated using media to expose the myth that a woman's success was only in domestic duties. Friedan, also, advocated for legislation that supported more equal opportunities for girls and women.

Friedan knew that the feminine mystique was a seductive trap for girls. By complimenting girls for feminine virtues, society gave girls an excuse to be lazy in their studies. Girls were given permission to fail to take responsibility for their futures. It took courage for a woman to realize she could pair the roles of wife and mother with other roles in society just as her husband paired his family role with another role. But Friedan believed that such courage was necessary for an authentic life as a human being.

Friedan's book became a best seller. In 1966, she began the National Organization of Woman, with the acronym NOW. The group advocated for a social revolution that would encourage cultivating girls to become educated and independent. The group also worked for specific political legislation that would aid women. NOW was joined by many women from different places in society.

Many Americans began to see the quest for equal rights for women as an important part of the larger civil rights movement. However, the gender existentialists insisted that the country needed a culture shift as much as a legislative one. Because gender existentialism presupposes that the definition of woman is constructed by culture, rather than given by nature, feminists with this theory of gender as their foundation were sharp critics of cultural influences that they believed promoted a confining and unhealthy gender construction for women. Women grouped together to create books, magazines, and advertising that they believed would work to liberate women psychologically. One example is Gloria Steinem's magazine *MS* which contained articles by and for independent working women. Steinem refused to cater to corporate advertisers who were used to a "'supportive editorial atmosphere'" in which journals would provide free advertising by including "articles that praise food/fashion/beauty subjects in order to 'support' and 'complement' food/fashion/beauty ads."[26] Instead, *MS* ultimately became an advertisement free magazine that stressed the need to free women from corporate influences. *MS* was in circulation from 1972–1987. Another example was the 1972 publication of *Our Bodies, Our Selves* by the Boston Women's Health Book Collective. This book strove to give accurate information about women's health while minimizing cultural bias concerning the nature and vocation of women. The book has gone through many editions and the current in-print edition was most recently revised in 2012. Many gender existentialist feminists continue to try to change culture by using media to portray what they believe is a more authentic view of a liberated woman.

Thinking Woman: Angela Davis

The historical construction of women's reproductive role . . . has been informed by a peculiar constellation of racist and misogynist assumptions.[27]

Biography

Contemporary philosopher Angela Davis was thrust into the national headlines in her twenties when her philosophical and political activism led to her imprisonment. Often times her thought is introduced by her life story as the manifestation of her philosophical ideals. Davis recognizes this and acknowledges that the patterns of her thought have been affected dramatically by her life experiences. Her life and her ideas are symbiotic. Moreover, Davis believes that in order for people to understand her thought they need to understand the life experiences of contemporary working class black women in the United States. Thus, she regularly responds to requests for autobiographical accounts of her life. She published her *Autobiography of Angela Davis* at the age of twenty-eight soon after her famous trial. Since then she has written many articles about her experiences in prison and has given many talks concerning the events of her life. Recently she participated in making the 2013 documentary *Free Angela and All Political Prisoners*. She asserts that most of her life experiences are products of her

26. Steinem, *Moving Beyond Words*, 133.

27. Davis, "Surrogates and Outcasts," *Angela Davis Reader*, 210.

race, gender, and class, and the biases that existed and exist in the society in which she lives. By telling the story of her life, she hopes to continue changing systems of oppression into systems that promote authentic human freedom.

Davis was born on January 26, 1944, in Birmingham, Alabama. She lived in government housing projects that she described as "a crowded street of little red brick structures" which rarely showed a patch of green and where "nothing could be planted to bear fruit or blossoms."[28] Yet there she had the experience of being surrounded by friendly neighbors. This changed in 1948 when she and her family moved to a traditionally white neighborhood on Center Street. They were the first black family to integrate the neighborhood. Here, she felt the hatred and hostility of the whites in her neighborhood, "their eyes heavy with belligerence."[29] As more black families began to move into the area, racist activity increased. Indeed, in 1949, black homes were targeted for violence by whites. "The bombings were such a constant response that soon our neighborhood became known as Dynamite Hill."[30] Davis and her family became accustomed to living in what amounted to a war zone. "So common were the bombings on Dynamite Hill that the horror of them diminished."[31]

From childhood, Davis experienced race as a fundamental part of her identity in society. As a black child in the South, Davis said she, like most Southern children, learned to read the words "colored" and "white" before any other. These words denoted the basic categories of human existence. Signs bearing these words carefully instructed children where they were allowed to play, sit, eat, and drink. At school she was taught that race was a natural category that placed people in a natural hierarchy. Indeed, in the 1950s Southern teachers and textbooks still taught children that before the "War of Southern Independence," slavery had been an institution that benefited white owners and black slaves alike.[32]

Yet, Davis's parents were determined to teach their children that racial segregation, oppression, hatred, and violence were unnatural and unnecessary. Davis was taught at home that racism was neither natural nor innate, but a structure caused by greater societal struggles. Davis's own

28. Davis, *Autobiography*, 77.
29. Ibid., 78.
30. Ibid., 79.
31. Ibid., 95.
32. Ibid., 100.

experiences taught her that racism was indeed merely a cultural construct. Her travels as a child to New York showed her there were places in the United States where segregation was less obvious. In New York, while she still experienced subtle racism, she recognized the possibility of an equality of all persons beyond the labels of "colored" and "white." With this recognition she began to fantasize about wearing the mask of a white person for a day in order to experience the benefits of white privilege in the South. She imagined at the end of the day, pulling off her mask to show her neighbors that only their own prejudice about the color of her skin made her different than white children.

Davis recounts that as a teenager she and her sister decided actually to try to do just this by creating a small social experiment. Davis, fluent in French, pretended to be a foreigner visiting Atlanta with her sister, who adopted a fake accent. They entered a store and posed to the white shopkeeper as foreigners. Davis narrates, "At the sight of two young Black women speaking a foreign language, the clerks in the store raced to help us. Their delight with the exotic was enough . . . to dispel their normal disdain for Black people."[33] Davis noted that the storekeeper did not sweep them to the back "colored" end of the store, but happily gave them first-rate service. The shopkeeper even introduced them to white customers as exotic foreigners. At the end of their visit, Davis and her sister stood up and announced, in English, that they were simply black girls from Alabama. Davis believed that she had demonstrated to the shopkeeper and the white customers how ridiculous their racist categories were.

Davis's commitment to un-doing racist categories became a major part of her life. In the hope of pursuing educational excellence without the constant constraints made for blacks in the South, Davis, encouraged by her parents, moved to New York for high school. With the aid of a scholarship from the American Friends, she attended Elisabeth Irwin High School. She was invited to live with a white progressive couple, the Reverend and Mrs. Melish, while attending this school taught by teachers who had been fired from public schools or blacklisted for their liberal, progressive, or socialist ideas. Here she learned about socialism and communism for the first time claiming, "*The Communist Manifesto* hit me like a bolt of lightning."[34] Engels's and Marx's text provided an answer to many questions that had plagued Davis about the origin of racism. Davis began to see the problems

33. Ibid., 86.
34. Ibid., 109.

of her family and other blacks as part of the context of the problems that affected all working people. She began to suspect that black liberation was linked to abolishing capitalism and emancipating the working class as a whole. In order to learn more about Marxism, she joined Advance, a Marxist-Leninist youth group.

Davis claims that as a teenager living in New York she often felt torn between continuing her education and returning home. In high school, while she was learning about Marxism with like-minded friends and teachers in New York, she often felt that she ought to return home to Alabama to help solve the problems of segregation and racism there. She was particularly attracted to the civil rights movement. However, her parents insisted that she finish her education and pursue every opportunity for further education.

After graduating high school, Davis received a full scholarship to Brandeis University. There she was one of only three black students in the freshman class. She reports feeling at the time "alienated, angry, alone."[35] At Brandeis she was exposed to French literature and more philosophy, especially the works of the French existentialist philosophers, Albert Camus and Sartre. She was further influenced by the work of author James Baldwin and philosopher Herbert Marcuse. Indeed, Marcuse was teaching philosophy at Brandeis at the time. At the end of her first year, she traveled to Europe for the first time to attend the Eighth World Festival for Youth and Students in Finland. There she was greatly impressed by the presentations on communism made by some of the Cuban student participants. Her global studies continued when she was accepted to study in the Hamilton College Junior Year in France Program. Yet, even as she was abroad, she was acutely aware of racism. This was especially acute in France where she witnessed the violent racism against Algerians.

While in Paris, she was reminded of the danger racism posed in America. In September of 1963, in a Parisian newspaper, she read the horrifying news of the bombing of the 16th Street Baptist Church in Birmingham. Reading the names of the murdered girls, she realized that she knew these four girls. They were friends of her family. Shocked and tearful, she realized that other students around her, both French and American, did not shed tears over the incident. They were not filled with the same sense of outrage or terror as she. Davis claims, that at this point she suddenly realized, "This act was not an aberration. It was not something sparked by a few

35. Ibid., 118.

extremists gone mad. On the contrary it was logical, inevitable. The people who planted the bomb in the girls' restroom in the basement of the 16th Street Baptist Church were not pathological, but rather normal products of their surroundings."[36] The racism of the United States had violently normalized the categories of race. The deaths of black girls were not mourned. This insight stayed with Davis.

When Davis returned to Brandeis, she decided to study philosophy as a major. She especially wanted to read Marx, his predecessors, and his successors. She was encouraged by Marcuse. After graduating *magna cum laude* as a member of *Phi Beta Kappa,* she went with a scholarship to study philosophy at the University of Frankfort. There she studied Kant, Hegel, and Marx in German with Jürgen Habermas and Theodor Adorno. Yet, she continued to keep abreast of the political situation in the United States. She was particularly interested in the Black Liberation Movement in America. She learned that activists, such as Huey Newton, Bobby Seal, and Bobby Hutton, had started the Black Panther Party for Self Defense. Davis felt torn between her desire to finish her doctorate under Adorno and her need to return home to work for civil rights. After two years of study in Frankfort, she decided to return to the United States and finish her doctorate at the University of California in San Diego. There she was able to study with her former professor, Herbert Marcuse.

As Davis worked on her doctorate in philosophy, she became politically and socially active in the black liberation movement. Witnessing the arrest of Huey Newton and the murders of many young black men by police, Davis decided to join the Black Panther Party. Soon after, she joined the Communist party. As a young woman in her mid-twenties, she was already known as an activist and a scholar throughout California. While she was still finishing her dissertation she was hired to teach at the University of California, Los Angeles.

Before she began teaching her first class at UCLA, an article in the *San Francisco Examiner* was published detailing a recent trip she had taken to Cuba to learn about Fidel Castro's regime. This article accused her of being a Communist. Suddenly this young philosopher became a national topic of interest. California's governor, Ronald Reagan, called the chancellor of the campus to ask if he had hired a Communist. Reagan claimed that there was a law on the books from 1949 that prohibited Communists from being hired at UCLA. Reagan demanded that Davis be asked about

36. Ibid., 130.

her political party affiliations. The philosophy department immediately and unanimously defended Davis. They stressed the need for academic freedom, proclaiming that party membership had never been asked during interviews for faculty at the University of California. However, Davis recognized that more than academic freedom was at stake. "I realized that the personal goals I had set for myself were about to collide head on with the political requirements of my life."[37] Rather than pleading that she did not have to answer questions about her political beliefs, Davis wrote a letter professing to be a Communist. Davis was immediately fired from her position. Massive protests were made across the country. When a judge ruled that the firing was illegal, UCLA rehired Davis. Her first lectures were attended by thousands of eager students. However, Davis knew that she was still at risk and that more than her academic career was at stake. First, a man violently attacked a philosopher in the department for being a supporter of Davis. Then, two police officers, claiming to have a warrant, broke into Davis's sister and brother-in-law's home. The officers pointed weapons at their infant and shot her brother-in-law in the shoulder. Davis's sister reportedly grabbed the gun away from the officer. She was subsequently arrested for attempted murder of an officer.[38] All of the charges against Davis's sister were dropped in court. But Davis became afraid for her family and her own safety.

Yet, Davis continued to teach philosophy and perform activist work. She watched the arrests of fellow activists and became used to frequent police interrogation. She became outspoken against the use of incarceration as a way to silence those who protested oppression. The most famous episode of her life began during this period of activism. In many ways, she felt her own imprisonment was inevitable considering the ideology of the times. She had been actively protesting the imprisonment of political prisoners, those who were incarcerated for their political philosophical views rather than for any specific crime. Particularly she was actively working to support the freedom of three men indicted for the murder of a white officer in Soledad Prison. The arrest of these men had come after a white guard named O. G. Miller had targeted and brutally murdered three black men with a sniper's gun in the prison exercise yard. When later a different white guard was found dead, three black prisoners, George Jackson, John Clutchett, and Fleeta Durango, were arrested for his murder. The case was made that they

37. Ibid., 217.
38. Ibid., 225.

had murdered this guard as an act of vengeance. However, there was little evidence in support of the arrest other than the fact that the men shared a history of reading anti-racist philosophical writing. Davis saw these men, thus, as political prisoners, falsely accused of murder because of their political beliefs and history of reading about civil rights. Her work on their behalf was the foundation of her own arrest.

The situation occurred in this way. On August 7, 1970, Jonathan Jackson, the seventeen-year-old brother of one of the Soledad prisoners, entered a court proceeding for James McClain, a political prisoner at San Quentin. Jonathan Jackson was armed; he directed those in the courtroom to stop the proceedings. Jackson, McClain, and two other prisoners attending the trial worked together to force the judge, the district attorney, and several jurors to a van outside. At this time, a San Quentin guard fired at the van. There was an onslaught of gunshots that left Jackson, McClain, the judge, and several others dead. More were wounded. After the scene had been investigated, the police announced that one of the guns that was in the possession of Jonathan Jackson had been registered in the name of Angela Davis. With no further evidence, Davis was accused of being the mastermind behind the attack. A warrant was issued for Davis's arrest for kidnapping, murder, and conspiracy. She was immediately placed on the FBI's ten most wanted list. Davis insisted on her innocence and denied being part of any conspiracy. However, she believed that she would be unable to obtain a fair trial. She was certain her political activism would be used against her as proof of her guilt. With the help of a wig and a number of friends, she was able to escape for two months before she was arrested inside a New York hotel. For nearly eighteen months, she was held without bail in jails in New York and then California waiting her trial. Her trial began on February 27, 1971. Global protests were made on her behalf by people who believed she was a prisoner because of her political beliefs. Indeed, the majority of evidence furnished by the prosecution had to do with her activism and political writing rather than any evidence of actual conspiring with Jackson. The only evidence that was produced concerned witnesses who had reportedly seen Jackson and Davis together on several occasions. However, these witnesses were deemed unreliable when they were unable accurately to identify Davis in court, mistaking her for another African American woman. On June 4, 1972, the judge and jury found her not guilty on all charges brought against her.

Throughout the 1970s Davis continued her activism, gave lectures, and wrote a number of essays about her experiences in prison. In the 1980s she wrote a number of important works in philosophy including *Women, Race & Class* and *Women, Culture, Politics*. She ran as a vice presidential candidate on the Communist party ticket that opposed Ronald Reagan in 1980 and 1984. She continued and continues to write and teach about racism, feminism, and politics. Currently, she is Distinguished Professor Emerita in the History of Consciousness and Feminist Studies Departments at the University of California, Santa Cruz.

Davis on Race, Gender, and Class

The significance of Davis's work in the theory of gender existentialism is her articulation of how cultural views of gender are created, manipulated, and promulgated by economics. While Beauvoir was certainly influenced by socialist thought, especially in her later life, and while Friedan was aware of the forces of advertising and marketing on the way women see themselves or are seen, Davis has a pointedly Marxist viewpoint. Her view is that the constructs of gender, as well as those of race and class, are purposefully constructed in order to solidify economic and political power in the hands of the wealthy. This perspective encourages her to look for differences in the way women are viewed, and the way women view themselves, depending on their race and socio-economic classes. Her work, like Beauvoir's, requires a thoughtful analysis of social history in order to uncover the roots of contemporary views of woman. Like Beauvoir, her philosophical hope is that understanding these roots will allow individuals to be freed from the passive acceptance of constructed gender roles in order that they might freely create their own authentic selves. However, Davis considers a revolutionary change in economic structure necessary for individuals to be able to claim their true freedom as human beings.

Davis presents a convincing analysis of how constructs of gender categories intersect with race and class constructs. Her work explains specifically how working class views of woman differ from the views of woman held by the wealthiest Americans. The difference in the constructs demonstrate both that the feminine essence of women is a cultural, not innate, construct; and that these constructs were formed with the particular purpose of solidifying economic power by the ruling class. The constructs change according to the needs or desires of the owners of the most wealth.

For example, in the nineteenth century in the United States, female slaves were considered equal in strength and working units of production to male slaves. Indeed, in 1850, 7/8ths of female slaves were doing the same field-work as men without gender distinction. "Strength and productivity under the threat of the whip outweighed considerations of sex. In this sense, the oppression of women was identical to the oppression of men."[39] In addition, Davis reminds her readers that many white European immigrants also shared the construction of gender neutrality as workers in factories. Factory workers were expected to work the same hours whether they were male or female. Women who worked in coal mines, iron foundries, and lumberyards had similar experiences to their male counterparts. In addition, few masters or work place managers modified their expectations for pregnant or newly delivered mothers. The children of slaves were expected to remain alone in slave quarters as often were the children of factory workers. Most poignantly, slaves were considered "not mothers at all; . . . simply instruments guaranteeing the growth of the slave labor force."[40] Slave masters often beat women who were working slowly post-partum until the blood and milk flowed together down their chests.[41]

Yet, while slaves and poor workers were expected to endure the same hardships whether they were male or female, white upper class women were considered to be radically different than white upper class men. Wealthy white women were considered far weaker than men and uniquely domestically oriented. The cult of motherhood instructed the wealthy woman that her role as mother made her uniquely fragile and important. White wealthy women were expected to remain in the home caring for their young as their natural vocation as "nurturing mothers, gentle companions and housekeepers for their husbands"[42] White wealthy men explained that women's role in democracy was only as wife and mother. They justified laws that did not permit women to have equal access to work, property, or suffrage as men as necessary because men and women were essentially different.

Davis points out that Sojourner Truth was one of the first women to publically uncover the different gender constructions for slaves and upper-class women in order to suggest that the concepts of woman as dependent

39. Davis, *Women, Race and Class*, 6.

40. Ibid., 6–9.

41. Ibid., 9. Davis suggests that the reader see Moses Grady, *Narrative of Moses Grady*, (1899).

42. Davis, *Women, Race and Class*, 5.

and woman as natural mother were cultural constructs not natural ones. However, equally important is Truth's recognition that gender neutrality does not, in itself, lead to the end of oppression. The equality of female slaves to male slaves did not end their oppression. Davis asserts, the equality of the female and male factory worker did not lead to their equality with the factory owner. True equality requires an end to the system of economic hierarchy.

Davis spends considerable time explaining the construct of gender in slave and upper class white society in order to make the point that the constructs were created and used in order to solidify power in the hands of those who already had it. She notes that slave men and women were treated equally for a variety of purposes that helped their wealthy male owners. For example, using men and women equally in the field doubled the master's free labor force. In addition, she notes that treating men and women as equals prevented a structure in which men felt responsible for or empowered to defend the women in their families. However, she notes that the unattended result was that both men and women slaves participated equally in acts of rebellion. In contrast, in white bourgeois society, there was a clear power differential between men and women which was meant to encourage obedience in women of the bourgeois class. Such women were taught that they were fragile and required the help of a man both physically and intellectually.

Davis notes that when wealthy white women began to protest their status and request political and economic rights, many centered their arguments around abolition. These women recognized that there was a common thread between slavery and misogynistic laws. The unity of these oppressed groups was divided after the civil war by those who used misogynism and racism to divide those who campaigned for black men's suffrage and women's suffrage. In addition, Davis notes that in the early part of the nineteenth century the labor movement was female-dominated. But misogynism and racism were used to divide the labor movement as it gathered strength. Davis's position is that racism and misogynism are purposefully constructed ideologies created and fueled by the bourgeois to keep the working class from uniting in a revolution that would create a truly egalitarian society. To repair these unfortunate divisions, Davis tries to explain women to each other by exposing the roles of differing social histories.

Davis's Discussion of Voluntary Motherhood

Many feminists, especially gender essentialists, consider motherhood as a unifying feature of women. Indeed, most of the first wave feminists of the nineteenth century assumed that most women would continue to value their biological role as mothers. In contrast, gender existentialists expose the idea of motherhood as a social construction rather than a biological category. Gender existentialists usually advocate that motherhood should be voluntary. Davis agrees with the idea of voluntary motherhood, but explains that this will mean radically different things to women of different races and classes.

First, Davis points out that many women have historically been refused the right to be mothers. Slave women were denied the label of "mother" and given instead the label "breeder" borrowed from animal husbandry. Slave women were often forced to leave their infants untended while they worked for the master, either in the field or factory. Some slave women were forced to abandon their own children and act as a substitute mother for the master's children. Slave women were not allowed to choose motherhood of their own children as their own vocation. Even after the civil war emancipated the slaves, many women of color were economically forced to work in the fields or were employed for the domestic care of white families. The closest most black women came to being traditional mothers was becoming "mammies" who were expected to nurture and care for the domestic needs of wealthy white families rather than their own.

White working class women also have been historically denied the right to voluntary motherhood. The history of the labor movement reveals the lack of protection for pregnant or newly delivered mothers of all colors in the workplace. Even today, contemporary legislation rarely advocates for working class mothers of any race. As a pointed example, welfare reform in the 1990s specifically targeted mothers who had chosen to stay home with their babies insisting that those who received welfare benefits had to find full time employment. Many poor women today are, thus, forced to leave their own children behind in order to work in childcare facilities for wealthier women. In addition, government subsidies for daycare costs for low income workers actually subsidize the companies who employ these women who would otherwise refuse to work for such a low wage. Davis explains that these women are not allowed to choose motherhood. Another contemporary example of not allowing women to choose motherhood occurs in incarceration. Women in jail awaiting trial and women in prison are disproportionately women of color or poor women. These women are stripped of their maternal rights to labor the way they wish, to stay with their new infants, and to mother their children.

Davis notes that while many white upper class feminists consider access to birth control and abortion as essential for voluntary motherhood, they need to consider the right for women to stay at home with their children as an important part of voluntary motherhood. In addition, Davis notes that the early movement for birth control and abortion access was marred by racism. On one hand, Margaret Sanger, who began Planned Parenthood, sought to increase women's ability to choose motherhood on their own terms after seeing many poor women die from botched illegal abortions. On the other hand, Davis also presents evidence that Sanger was heavily influenced by racist propaganda that encouraged her to urge women of color to have as few children as possible. Outside of Sanger's movement, there were many cases of poor women of color who were sterilized by doctors without their knowledge or consent in the 1960s and 1970s. These cases in the context of centuries of denying black women the rights of motherhood have spread skepticism in many minority communities concerning birth control and abortion. Davis notes that while wealthy women want freedom not to be mothers, many poor women of all races want more freedom to be mothers.

Yet, Davis is attentive to how the concept of motherhood "ideologically incarcerated" upper-class white women to "their biological reproductive role."[43] While minority and poor women were forced to refrain from any real role of mothering, white wealthy women were categorized as mothers with no other identity. While fatherhood was and is considered a minor role in the life of the autonomous man, motherhood was considered the only role for the white wealthy woman. Ironically, many of these white wealthy women hired black women to perform the domestic duties often associated with mothering for them. Similar issues still arise today, according to Davis. New reproductive technologies could increase opportunities for voluntary motherhood. Too often they are being manipulated by the same capitalist interests that have oppressed people for centuries.[44] In contemporary American society Davis sees wealthy women still being told that they must be mothers. Some of those who wish to free themselves from the duties of biological motherhood use egg donors, surrogate mothers,

43. Davis, "Surrogates and Outcasts," *Angela Davis Reader*, 212.
44. Ibid., 210.

and adoption. If this is done with authentic choice, this can be a path of voluntary motherhood for these women. The problem is that many of these women are still working under a Victorian construction of their identity as mothers being primary. Worse, they, perhaps unintentionally, expect working class women to sell their fertility, bodies, and domestic duties in order to survive economically.

Davis does support voluntary parenthood. She believes that giving all people real economic freedom will help all people make free choices about motherhood. She hopes for a system in which families can foster the ideal of nurturing and raising children. But she believes that further philosophical analysis must be done and that there must be a radical economic change in order for this to happen. Only then will individuals be able—authentically and autonomously—to choose or not choose mothering.

Davis on Rape and Women's Oppression

While many gendered experiences are culturally specific, sexual assault is a pervasive weapon against women and a common instrument of control. Rape has systematically been used to reinforce the identity of women as vulnerable to a unique form of attack. Rape is used as a way to undermine woman's agency and sense of independence. Davis has explained how rape was used to control woman slaves as "an uncamouflaged expression of the slave holder's economic mastery and the overseer's control over Black women as workers."[45] Similarly sexual harassment and rape have been used as a way to express power over female workers by factory owners. Particularly chilling is her recollection, pointed out by many other feminists in the 1970s, of how the United States Army instructed soldiers to use rape as a weapon against communist women in Vietnam.[46] Davis argues that this was sanctioned as a particular weapon against women who were learning to see themselves as equal to men under communist rule. Sadly, Davis says, most social outrage concerning rape only occurs when it threatens to undermine men of the upper economic classes who wish to protect their wives and daughters as property. As a result, "what happens to working class woman has usually been of very little concern to the courts."[47] Yet, rape and sexual assault is of great concern to feminists for such assault oppresses

45. Davis, *Women, Race and Class*, 7.

46. See ibid., 29.

47. Ibid., 172.

and silences women of all classes, keeping them from full participation in society. This is harmful both to the assaulted women and the society to which they might otherwise have contributed.

Davis's View of Women's Liberation as the End of Economic Oppression

Davis argues that the end of female oppression requires the end of all economic oppression. She believes that feminists must not work only for female liberation but for universal liberation. She quoted Angelina Grimke's comments from the era of the Civil War,

> The war is not as the South falsely pretends, a war of races . . . but a war of Principles, a war upon the working classes, whether white or black. In this war, the black man was the first victim, the working man of whatever color, the next; and now all who contend for the rights of labor, for free speech, free schools, free suffrage, and a free government . . . are driven to do battle in defense of these or to fall with them, . . .[48]

Davis says her position is similar to Grimke's. She believes that oppression is a tool of the economic elite and will be used against anyone of any gender or color. Davis explains the reason women waited for so long for suffrage was not because men were particularly, or naturally, misogynistic. "But it was not so much because they were men, it was rather because, as politicians, they were beholden to the dominant economic interests of the period."[49] Davis's claim is that it is economics that drive the definitions and structures of gender, race, and class. She has articulated that racism was and is "consciously planned by the representatives of the economically ascendant class."[50] As way of an example she discusses the race riots at the turn of the century in working class cities that were "orchestrated precisely in order to heighten the tensions and antagonism within the multi-racial working class."[51] She explains that racism and sexism nourish each other in order to continually divide oppressed groups who might otherwise work together for liberation.

48. Quoted from Lerner, *Grimke Sisters*, 354. In Davis, *Women, Race and Class*, 68.

49. Davis, *Women, Race, and Class*, 74.

50. Ibid., 124.

51. Ibid.

Feminist Merits of Davis's Gender Existentialism

Davis's remarkable philosophical achievement is her deep analysis of the differing impacts of gender roles for women of different races and socio-economic classes. Davis exposes the fact that the cultural construct of woman for African American slave women was radically different than that for white upper class women in the nineteenth century. She explained that racialized constructs remain in place today as well. Thus, Davis demonstrates the fluidity of gendered roles. More importantly, Davis explains the economic reasons why gendered and racial constructs are created and enforced. Her critique of capitalism unmasks the way corporate interests create constructs in order to oppress the working classes and increase bourgeois wealth and power. Davis insists that just as gender can be deconstructed, so can race and class. She continues to advocate that people who suffer oppression must work together to liberate all people physically, politically, economically, and psychologically.

Thinking Woman: bell hooks

Feminism is a movement to end sexism, sexist exploitation, and oppression.[52]

Biography

bell hooks is one of the most prolific feminist writers today. Born September 25, 1952, in Hopkinsville, Kentucky, she was named Gloria Jean Watkins. She has chosen to publish under the pen name bell hooks. This use of the uncapitalized form of her grandmother's name is intended to emphasize the ideas in the text rather than call attention to the particular author. Growing up in a working class African American family, hooks speaks of the constant pressure to do domestic work rather than intellectual work. Time and space for quiet private reading, writing, and thinking were rare. Taking that time or making that space was often considered an act of selfishness. As a result one of hooks's major points of activism is to convince women, especially women of color, that intellectual work is important work; as loving as domestic work, as valuable as paid work, and as

52. hooks, *Feminism Is for Everybody*, viii.

politically necessary as community work. She suggests that women need to advocate for themselves and their daughters to have access to thoughtful and critical education as well as to the space and time necessary for learning, reading, and writing.

bell hooks attended racially segregated public schools as a young child. As the schools were integrated, she moved from all-black institutions to those that were dominated by white teachers and administrators; she noticed there was a difference in culture and concepts. After graduating from Hopkinsville High School, hooks attended Stanford University as an undergraduate. There she felt isolated by her ethnicity. In her classes, she frequently experienced being marginalized. She graduated with her B.A. in 1973. When she finished her Masters at the University of Wisconsin in 1976, she was hired to teach ethnic studies in the University of California system.

While teaching and working on her PhD at the University of California, Santa Cruz, she published a book of poems titled *And There We Wept* (1978) and a major work of feminist philosophy titled *Ain't I a Woman? Black Women and Feminism* (1981). hooks had begun writing this book as an undergraduate when she felt marginalized by the academic feminism of the early seventies. In the book, she explains social roles and stereotypes that affect black women's sense of identity. hooks's hope was to explain some of the issues affecting women of color to white feminists in order to broaden the scope of academic feminism. The book was her first attempt to help form an active feminist sisterhood of women stepping across the boundaries of race and class in order to work together to end the oppression of all people.

In 1983, hooks finished her PhD with a dissertation on the literary work of Toni Morrison. Since then, hooks has taught at many different colleges and universities including Yale University, Oberlin College, the City College of New York, and the New School. She has published thirty-two books on feminism and feminist activism. Currently, she is Distinguished Professor in Residence in Appalachian Studies at Berea College in Kentucky. Her career as an academic teacher and a public intellectual has been rooted in the philosophical stance that studying the history of ideas, thinking deeply, and discussing with a wide variety of other people are essential ways to work to end oppression.

bell hooks's Theory of Gender Existentialism

bell hooks's understanding of women is that of a gender existentialist. She asserts that to be a woman in Western society is to be a human being whose identity has been constructed by the system of *white supremacist patriarchy*. Unlike Angela Davis, who claims racism and sexism are symptoms of capitalist oppression, hooks claims that white supremacist patriarchy is itself a cause of oppression that can and does exist in both capitalist and non-capitalist economic structures. hooks prefers to speak specifically of *white supremacist patriarchy* rather than generally of racism and sexism because she wishes to expose the specific bias that claims white characteristics are supreme and that white men are the natural authorities. Under this bias, people of color and women are considered secondary, the *Other*. Importantly, this is not a particular bias of white men, but is internalized by all members of society. hooks writes, "[A]ll of us, female and male, have been socialized from birth on to accept sexist thought and action."[53] Once the bias of white supremacy takes hold, the bias becomes a cause of further oppression. hooks writes, "Initial imprints seem to over determine attitudes about race."[54] These imprints of white supremacist patriarchy cause people to think and act in unhealthy and inauthentic ways. As just one small example, the beauty bias of white supremacy causes black women to use unhealthy chemicals to straighten their hair and the hair of their young girls. This same beauty bias causes woman of all ethnicities to diet excessively and wear restrictive and uncomfortable clothes in order to feign fragility and weakness. Defined as immanent body, sexualized object, and natural mother rather than transcendent human being, "all females no matter their age are being socialized either consciously or unconsciously to have anxiety about their body."[55] This anxiety keeps them from taking on the identity of free subjects who can determine the scope of their own lives. This anxiety leads to self-hatred and internal oppression, as women, particularly women of color, consistently see themselves as secondary citizens.

53. hooks, "Feminism is for Everyone," viii.
54. hooks, *Teaching Community*, 26.
55. hooks, *Feminism is for Everybody*, 35.

hooks's Theory of Philosophical Thinking as Feminist Activism:

bell hooks's argument for intellectual feminism hinges on her philosophical stance that all action is rooted in thinking. Women must first understand the ideas that underlie the current system in order to use new ideas to change the system. hooks believes that one of the main objectives of feminism is to unmask the bias of white supremacist patriarchy as it exists in both men and women. This requires deep thinking. Women must "unlearn female self-hatred . . . [and] break free of the hold patriarchal thinking had on our consciousness."[56] She believes that this freedom will be more authentic and healthier for all members of society. This includes men who, she insists, will "find in feminist movement the hope of their own release from the bondage of patriarchy."[57]

hooks believes deeply in the possibility of real freedom for individuals. While she insists that a strong white supremacist patriarchal bias pervades Western culture, she also insists that individuals can choose to resist this bias once it is exposed to them. In her book, *Teaching Community*, she writes, "No one is born a racist. Everyone makes a choice."[58] She continues, "While it is a truism that every citizen of this nation, white or colored, is born into a racist society that attempts to socialize us from the moment of our birth to accept the tenets of white supremacy, it is equally true that we can choose to resist this socialization."[59] This radical view of freedom, she shares with the French existentialists. Once a bias is uncovered, once the mind is decolonized, the individual can freely think and freely become who she wishes to be.

Feminist Merits of hooks's Work toward the Nonviolent End of all Oppression

According to hooks, a major part of the pattern of white supremacist patriarchy is the concept that "it is acceptable for a more powerful individual to control others through various forms of coercive force."[60] Patriarchy's foundation, according to hooks, is that violence justifies authority. In order to

56. Ibid., 14.
57. Ibid., ix.
58. hooks, *Teaching Community*, 53.
59. Ibid., 56.
60. hooks, *Feminism is for Everybody*, 62.

end patriarchy and white supremacist thinking, feminists must advocate a new understanding of power that does not come from coercion. Feminism should certainly work to provide equal opportunities for women and men within their defined social classes, but should, also, seek to end all oppression with a commitment to equality of all people and the end of all violent coercion. Feminists cannot win by simply becoming mighty.

Importantly, ending oppression and coercion in order to allow autonomy does not mean that individuals are given an arbitrary kind of freedom. Indeed, hooks frequently takes a stand against those writers who suggest that any woman is a feminist as long as she is proud of who she is. hooks has written, "Obviously this way of thinking has made feminism more acceptable because its underlying assumption is that women can be feminists without fundamentally challenging themselves or the culture."[61] The problem with this way of thinking is that it mistakes freedom with arbitrary choice without requiring the individual analyze what bias might be active in her choice. For example, hooks believes that feminists must be politically pro-choice, because uncovering the oppressive "notion that a woman's reason for existence was to bear children" requires an acceptance that woman should be allowed control over her body to make reproductive choices.[62] In addition, while hooks does not make the same Marxist critique of capitalism as Davis does, hooks does claim that poverty is a feminist issue. Because the bias against woman has caused the majority of people in poverty to be women, she believes the fight against poverty is a fight feminists must make. hooks's point is that a diverse group of people with different cultural perspectives must join together for philosophical discussion to create a better system for all people.

The way to move people towards a feminist perspective without violence, according to hooks, is to encourage rich intellectual dialogue among a diverse crowd of people. The more people interact, teach, and learn from individuals of different genders, races, and classes, the more people will come to recognize the diversity of human being as well as the universality of human dignity. To this end, hooks advocates using diverse images in the media, encouraging diversity in leadership roles, and teaching full accounts of human history, not just the history of white supremacist patriarchy. In addition, hooks is very serious about the need for feminists to publish intellectual books for the general public, not just highly literate, well-educated

61. Ibid., 6.
62. Ibid., 27.

and materially privileged academics. Feminists must also have discussions with themselves and with others outside the movement. This reveals that hooks firmly holds a philosophical stance that bias can be unmasked and truth can be recognized through reading, thinking, and talking in community. Her own books, lectures, and essays have influenced a wide variety of readers from many different disciplines.

Problems with Gender Existentialism

Gender existentialists promote a view of authentic human nature as essentially free. This leads to three major critiques made by feminists who call themselves *third wave feminists*. These third wave feminists are not unified by theory, but by their sense that they come after the second wave writers and have recognized flaws in their work. Third wave feminists offer a diversity of solutions and do not see themselves as a single movement.

First, some third wave feminists argue that any attempt to define a universally authentic identity denies individuals their true freedom. For example, hooks is accused of creating too narrow a definition of feminism in denying the possibility of pro-life feminism, militant feminism, or any feminism that is not actively anti-racist or anti-classist. Some of her third wave critics suggest that she needs to allow each woman to define her own sense of identity.

Other third-wave feminists offer the critique that what many gender existentialists promote as universal human authenticity is actually a Eurocentric male bias about freedom. Indeed, Beauvoir, Friedan, and Davis have been criticized as advocating a view that claims femininity is a psychosis that needs to be cured in order to help women be more male. Specifically, Beauvoir is accused of promoting the masculine view of Sartre that encourages individual freedom at the expense of the family. Friedan is accused of promoting the male capitalist view that a human being needs a career in order to be authentic. Davis is accused of accepting a male view of the inevitable need for violence in order to create power. Generally, third wave gender essentialists, including womanists and those who advocate an ethics of care, suggest that gender existentialists ought to consider the real value of the feminine perspective. These feminists, discussed in chapter 1, advocate what they call *difference feminism*, which is a contemporary version of gender essentialism.

Another critique of gender existentialism is that defining human nature as essentially free promotes a philosophical claim that there are no objective standards for thought or behavior. If freedom is the absolute goal, philosophers cannot define how·that freedom is to be used. Such a claim, says critics, makes activism impossible. These critics argue that there needs to be firmer common ground that defines wellbeing, health, or authentic living for human beings. Some third wave feminists, thus, argue for grounding feminism in Marxism, Christianity, or Buddhism.

A final critique of gender existentialism is that the proponents of this theory do not go far enough to deconstruct the gender binary. These critics suggest that not only is gender a social construction that limits the freedom of individuals, but also biological sex. These critics are proponents of *queer theory*, which will be the subject of the next chapter.

Conclusions

Despite the emergence of critiques from the third wave of feminism, the existentialists are widely regarded as having provided an extremely important theory of woman. Unlike the gender essentialists, they do not tie a woman's destiny to her biological sex. They argue for the equal potential in all realms for men and women. Yet, unlike liberal feminists who propose gender neutrality, second wave feminists acknowledge that gender constructs have limited the potential of women to see themselves as fully active, conscious human beings. They also note how race and class stereotypes further limit an individual's potential. Unlike the proponents of gender neutrality, the gender existentialists acknowledge that legal equality will not free women's minds unless there is a change in the way the gender binary is constructed. Culture created gender categories do not fall away just because of legislation. Women's desires, tastes, and sensibilities have been cultivated in specific ways, depending on where and how they were raised. By recognizing the ways women have been cultivated, women can free their minds from harmful stereotypes and live more authentic and healthy lives.

The work done by gender existentialists to deconstruct the gender binary has radically influenced the way media portrays women, corporations advertise to women, and schools educate girls. Moreover, many contemporary women continue to find the experience of reading the works of twentieth-century gender existentialism a helpful psychoanalytic task that helps unmask their selves to themselves. Contemporary gender existentialist thinkers such as Davis and hooks continue to lecture to large audiences that are encouraged by their ideas of authentic human freedom.

4

Gender Fluidity

The very subject of women is no longer understood
in stable or abiding terms.

—JUDITH BUTLER[1]

Parents often expect that the first pronouncement about their newborn will announce the child's sex. However, there are times when the newborn's body is not easily characterized as male or female. Indeed, statistics show that the external genitalia in at least 1 in 2000 babies are ambiguous or difficult to classify.[2] In other cases, the results from prenatal genetic testing do not match the phenotype of the newborn baby, as when a child has the genetic code for one gender but the physiological appearance of the other. At other times the genotype itself is ambiguous, neither XX nor XY. When all is taken into account, careful studies of medical literature demonstrate that the sex is ambiguous in as many as 1 in 100 newborns.[3]

1. Butler, *Gender Trouble*, 4.

2. See Dreger, *Hermaphrodites*, 41–43.

3. See ibid., 42. Importantly, Dreger notes "In conclusion, it is not possible to provide with any great certainty a statistic of the frequency of births in which the child's sex falls into question. . . . such a statistic is always necessarily culture specific. It varies with gene-pool isolation and environmental influences. It also varies according to what, in a given culture, counts as acceptable variations of malehood or femalehood as opposed to forms considered sexually ambiguous."

In still other situations, babies who were labeled one sex at birth begin to develop the physical characteristics of the opposite gender as they mature. Also, some adults are surprised to discover during a medical exam that their bodies have hormonal balances, genetic traits, or internal organs that do not correspond to the medical definition of the sex they believed themselves to be. In addition, there are a number of people who find that they psychologically do not identify with their sex as biologically defined. And of course, as the earlier chapters have suggested, there are many people who find the categories of sex and gender too constrictive to explain their own talents and desires. With all of these situations in mind, a new theory of sex and gender called *queer theory* began in the 1990s.

This chapter is an exploration of what *queer theory* and its theory of *gender fluidity* say about being a woman. In contrast to all the previous theories, queer theorists deny that there is any essential, natural, or static definition of the word "woman" psychologically, spiritually, or even biologically. However, queer theorists would deny that the word "woman" is meaningless or unimportant. Rather, queer theorists analyze language and culture in order to investigate what it means to act or perform as a woman in society. Queer analysis exposes the constructed nature of the definition of woman in order to highlight both what is helpful and what is problematic in the contemporary definition. This theory is used by many feminists who wish to critique and disturb society's understanding of what it means to be a woman in order to better recognize and care for all individuals.

What Is Gender Fluidity and What Is Queer Theory?

Gender is defined as the classification of male or female that includes social, psychological, emotional, and intellectual characteristics. *Fluidity* is a term that suggests that a category is in the process of change and that individuals who belong to the category may flow in and out of that categorization. *Gender fluidity* is the theory that claims the categories of gender are fluid. Importantly, according to this theory, biological sex is as fluid as gender. This means that the biological categories of male and female are human constructs not natural constructs. The way medicine and science constructs biological sex depends on how culture has already constructed gender. In Western culture much of the categorization of both sex and gender comes from cultural ideas about sexuality and sexual attraction. A theory of gender fluidity insists that all of these categories need to be continually engaged and re-thought in order to most accurately account for the variety of human life experiences. Moreover, a theory of gender fluidity suggests that individuals flow in and out of sex and gender categories. For example, this theory accepts the possibility that a baby with the biological sex of male might develop into a biologically female person. This theory also considers the possibility that a baby with the biological sex of male might perform as a gendered male or as a gendered female at different points in its life. This theory also insists that sexual desire is also fluid. An individual's sexual desire may or may not follow the rules of heterosexuality.

Queer is an adjective that describes anything odd or strange. In the twentieth century, the word queer was often used as a slur against homosexuals. In order to re-appropriate that term, gender theorists as well as individuals in popular culture have begun to use the word *queer* to denote concepts, characteristics, or bodies that transgress or defy the boundaries which are considered to mark the male from the female and vice versa. The use of the word *queer* as a verb means to take a word, concept, category, or story and use it to disturb the boundaries between male and female.

Queer theory at its most fundamental level is theory that takes into account all those bodies, ideas, and ways of life that do not fit the gender binary and, thus, are considered *queer*. *Queer theorists* analyze the concepts of sex and gender in order to expose them as fluid concepts with permeable boundaries. The theory has philosophical, scientific, and sociological roots. The theory's interdisciplinary nature lends it a vigorous intellectual and popular force.

Queer Theory and the History of Philosophy

There are deep philosophical roots to queer theory in post-Enlightenment philosophy. In order to understand queer theory, it is helpful to have some introduction to these roots. Philosophically, queer theory espouses a view of gender and sex as radically inessential. This theory of gender suggests that not only is gender a cultural construct as the existentialist theory of gender asserts, but that, also, sex and sexuality are constructs. This theory claims that culture and language have created the constructs of the gender/sex binary. The words, "masculinity," "maleness," "femininity," and "femaleness" are names that are meaningful only in the context of specific languages and cultures. This view stands opposed to any theory of natural law that claims sex is part of the natural world. Rather than looking at nature in order to understand the natural structures of sex, queer theory insists that language, not nature, created sex. This theory is indebted to the dominant Western philosophical traditions that followed the Enlightenment: the nineteenth to twenty-first-century philosophical systems of idealism, phenomenology, existentialism, analytic philosophy, and deconstructionism. These modes of thought highly influenced the main architects of queer theory.

The philosophical innovations of the nineteenth and twentieth centuries are varied and complex. Here is only a brief synopsis in order that the reader might be better orientated towards the advent of queer theory. Throughout the late eighteenth and the whole of the nineteenth century there arose a philosophical movement counter to the Enlightenment's assurance that reason and experience could lead interested individuals to uncover the truth of nature. This post-Enlightenment thinking is sometimes categorized as the earliest beginning of *postmodernism*. Postmodernism is the period of philosophy after the modern period. The first thinkers in this very early postmodern movement were influenced by the German philosopher Immanuel Kant, who suggested that a human observer cannot see the world as it really is but only as the individual's mind sees the world. While Kant had declared that there was a *noumenal* world, or a world that exists in and for itself, he made it clear that a human observer only had access to the world of her experience, the *phenomenal* world. His philosophical work amounted to a philosophical revolution, the Kantian revolution. European philosophers after Kant had to acquiesce that human access to the truth about nature is unavoidably limited. This view that humans see the world according to the categories created in their minds led philosophical *idealists* to suggest that reality, at least as far as human beings know it, is a construction of the mind. *Idealists* suggest that the world human beings experience is the immaterial world of ideas that exists in the mind. Thus, the nineteenth-century idealists claimed that philosophers ought to study the structures of the mind rather than attempt to access the inaccessible structures of reality.

Idealism influenced the creation of three new strains of philosophy: *phenomenology*, *existentialism*, and *analytic philosophy*. First, the *phenomenologists* maintained that phenomena, or appearances, should be the object of philosophical inquiry. These philosophers insisted on studying the experiences of human beings rather than any reality beyond experience, as such reality is inaccessible. This was the approach of philosopher Edith Stein, who was discussed in the first chapter. As many philosophers began to be most interested in ideas and experience, throughout the late nineteenth and early twentieth centuries, *existentialists* reminded readers that human beings and their experiences in the world are always changing. Thus, existentialists asserted that both individuals and their ideas are constantly becoming something new rather than remaining fixed. Existentialists denied the existence of fixed essences and emphasized the possibilities of freedom. This theory grounded the gender existentialists discussed in the previous chapter. Phenomenology and existentialism were prominent across the continent of Europe, especially in Germany, Scandinavia, and France. At the same time a different response to idealism arose in Austria and England, that of *analytic philosophy*. Analytic philosophers claimed the project of philosophy ought to focus on analyzing human language in order to gain clarity about human experience of the world. To conclude, most of these types of thinkers hoped to find some access to truth. Many phenomenologists hoped that their studies would reveal the underlying structure of reality. Many existentialists trusted that an individual could use their theories to discover an authentic way of life. And most analytic philosophers believed that underlying language there were fixed realities that the human mind could discover. Yet, all three types of thinkers were influenced by idealism's view that human access to truth, reality, and nature was limited by the human mind.

A key thinker in the early twentieth century, the Austrian philosopher Ludwig Wittgenstein, had an important role to play in this philosophical history. Wittgenstein insisted that philosophers needed to admit that they had no reason to believe that human ideas, experiences, or language correlated to any real truths. Wittgenstein argued that philosophers who wished to get clear about language could solve linguistic problems but not philosophical problems. For example, a philosopher who wished to understand the true nature of "pain" by examining how the word is used in English would be ignoring the fact that the word "pain" was an invention of language, not nature. Thus, the philosopher could only get clear about how speakers of a particular language use the word "pain" and could not gain access to what pain truly is. Indeed, Wittgenstein suggested that there may be no true reality under the word at all. This radical *nominalism*, the view that names are human constructs that may or may not correspond to real essences, led many later twentieth-century scholars across the disciplines to adopt *deconstructionism*, the project of analyzing the way language is used in order to de-construct the categories that once appeared fixed. The project of many thinkers, thus, became to free readers from constrained thinking rather than to discover truths.

Queer theory inherits this philosophical viewpoint. Unlike most of the thinkers discussed in the first three chapters, queer theorists do not try to get clear about the true nature of women. Rather they suggest that the concept of woman is a constantly changing cultural idea. These thinkers deny that there is any actual real nature of woman that exists separately from human language and thought. Contrary to gender essentialists, queer theorists deny the possibility of discovering a true natural essence of women. Contrary to first and second wave feminists they also deny the possibility of uncovering or freeing an authentic un-gendered mind through the use of reason or self-analysis. But the queer theorist does have a goal. Queer theory raises questions and creates new ideas in order to compel the reader to analyze and de-construct what gender and sex mean in culture. After this deconstruction of culture's ideas, queer theorists advocate inventing new concepts about gender that are more inclusive and useful than the previous ones.

Queer Theory and the History of Science

Queer theory is also indebted to the scientific revolutions of the twentieth century. Evidence collected by geologists and biologists of the nineteenth and twentieth centuries led to the acceptance of a worldview that mountains, valleys, and species are not fixed but fluid. Evidence gathered by chemists and physicists led to a worldview that the smallest building blocks of the cosmos do not obey the linear laws of mathematics suggested by Isaac Newton. The new theories that were adopted led to the acceptance by many scientists of *scientific anti-realism*, a theory that scientific theories are human constructs biased by the culture of the scientific community.

Werner Heisenberg, an Austrian physicist, was one of the first physicists to assert that the role of the scientist cannot be to describe the world as she thinks it really is but simply to provide useful mathematical models that describe the behavior of the objects of human observation.[4]

4. See Cox and Forshaw, *Quantum Universe,* 12–13. "In July of 1925, Heisenberg published a paper . . . and ushered in an entirely new approach to physics. . . . Heisenberg is saying that the underlying mathematics of quantum theory need not correspond to anything with which we are familiar. The job of quantum theory should be to predict directly observable things. . . . It should not be expected to provide some kind of satisfying mental pictures for the internal workings of the atom, . . . In one fell swoop, Heisenberg

Importantly, this new way of thinking about the role of the physicist allowed for a number of breakthroughs in physics that would not have been possible had scientists been constrained by the attempt to describe the real behavior of particles. Quantum physicists have discovered that quantum particles do not behave in ways that seem realistic or even logically possible. The revolutionary new ideas of quantum mechanics led to new debates between *scientific realism* and *scientific anti-realism,* debates between those who consider science the enterprise of discovering natural laws that describe reality and those who consider science the enterprise of creating theories that describe what humans observe. In response to these debates, the physicist Thomas Kuhn wrote the *Structure of Scientific Revolutions* in 1962. This groundbreaking work asserted that scientific theory is a construction of human minds that becomes the lens through which scientists and the general public view the world. As an example one might consider Galileo's discovery of the moons of Jupiter, which is often considered a key discovery by which Galileo "proved" that not all celestial bodies orbit the Earth. Kuhn's theory proposed that Galileo discovered the moons of Jupiter only because he already knew about the heliocentric theory of Copernicus. Because Galileo had read Copernicus he was open to the possibility that all objects in space do not orbit the earth. Because he was open to the idea, he was able to see Jupiter's moons as Jupiter's satellites. Before Galileo could use a telescope to look in the night sky, he needed a reason to do so. Moreover, even the moons being present in Galileo's field of vision was not enough. Galileo needed a theory in his mind that would allow him to see the moons. Indeed, after Galileo's work was widely published, many new discoveries were suddenly made. The theory opened the door to the observation. Kuhn's point is that a new theory changes the way the world appears to scientists and eventually the public. Evidence is only seen if a new theory allows one to see it.

This view of science is deeply embedded in queer theory. One of the foundational thinkers of queer theory, Donna Haraway, began and continues her career in biology. Her doctoral thesis explored the way linguistic metaphors determined the design of scientific experiments. She used empirical evidence to prove that the language use of a scientist affects the empirical evidence the scientist is able to see. This means that scientists are often limited in their pursuit of knowledge by their language and cultural

---

removed the conceit that the workings of Nature should necessarily accord with common sense." See Heisenberg, "Über quantentheoretische."

bias. Furthermore, scientists, also have the power to construct bias as they create categories and collect empirical evidence that is used to cement those categories. This is seen in the way eighteenth-century Swedish biologist Carl Linnaeus created the modern taxonomy of animals as mammals, reptiles, fish, birds, and amphibians. This is also seen, according to Haraway, in the way medical doctors named and created sex categories as a binary of male and female.

Queer Theory and Sociology

Finally, the philosophical and scientific revolutions after the Enlightenment are reflected in sociological trends. Simultaneously in philosophy, science, and culture there arose a skepticism concerning fixed essences and values that were once believed to come from nature or the Divine. Throughout Western culture from the late nineteenth century to the early twenty-first century, popular belief claims truth is a cultural construct. However, sociologists note that cultural constructs can have authority within their culture. Indeed, they dictate the way individuals in a culture think and behave. Often times there appears a *hegemony* of thought in a culture, a way of thinking that is so dominant that it is difficult to see the way of thought as a construct rather than a fixed truth.

As a marked example, the queer theorist Judith Butler notes that while many people in Western culture today accept a diversity of ideas about the Divine, these same people are incapable of accepting a diversity of ideas about sex and gender. She asserts that there exists in Western culture a *hegemony* about sex and gender. Trained to see fixed gender ideals, individuals see these stereotypes as essential and real. The individuals then force themselves and their friends and relatives to behave according to the stereotypes. Thus, the acceptance of the stereotypes actually creates what looks like empirical evidence that the stereotypes are true. Yet, these ideas and the evidence that substantiates them are constantly changing according to queer theory. This can be seen in the inconsistency of the societal standards of masculine and feminine. Queer theory suggests that changes in society demonstrate that sex is a construct not a natural structure. Yet, queer thinkers acknowledge that sex is a construct that has great authority in Western culture.

Queer theory has developed from philosophical, scientific, and sociological trends in the last two centuries. Importantly queer theorists suggest that the way people think and talk about sexuality, sex, and gender affects how people see the world and how people act in the world. Thus, the way people think actually changes the world. Thus, to suggest that gender roles no longer function as they once did does not simply mean that people have changed their minds. Rather, this suggests that sexuality, gender, and sex are actually different in the twenty-first century than ever before. Queer theorists both desire to help expose the way gender and sex fluctuate and to encourage a consciousness about sex and gender that exposes diversity and creates value for that diversity.

Thinking Woman: Donna Haraway

> Once upon a time, in the 1970s, the author was a proper, US socialist-feminist, white, female, hominid, biologist, who became a historian of science to write about modern Western accounts of monkeys, apes, and women. . . . But . . . she has turned into a multiply marked cyborg feminist.[5]

Biography

Donna Haraway, scientist and philosopher, is considered one of the main architects of queer theory, along with philosopher Judith Butler and literary theorist Eve Kosofksy Sedgwick. Donna Haraway was born in 1944 in Denver, Colorado. Her Colorado upbringing included exposure to Native American sensibilities, symbolism, and culture. She also claims that she was deeply influenced by her Roman Catholic upbringing. She says about Roman Catholicism, "I learned it. I studied it. It is deep in my bones."[6] When she voiced questions about her faith at age twelve, her priest urged her to read Thomas Aquinas. While she claims that she did not understand Aquinas's words, her relationship with her priests introduced her to the theological framework of Catholicism, "the theological tradition that focuses on unnameableness."[7] She claims this was powerful to her as a child, especially "the idea that if you seriously are trying to deal with something that is infinite, you should not attach a noun to it, because then you have

---

5. Haraway, *Simians, Cyborgs, Women*, 1.
6. Haraway, "An Interview with Donna Haraway," *Donna Haraway Reader*, 334.
7. Ibid.

fixed and set limits to that which is limitless."[8] After high school, she studied philosophy and theology at the Fondation Teilhard de Chardin in Paris on a Fulbright Scholarship. While Haraway claimed in 1999 to be "a committed atheist and anti-Catholic, anyway at some level," she continues to see the Catholic theological tradition as part of her "very deep inheritance."[9]

When Haraway returned from Paris, she enrolled at Colorado College where she triple-majored in zoology, philosophy, and literature. She went on to study at Yale University where she received her PhD in biology with a dissertation on the use of language and metaphor in experimental biology. Interested in interdisciplinary work, she taught both science and women's studies at the University of Hawaii from 1971–74. She moved to John Hopkins University in 1974 and taught for six years in the Department of the History of Science. In 1980 she moved to the University of California, Santa Cruz, where she is a professor in the History of Consciousness Program. She has also taught as Professor of Feminism and Technoscience at the European Graduate School.

Haraway has written several important and influential works on gender, on human nature and on the philosophy of science. Particularly, she is known for groundbreaking work in feminism, primatology, and philosophy of technology. The link between the three is seen in her *Cyborg Manifesto,* an essay she began in response to a call for articles on the future of socialist feminism by *the Socialist Review* in 1983. This essay discusses ways in which categories are constructed by scientists and by culture. Specifically, Haraway speaks of how women are constructed like cyborgs. Often these constructions have been done to serve patriarchy and capitalism, according to Haraway. However, she opens the possibility that these constructions could be re-constructed to benefit individuals giving them increased pleasure and increased responsibility in their lives. The radical idea that human beings are actually cyborgs, beings who have transgressed the boundaries of nature, has become a revolutionary philosophical concept. Haraway has continued to deconstruct philosophical concepts of "nature," "woman," "sex," "dominance" and "human nature" in her many essays and books such as *Primate Visions* (1989), *Simians, Cyborgs, and Women: The Reinvention of Nature* (1991), *Modest_Witness @ Second_Millennium.FemaleMan* © *_Meets_OncoMouse™: Feminism and Technoscience* (1997), and *The Donna Haraway Reader* (2004).

8. Ibid.
9. Ibid.

Donna Haraway's Theory of Woman as Cyborg

> I want my writing to be read as an orthopedic practice for learning
> how to remold kin links to help make a kinder and unfamiliar
> world.[10]

Donna Haraway's major philosophical innovation is her articulation that the boundaries between the natural and the artificial are themselves artificial. There is no natural versus artificial world, according to Haraway, no human nature versus human artifice, no natural woman versus female construct. In her view all of nature is artificially constructed, and all construction is part of nature. Every woman is a cyborg.

Haraway's view is rooted in her philosophy of science. She repudiates the view that science can discover the truth about nature. She believes that science is a construct.[11] With empirical evidence and philosophical argument, she demonstrates that this is true in her own field of primatology where she has witnessed many scientists who believed that they were able to uncover certain knowledge of human nature by studying apes. Haraway insists that a scientist who wishes to get beyond her bias when looking at a primate is attempting an impossible project. The scientist is affecting the primate by her observation and influencing the primate. Moreover, the primate is influencing the other primates, the surrounding environment, and the observer herself. All of this is affecting the scientist who is, of course, looking through a lens formed by her own experiences and language. There is no natural world for the human observer to observe, there is only the observed world in relationship with the observer. Failure to acknowledge this leads scientists to report data without contextualizing that data in terms of the type of experiments done and the bias of the scientist herself.

As just one example of many, Haraway speaks of the famous experiments done by Harry Harlow with rhesus monkeys that "proved" the need for primates, including humans, to have an intimate loving physical relationship with their mothers. Haraway explains first the cultural bias of Harlow, who was open about his ambivalence towards working wives and mothers who "threaten to displace the American man in science and

---

10. Haraway, "Introduction," *Donna Haraway Reader*, 2.

11. For a full explanation of Donna Haraway's understanding of humanist scientific anti-realism see chapter 4: "In the Beginning was the Word; The Genesis of Biological Theory," *Simians, Cyborgs, and Women*, 70–80.

industry."[12] Haraway recounts the experiments themselves. She explains ways in which the results of the experiments may have been skewed by what might be called the sadism of Harlow's experiment, especially the artificial insemination of the female monkeys on what Harlow named "the rape rack" and some of the constructions of the metal surrogate "mother" that froze, spiked, shook, or shocked the infant monkeys that clung to it. Neither the biological mothers nor the infant rhesus monkeys were in a neutral or natural environment. They were in an artificially constructed environment that could be described as one of terror. However, the effect of the environment was not considered significant in altering the infants' ability to thrive without their mothers. Indeed, these experiments have been used in a great variety of arguments as proof of the need for a warm, caring, and gentle mother for all primate infants, including human infants. The experiment's bias and method certainly does not mean that the opposite of its conclusions are proven. Haraway does not mean to suggest that infants do not need loving support, but she does wish to point out how this experiment by Harlow does not prove the natural need of a specific type of mother as Harlow claimed.[13] Importantly, Harlow's failure to observe and report on real natural motherhood is not simply because of his particular bias or experimental design. Haraway insists there is a bias in every human scientist who seeks to uncover a truth of natural motherhood or even human nature. Scientists see what they observe. The observed is always an artificial construction of the mind of the observer.

Haraway's scientific background significantly affects her views about human beings and women. Haraway insists that the human being is a construction with no clear boundary between the natural and the artificial. Haraway explains that "we are chimeras, theorized, and fabricated hybrids of machine and organism; in short, we are cyborgs."[14] Pacemakers, implants, hormone patches, medications, vitamin supplements, and other technologies exist, literally, inside human bodies. Piped music, flashing billboards, and ringing cell phones are taken in through the senses and become part of the neurological structure of the mind. There is no human being that is not vitally formed by technology.

This, too, is true of female human beings. The woman, even more than the general human being, is a cyborg according to Haraway. Many

---

12. Harlow and Mears, *Human Model*, 125; quoted in Haraway, *Primate Visions*, 236.

13. See "Metaphors into Hardware," in Haraway, *Primate Visions*, 231–44.

14. Haraway, "A Manifesto for Cyborgs," *Donna Haraway Reader*, 10.

contemporary feminists, influenced by gender existentialism, have articulated the need for women to uncover what is essential to womanhood and what is culturally imposed upon them. But Haraway believes that these feminists are creating a false dichotomy. Contemporary people, whether they are classified as men or women, have all taken technology and biotechnology into their bodies, both consciously and un-consciously. Some women consciously take female hormone therapy to restore their natural balance, albeit artificially. Other women unknowingly ingest hormones in the milk they drink and meat they eat. Some women consciously use hair-dyes, make-up, and surgery to create an appearance that they believe is more natural. Others unconsciously use diet and exercise to conform to an image they do not even realize they desire. Some women use medical technology to live longer lives, to conceive more or fewer children, and to ease specific pains. Other women are denied access to this technology because of the conditions imposed by the companies for which they work or the governments under which they live. Haraway insists both sets of women live according to artificial technologies, boundaries, or standards. Yet, too, both sets of women are natural women. Haraway does not simply ask feminists to consider that all women are artificially constructed, but also to consider that all "artificial" construction is part of nature.

> If the world exists for us as "nature," this designates a kind of relationship, an achievement among many actors, not all of them human, not all of them organic, not all of them technological. In its scientific embodiments as well as in other forms, nature is made, but not entirely by humans; it is a co-construction among humans and non-humans.[15]

Haraway thinks the best philosophical solution to the question of "What is a natural woman?" is in admitting that there "is no fundamental, ontological separation in our formal knowledge of machine and organism, of technical and organic."[16] Further, she insists that seeking the "natural law" is a philosophical error that "misses most of reality, probably always, but certainly now."[17] For Haraway, there is no distinction between the artificial and natural.

15. Haraway, "The Promises of Monsters," *Donna Haraway Reader*, 66.
16. Haraway, "A Manifesto for Cyborgs," *Donna Haraway Reader*, 35.
17. Ibid., 39.

Feminist Merits of Donna Haraway's Queer Theory

Haraway rejects the view that natural women exist. But she does not reject the feminist project of increasing the rights of those who are labeled women. The ethical and political solution for feminists cannot require uncovering and revering the "natural" woman. But, feminists can and ought to advocate for the "utopian dream of the hope for a monstrous world without gender."[18] Haraway insists that feminists can and should attempt to create new definitions and categories that increase pleasure and responsibility for all stakeholders rather than serving capitalism and patriarchy.[19] To free women, feminists ought to embrace the scientific and philosophical arguments that destroy the tenets of natural law that created the category of woman and the subsequent boundaries and constraints for those categorized as women. Feminists need a new way of talking that self-consciously recognizes the creative power of language. Haraway suggests this will be a "cyborg language" that does not create a new *hegemony*, or coercive way of thinking. Rather she hopes for a new and common language that is "a powerful infidel heteroglossia . . . a feminist speaking in tongues."[20] She advocates for a new way of speaking, seeing, and being in a world beyond gender.

Thinking Woman: Judith Butler

The efforts to denaturalize sexuality and gender have taken as their main enemy those normative frameworks of compulsory heterosexuality that operate through the naturalization and reification of heterosexist norms.[21]

Biography

Judith Butler is one of the central philosophical architects of queer theory. Butler was born in 1956, in Cleveland, Ohio. Her Jewish family was of Hungarian and Russian background. During her childhood, memories of the Holocaust were still fresh for her family. Many of Butler's mother's family

18. Ibid.

19. See Haraway, *Simians, Cyborgs, Women,* 68 and 150.

20. Haraway, "A Manifesto for Cyborgs," *Donna Haraway Reader,* 39.

21. Butler, *Bodies that Matter,* 93.

had perished in concentration camps. Butler claims her Jewish heritage provided some of her intellectual foundation and many of her values about speaking her mind.

Butler recounts her introduction to philosophy in an essay in which she advocates for the discipline. She presents herself as a young teenager in her basement, with the door locked, in order to smoke and be alone. Looking up at the bookshelf she noticed a book with a title that roused her to take the book and read. The book was one of her mother's old college books, a copy of Spinoza's *Ethics*. Soon afterwards Butler discovered two other books on the shelf, Søren Kierkegaard's *Either/Or* and Schopenhauer's *The World as Will and Representation*. These had been given to her father by an old girlfriend years before he met her mother. Butler found the three texts rich in ideas. She claimed Spinoza, particularly, gave her teenage self a profound and clear way to understand her own passions and emotions.[22]

During those same teenage years in which she was reading philosophy in her basement, she was also attending Hebrew school classes at her local synagogue. The topics that most interested her were morality and human responsibility. In the class she persisted in asking questions, for example, why the philosopher Spinoza had been expelled from the synagogue in his own day. Her instructor labeled her as defiant. As punishment, she was assigned readings by Jewish philosophers and a weekly tutorial in ethics with her rabbi. The tutorial profited her by encouraging her questioning and deep thinking. To this day, Butler credits her Jewish heritage for her ability to ask difficult questions and for the courage to raise them.

Her interest in philosophy continued when she went to Bennington College. But her initial contact with a course by Professor Paul de Man on Nietzsche gave her a marked experience of groundlessness. She claims that she had to steady herself literally against the handrail after the initial class period, proclaiming "with alarm, that he did not believe in the concept, that de Man was destroying the very presumption of philosophy, unraveling concepts and metaphors, and stripping philosophy of its powers of consolation."[23] She refused to return to the class, although she claims she frequently stood outside the door listening. Butler, self-aware, says that she has seen the same reaction in people who listen to her or read her books. She understands their reaction.

22. Butler, *Undoing Gender*, 235.
23. Ibid., 238.

Butler received a B.A. in philosophy from Bennington College in 1978. In 1979 she studied at the University of Heidelberg on a Fulbright scholarship. She finished her PhD in philosophy from Yale in 1984, writing her dissertation on how the philosophy of desire put forth by the nineteenth-century German philosopher G. W. F. Hegel was appropriated by twentieth-century French philosophers. Her first book was a revised version of her dissertation. It was published in 1987 under the title *Subjects of Desire: Hegelian Reflections in 20th Century France.*

It is important to note the role of Hegel's thought in Butler's work. Hegel was one of the great system-building thinkers of Western philosophy. A German idealist, he proposed that all of history was the project of a great consciousness, a *Weltgeist,* (or world spirit) trying to understand itself. Hegel's concept of the world as the unfolding of consciousness plays into Butler's conception of reality as determined by the collective process of thinking minds. This is a markedly different standpoint than the Enlightenment position that the nature of reality can be known by using reason to analyze experience. More importantly, this is a markedly different view than that held by the average Western contemporary person who considers that the material world gives rise to the experiences of the human thinker. Understanding Butler's framework requires the reader to consider the role of the mind as greater than the role of the material world in giving rise to experience. As such Butler is often accused, and even accuses herself at times, of being radically anti-materialist.[24] In an age of materialism and scientific reductionism in which many thinkers suggest all experience can be explained by understanding the neural structure and chemical composition of the brain, Butler makes a radical counter-claim. Science, like all theory, is a product of communal consciousness. This shift in thinking is difficult for many readers to consider, although some might find parallels in contemporary appropriations of Jungian psychology or even of Buddhist thought.

Hegel's understanding of the way consciousness unfolds also influences Butler's thinking. Hegel's view is that the history of ideas is a history of dialectic: the process of statement, counter-statement, debate, and synthesis. This view is clearly adopted by Butler who stresses the role of the history of ideas in creating new ideas. Also, this view defines Butler's concept of the philosophical activist who questions, debates, and parodies concepts in order to expand them and with them the experience of the

24. See Butler, *Bodies that Matter,* ix–xii.

world. Importantly, Butler has been keenly interested, as was Beauvoir, in Hegel's famous passage labeled "The Master-Slave Dialectic." This text claims that a conscious mind always seeks domination, power, and control over other conscious minds. While Butler explains the history of *hegemony*, of dominant strains of thought, in terms of such desire for domination, Butler does not assert that the desire for domination is a necessary trait of the individual conscious mind faced with the "Other." Butler instead seeks to de-construct both the concept of the individual and the concept of domination in order to understand better what happens when modes of thought transplant one another.

Butler's work and thought is also influenced by many strains of philosophy that came after Hegel, especially phenomenology and existentialism, as her interest in the role of perception and consciousness is paramount to her philosophical work. She is also heavily indebted to French *poststructuralism*, the philosophical stance that philosophy must acknowledge its inability to uncover real essences or structures of reality and turn its project to de-constructing the false structures that currently limit human thinking and creativity. Particularly, she claims to be heavily influenced by the writings of Nietzsche, Freud, Heidegger, Merleau-Ponty, Beauvoir, Monica Wittig, Michel Foucault, and Jacque Lacan.

Judith Butler's first major work on gender, *Gender Trouble,* was written for an audience of postmodern academic feminists who considered the definition of woman to be a fixed, easily recognized term. These feminists wanted to empower women, and they were confident that they knew who these women were. Butler wanted to de-construct the construct of woman in order to demonstrate where the term was failing to be honest or helpful. She anticipated a readership of one to two hundred academics who had been previously immersed in postmodern thought and contemporary feminism. She hoped gently to sway these few thinkers to a broader sense of questioning about sex and gender. But *Gender Trouble* sold over one hundred thousand copies, spilling into a more general audience. Many readers were introduced for the first time to contemporary philosophical thought as well as to Butler's ideas about gender. Her influence on academic feminism was more profound than she anticipated. Even those feminists who disagreed with her recognized that they must account for the problems she had raised and the questions she had asked. Even more significantly, Butler's "troubling" of traditional views on gender entered public discourse, making her one of the few academic philosophers whose name is recognized by thinkers in a wide variety of disciplines and who is featured in popular internet blogs and chat sites. Her troubling ideas about "women" have become part of the pop culture of gender.

Butler followed *Gender Trouble* with *Bodies that Matter: On the Discursive Limits of "Sex"* in 1993. These two works have been foundational for all subsequent gender studies work. In 2004, she published the provocative *Undoing Gender* in order to explain the evolution of her thought to an even wider audience. In addition, she has written many other important books and articles on literature, disability rights, and politics. In 2012, her groundbreaking work in critical theory was awarded the prestigious Adorno Prize for excellence in philosophy, theater, music, or film.

Currently she is the Hannah Arendt Professor of Philosophy at the European Graduate School in Switzerland and the Maxine Elliot Professor of Rhetoric and Comparative Literature at University of California, Berkeley. She continues to write on gender, race, and disability as constructions that need regular critique. In addition, she is active in political and social movements that call for the universal acceptance of human rights and which advocate for peace.

Judith Butler's Theory of Woman as a Fluid Construct

Realness is the ability to compel belief.[25]

Butler's theory of woman begins with her conviction that the definition of woman is constructed by language and culture, not by nature. Thus, whether a person is a woman depends on how the word "woman" is used and how the person conforms to that word-use. Specifically, Butler sees the use of gendered words like "woman" and "female" as part of what she calls *the heterosexual matrix*, a way of thinking that identifies individuals by their place in heterosexual relationship as culturally defined. As such Butler rejects not only gender essentialism, but also the view of the Enlightenment feminists and gender existentialists who suggested that while biological sex is fixed, gender characteristics are fluid. Butler's position is that biological sex is itself a construct formed not by nature, but by a cultural *hegemony* of thought that enforces a heterosexual ideology and a corresponding sex binary from conception to grave. To explain, while in some cultures the division of the sexes is explained in religious language,

25. Butler, *Bodies that Matter*, 129.

in contemporary Western secular society, sex is considered a scientific fact. Humans are taught to expect that every individual is either naturally male or naturally female. Further, people are taught that the process of evolution developed this division for the survival of the species. People are taught that biological fitness is based on heterosexual attraction and reproduction. Darwinian evolutionary theorists work to explain how various feminine and masculine traits, both physical and psychological, evolved in order to secure the survival of the species. Butler explains that in this way the cultural ideas about heterosexuality are written into scientific theory. For example, the male is defined as the stronger, more aggressive and more dominant partner to a weaker, softer, more yielding female. The scientific theory then imbues cultural rules about sexual difference with a powerful religious-like transcendence. However, Butler insists that these laws are human constructs, not divine dictates nor elements of natural law.

The origin of the concept of woman, both in terms of sex and gender, is not divine nor is it natural, according to Butler. In the same way that many gender existentialists, such as Simone de Beauvoir, Betty Friedan, Angela Davis, and bell hooks, suggested that the concept of the feminine grew out of culture, so does Butler suggest that the whole of the concept of the woman comes from culture. But unlike Friedan, Davis, or hooks, Butler does not name specific culprits or motives. She does not blame corporate advertisers, capitalists, factory owners, or slave traders for creating these concepts consciously or maliciously. Rather, Butler argues that categories and concepts come from communal thinking and speaking about sexuality. Infants are not indoctrinated into a false set of concepts about femininity and masculinity in order that certain corporations can sell clothes, make-up, or toys more easily. Infants simply learn to talk, and through learning language, learn to think using concepts that come from the communal culture that is dominated by heterosexual thinking. Learning to speak teaches children how to organize their thoughts, how to experience the world, how to categorize those experiences, and how to behave in that world they experience.

Children and adults see, think, and behave only within the limits of their language and culture. In contemporary Western society, as well as in many other societies, language and culture have been built around certain concepts of woman. Butler believes that the primary concept of woman in Western culture is that a woman is the human being who is sexually desired by men, submits to men, and conceives children through this desire and submission. For Butler, there is no nature, no reality, separate from the thinking about it. So, of course, individuals, including scientists, see their observations of the natural world as substantiating the existence of biological sex. Scientists see bodies as divided into male and female based on their reproductive role and their role in the sexual hierarchy. Their observations of the natural world are done necessarily within the modes of thought through which they experience and think about the world.

And yet, linguistic, cultural, and scientific revolution is possible. New strains of thought appear and allow a new way of observing the world to be possible. Butler's most convincing argument, at least to the lay public, lies in part with her descriptions of evidence of medical records and sociological observations which demonstrate the social construction of sex and gender. Subversive stories of the bodies and lives of hermaphrodites, of accounts of the medical structure of sex and gender, and of contemporary individuals who defy the cultural norms of sex, gender, and sexuality give Butler's words culture-changing power. After analyzing *Gender Trouble,* the reader can no longer see the world according to the old fixed constructs of man and woman.

Butler's Use of Subversive Stories

The story of Herculine Barbin was introduced to Butler through her reading of Michel Foucault's *History of Sexuality.* Herculine was a nineteenth-century hermaphrodite with a small penis/enlarged clitoris, a shallow vagina, and no breasts. Foucault had used excerpts from the journals of Herculine in order to present an example of an individual whose anatomy allowed freedom from the categories of sex. Foucault highlighted Herculine's sexual relationships as free and even utopian, as they were not constrained to the rules of heterosexuality. Yet, Butler found the journals to tell a different story, the story of a person stranded without identity. Herculine's story, according to Butler, is a tragic history of a person "who lives a life of unjust victimization, deceit, longing, and inevitable dissatisfaction."[26] Butler notes that Herculine speaks about his/her "metaphysical homelessness, a state of insatiable desire, and a radical solitariness" that causes rage and finally suicide.[27] Butler's account introduces the reader to a body that does not fit any standard taxonomy of sex but is clearly a body that should matter.

26. Butler, *Gender Trouble,* 124.
27. Ibid.

Herculine's inability to conform to the role of man or woman kept him/her from mattering to herself/himself and her/his contemporaries. Butler's inability to find a pronoun that fits Herculine, demonstrates that contemporary Western culture is still unable to give an identity to the hermaphrodite. Herculine's journals count as evidence that the sex binary remains both inadequate and harmful for some individuals.

Moreover, Butler's work demonstrates that Herculine is not an isolated example; no matter how isolated he/she might have felt. This is because the biological definition of "woman" is nothing other than a human construction, a "gathering of attributes under the category of sex."[28] According to Butler, the biological definition fragments whole bodies and reduces them to gender categories aligned to a few body parts attributed to heterosexual desire and sexual reproduction. As a result many individuals feel marginalized by gender categories.

Butler highlights the persistent insistence by the scientific community and the general public that sex is a fixed natural category, even as the definition of sex continually changes. As one example, Butler gives a lengthy explanation of a study in 1987 made by researchers at Massachusetts Institute of Technology. These scientists hoped to study DNA to find "the secret and certain determinant of sex."[29] The research was considered necessary because previous study had revealed that

> a good ten percent of the population has chromosomal variations that do not fit neatly into the XX female and XY male set of categories. Hence, the discovery of the "master-gene" is considered to be a more certain basis for understanding sex determination and hence, sex-difference, than previous chromosomal criteria could provide.[30]

In other words, the previous categorization of female for individuals with XX chromosomes was not compatible with other categorizations of female that involved examination of genitalia and hormones. The study was done on four individuals who had been categorized as males but had XX chromosome and on two individuals who had been categorized as females but had XY chromosomes. Butler noted that David Page, the lead researcher, made an initial assumption that categorizing people according to phenotypical gendered characteristics was legitimate. For example, Page

28. Ibid., 146.
29. Ibid., 136.
30. Ibid., 137.

assumed that the XX males *were* males because they *looked* like males. Page assumed the XY females *were* females for the same reason. He did not consider that the impression of what a male looks like is actually a cultural, rather than a scientific, concept. His hypothesis was that there was a genetic switch present in males and not females or at least active in males and not females. This switch, he assumed, sparked the development of male attributes whether or not a Y chromosome was present. As is often the case in Western philosophy and science, the male was assumed to have something that the female lacked. Page did not consider looking for a genetic switch in the female that was absent in the male. Moreover, the switch Page was looking for was one that would cause an embryo to develop a penis and testicles, as these were considered by Page to be the marker of maleness. Any individual lacking this marker was deemed a female. The female was defined as that which lacks the phallus, rather than as that which possessed ovaries, a vagina, or any other specific attribute. As Butler explains, the key to sex was not being discovered, but was already defined in a very specific and culturally gendered way. Yet, interestingly, the researchers still could not find a definitive genetic key to "maleness" in this study. There did not appear to be a simple genetic switch after all.

The sexually ambiguous body is hardly rare. As noted previously, statistics show that at least one in two thousand newborns require a specialist to assign the child's biological sex. Such a statistic requires the reader to consider that every newborn is examined and categorized by someone. That category is considered essential. The category assigned dictates the identity of the individual. Indeed, without the category of sex, the infant remains an "it," relegated linguistically as an object rather than a human person.

An infant named as male will be expected to perform as a male in dress, play, and speech. He will be encouraged to dress, eat, and exercise in ways that present and form his body to be what is considered a masculine body: strong, tall, large. If a US citizen, he will be required to register for the draft. If he is Roman Catholic, he will be allowed to consider the priesthood. If he is not called to a celibate life, he will be encouraged to marry a woman. In many countries, he will only legally be allowed to marry someone who is categorized as female. Indeed, Butler suggests that all of the expectations of him as male are based on the expectation that he will be in heterosexual relationship. He will be considered deviant if he wishes to wear dresses and lipstick. He will be accused of going against nature if he takes estrogen supplements or has surgical breast implants.

In contrast, an infant named as a female will be expected to perform as a female in dress, play, and speech. She will be encouraged to dress, diet, and sculpt her body in ways that present and form her body as a feminine body: small, thin, soft. If she is raised in a conservative Amish, Jewish, or Muslim home she will be required to cover her hair, her knees, and her shoulders in all public places. She will be encouraged to marry a man; and in many countries she will not be legally allowed to marry a woman. She will be encouraged to take supplements if her estrogen levels are considered low and to have implants if a surgical approach to cancer must remove her breasts.

According to Butler, it is the labeling of a child's sex that creates the child's sex. The label will form the way the child will develop both psychologically and physically. Any child, or adult, who fails to develop as expected, especially in terms of sexual desire, will be considered subversive to the categories, and there will be medical and social attempts to normalize the individual, for example through social pressure, psycho-analysis, hormone therapy, or surgery. A child labeled as a girl will be encouraged to date and desire boys. She will be examined by psychiatrists if she seems "gender-confused." If she does not menstruate by a certain age she will be given doses of estrogen and progesterone. If her clitoris is too large, she may have it surgically altered. Other ways of non-conforming may be explained by giving her a new label: lesbian, gender-confused, transvestite, transgendered, transsexual, or intersex. Very often the individual will be pathologized, although the only disease is that the sex label given to her does not seem to fit who she is.

For Butler, the sum of these subversive stories demonstrate that sex and gender are not natural norms but cultural norms. Butler suggests, instead, that "the strange, the incoherent, that which falls 'outside' gives us a way of understanding the taken-for-granted world of sexual categorization as a constructed one, indeed, as one that might well be constructed differently."[31]

Butler's View of Gender as Performance

When people meet each other for the first time, they often instantly recognize each other as a male or female. When a person recognizes an individual

31. Ibid., 140.

as a "woman," the person rarely is looking at the genitalia, the genes, or the hormone levels of the individual. Instead, when a person recognizes an individual as a "woman," there is a recognition of the individual as performing as a woman, dressing like a woman, speaking like a woman, and moving like a woman. This makes sense, says Butler, for to be a woman is to perform as a woman given the performance requirements made by society. No one's performance is natural. Butler insists that all people perform their sex and their gender. All people train themselves to perform their gender roles, not just those who are labeled as transvestite or transgendered. If an individual with an XY genotype, male genitalia, and an abundance of testosterone wears a dress, high heels, and make up, society might label this as unnatural. But it is obviously no more natural for an individual with an XX genotype, female genitalia, and an abundance of progesterone and estrogen to wear a dress, high heels, and make-up. The dress is a costume worn by a performer in either case. As Butler says, "all gender is drag."[32]

Butler does not argue that gender is separate from sex. As such, she sees sex as also a type of performance, although not necessarily one chosen by the individual. Indeed, naming a child's sex is an act that "creates and legislates social reality" for that child.[33] The pronouncement of sex will determine social attitudes towards the child ever after that moment of pronouncement. A variety of duties and prohibitions will go into affect when the sex is announced. These duties and prohibitions will demand a performance of sex and gender. The adult whom that baby becomes will be shamed as "contrary to nature" if he or she disagrees with the original sexual label. The "gender-confused" will be labeled as pathological. The cure that will be suggested may either be psychoanalysis intended to integrate the individual to his or her sex role or gender re-assignment. Either way the assumption is that each individual has a true sex and corresponding gender that must be discovered by looking at specific bits of the physical and psychological make-up. In contrast to this assumption, Butler raises the antithesis: sex is a social category not a biological one. Sex is an act, a "performance." To be real or natural is to be able to compel belief that one's performance is real or natural. The body of the individual is part of the performance. Butler writes that "no anatomy enters gender without being "done" in some way."[34]

32. Butler, *Bodies that Matter*, 125.
33. Ibid., 147.
34. Butler, *Undoing Gender*, 143.

Butler's statement is radical. She is not just talking about the way female models are photo-shopped or the way most American women shape their bodies with undergarments, make-up, and dieting. Butler maintains that under all the masks a woman wears there is no "real body" that can be accessed. A woman's body, like all bodies, is a projection of her mind. She recognizes her body only insofar as her mind projects it, and her mind projects it only insofar as discourse legislates it. This might seem to some readers as the kind of view that gives philosophers a bad name. And many philosophers see Butler as ignoring the positive arguments of materialism. But in the poetic article *How Can I Deny These Hands and This Body are Mine,* Butler speaks of the dream body projected by the sleeping mind and the hallucinated body of the psychotic patient with such clarity that the reader finds Butler's anti-materialism to be epistemologically honest.[35] In *Bodies that Matter: On the Discursive Limits of Sex,* Butler argues that the boundaries of an individual's body, like the sex of the body, are often culturally and linguistically prescribed. Butler does not deny the existence of the body, but she is convinced that the experience of bodies is limited to the mind's ability to think and talk about them. The limits of language prescribe the limits of bodies and the world.

Butler's Concern that Sex and Gender are a Constraint

The limits of language then also limit the freedom of individuals to define themselves. Thus, while sex, gender, and sexuality are constructs according to Butler, they are constructs that constrain and bind individuals. Indeed, one of Butler's main critiques of both liberal Enlightenment feminism and existentialism is the over-emphasis on the possibility of individual freedom to transcend the cultural constraints of gender, sex, and sexuality. "For sexuality cannot be summarily made or unmade, and it would be a mistake to associate 'constructivism' with 'the freedom of a subject to form his/her sexuality as s/he pleases.'"[36] Indeed, Butler's point is that language creates the reality that individuals experience. The individual is caught in the constraints of that culture, sometimes painfully. Furthermore, the individual only exists insofar as s/he is sexed. "For there is no 'I' prior to its assumption of sex," explained Butler in *Bodies that Matter*.[37] The attempt to live outside of the gender binary is an attempt to live an unlivable life.

35. See Butler, "How Can I Deny."
36. Butler, *Bodies that Matter*, 94.
37. Ibid., 99.

In *Undoing Gender*, Butler explains the way gender categories "undo" or destroy certain individuals who are unable to perform according to the culture's gendered regulations. The question of why these individuals are unable to perform is left unanswered by Butler. She rejects the argument that there is an underlying natural disorder that causes some individuals to be unable to perform gender as society dictates. But she also rejects the possibility that individuals freely choose to perform or not to perform. For example, she denies that it is a pathology for women to desire other women sexually, rather than men. And she denies that sexual desire is a lifestyle choice.[38] Perhaps, differing types of sexual desire come from interactions with the parents; perhaps, they come from reactions to the taboos against them, as Freud once suggested. In any case Butler's point is that neither heterosexuality nor homosexuality is "real" or "natural" in any person or species. These are constructed labels. After all, if biological sex is an artificial construct, labeling certain sexual desire as natural or unnatural is problematic. But that does not mean that the object of sexual desire is freely chosen.[39] The experience of the desire is that it is unthinkable to desire otherwise, that one is compelled by the desire. When one's compulsion, one's desire, is labeled as unacceptable, as marginal, as taboo, one's experience as a person is that one's very self is unacceptable, marginal, and taboo. Then one experiences one's life as unlivable.

In such a way are individuals undone by the labels of gender. Unable to perform as society dictates, they fail to see their own lives as valuable, as livable. Such a person was Herculine. Another such person, famous in contemporary headlines, was David Reimer, whose story Butler recounted in *Undoing Gender*. As an infant, Reimer's penis was accidentally severed during a surgery to remove a piece of his foreskin. Urged by doctors who suggested that performing as a male was impossible without a sizable penis, his parents decided to raise him as a sister to his identical twin brother. The child was renamed Brenda. A doctor and researcher, John Money monitored Brenda and her brother's development and encouraged practices that would "feminize" Brenda, for example forbidding her from playing with toys made for boys. Money's own psychological work with Brenda has been

---

38. "The 'activity' of this gendering cannot, strictly speaking, be a human act or expression, a willful appropriation, and it is certainly *not* a question of taking on a matrix." Ibid., 7.

39. "The radical unthinkability of desiring otherwise, the radical unendurability of desiring otherwise, the absence of certain desires, the repetitive compulsion of others, the abiding repudiation of some sexual possibilities . . ." Ibid., 99.

criticized as abusive, for example he required session in which the twins were forced to examine each other's naked bodies and simulate hetero-sexual intercourse in order to socialize Brenda into her role as a female in a heterosexual relationship. Surgeries and hormone therapies were advised in order to fully feminize Brenda. Money believed that the experiment was a success. He published articles on his experiment asserting the ease at which children could be re-assigned gender. Despite being the subject of numer-ous public interest pieces as well as medical articles, Brenda was never told of her history or that she was a subject in a popularly known study. As a teenager Brenda learned her own story and claimed that she wanted to be re-assigned as a man. New surgery and hormone therapy completed the process of re-masculinizing David. The press cited this as proof that sex was real and could not be changed by upbringing, even as Money continued to claim the opposite account. At age 38, David Reimer, for reasons unknown committed suicide. Butler writes that the history of David Reimer, a person subjected to many different influences, physical, chemical, cultural, from many different sources, can reveal nothing about the natural reality of sex or gender. But the reader is left with the recognition that the story certainly reveals a life made unlivable.[40]

Judith Butler, Queer Theory, and Ethics

What makes for a livable world is no idle question.[41]

In 1999, Judith Butler insisted that her written work "does not and can-not take the form of a prescription."[42] Butler insisted that her work was a work of de-construction. She believes that good thinkers need to subvert the categories of sex and gender that are constraining individuals and keep-ing them from livable lives. She has raised examples of individuals driven to suicide, and she has noted the lack of public support for AIDS research in the 1980s as evidence that certain cultural constructs have literally de-nied life to certain individuals. Yet she refuses to declare ethical norms or metaphysical guidelines about what counts as true goodness, or even true health. This has inspired criticisms from many thinkers.

40. For Butler's discussion of David Reimer see the whole of her essay "Doing Justice to Someone: Sex Reassignment and Allegories of Transexuality," *Undoing Gender*, 57–74.

41. Ibid., 17.

42. Ibid., xxi.

For example, philosopher Martha Nussbaum raged against Butler in an article in the *New Republic* accusing her of both *quietism* and *sophistry*. The ancient Greek sophists were teachers who claimed that truth was a human construct. In this way, they were similar to Butler. But the sophists were *quietists*; they advocated keeping the status quo, and they did not search to uncover truth. Sophists simply played a game with language and taught their students to do likewise. They were hired to train wealthy men's children to become lawyers and advertisers, to use words to their own advantage. And while they had a bad reputation, they rarely caused political upheaval. Indeed, the only thinker executed for sophistry in Athenian history was Socrates, a man honored by Nussbaum in the very same essay for his humble questioning spirit.[43] Butler is more like Socrates than any of the other Greek philosophers or sophists. She certainly does not follow the status quo. She asks questions that make believers in the status quo uncomfortable. True, Butler's readers are not given a formal path to goodness or even health. But like the followers of Socrates, who called himself a societal gadfly, Butler's readers are not able to continue arrogantly on their old path of thinking.

Yet, Butler's resistance to putting forth any normative structures continues to anger some feminists who question if academic writing about language can make any real impact on women's lives. This anger is summed up in Nussbaum final condemnation of Butler's work:

> Hungry women are not fed by this, battered women are not sheltered by it, raped women do not find justice in it, gays and lesbians do not achieve legal protections through it. . . . Judith Butler's hip quietism is . . . a bad response. It collaborates with evil. Feminism demands more and women deserve better.[44]

However, Butler's academic work has influenced many non-academics and has inspired action. Butler asserts that her own goal in her books is to present a "radical rearticulation of what qualifies as bodies that matter, ways of living that count as 'life,' lives worth protecting, lives worth saving, lives worth grieving."[45] While she cannot provide the reader with the truth about sex and gender, she has de-constructed the constructs that make life unlivable. This is a kind of activism. She explains,

43. Nussbaum, "Professor of Parody," 40.
44. Ibid., 45.
45. Butler, *Bodies that Matter,* 16.

> To problematize the matter of bodies may entail an initial loss of epistemological certainty, but a loss of certainty is not the same as political nihilism. On the contrary, such a loss may well indicate a significant and promising shift in political thinking. This unsettling of "matter" can be understood as initiating new possibilities, new ways for bodies to matter.[46]

By de-constructing the heterosexual matrix, and its hierarchy of gender, Butler believes that there will be more room for individuals who were formerly "undone" by gender constraints such as homosexuals, intersex people, and battered and impoverished women.

Feminist Merits of Butler's work: Destabilizing the Hegemony of Heterosexuality

Particularly, Butler wants the reader to examine what is at stake in maintaining *the heterosexual matrix:* a systematic way of thinking that enforces heterosexual sexual relationship as the ideal. As many of the first and second wave feminists asserted, Butler emphasizes that what is often considered as normal heterosexual relationship is actually a relationship based on a culturally constructed sex hierarchy. Too often, heterosexuality is described in terms of a distinct sex binary with the male as the active agent and the female as the passive and yielding partner. Thus the heterosexual matrix is less about natural laws of reproduction and more about constructed laws of domination. Individuals who defy the heterosexual matrix with their bodies or their behavior destabilize that matrix by revealing it as a matrix. By highlighting these subversive individuals and their subversive stories, Butler has done her own share of work in destabilizing the heterosexual matrix. In part, because of queer theory at the academic level and at the popular level, there has been a marked change in the cultural construction of homosexuality and bisexuality as forms of deviance. Nussbaum was wrong to say Butler's work would not help gays and lesbians achieve legal protections. In addition, because of Butler and other queer theorists, more people are considering the naturalness of many aspects of the construct of woman including her biology, her psychology, her sexuality, and her place in the social and sexual hierarchy. In this way, one could argue that women have begun to appear as less rape-able, beat-able, and starve-able because of this de-construction. Butler's naming of gender trouble has changed

46. Ibid., 30.

the discourse about sexuality, gender, and sex in contemporary Western society.

Queer Theory and Gender Fluidity in Contemporary Issues

Gender Fluidity and Health Care

One of the most powerful arguments for gender essentialism in the twenty-first century is its call for focus on the health care needs of women. Queer theorists certainly do not object to an increased focus on health care for bodies that menstruate, gestate, and lactate. Nor do they object to calls for more funding for research on breast cancer, birth control, menopause, or other areas that are traditionally considered women's health issues. However, queer theorists do ask that the medical community consider analyzing and questioning their views on the definition of health, particularly as it applies to gendered health.

First, queer theorists urge doctors to consider and admit the constructed and fluid nature of the norms for ideal female health. Cultural definitions of the ideal female body play into the way both doctors and patients see the role of nutrition and exercise for a healthy lifestyle. Cultural definitions of the goals of female life create rivaling views about the role of birth control, fertility treatments, and abortion in health care. Constructed definitions of female strength and beauty create differing norms for the use of hormone therapies, physical therapy, and cosmetic surgery in health care. Stereotypes of motherhood affect the way women are urged to use or avoid anesthesia in childbirth, to breastfeed or bottle feed their babies, and to wean or to suckle their toddlers. Queer theorists do not have a normative framework that they wish the medical community to adopt, but instead simply raise questions they believe are important to consider.

Second, queer theorists demand an investigation into medical practice as it applies to those whose bodies transgress sex categories. Queer theorists raise questions about the mainstream practice of "normalizing" intersex infants, children, and adults. Often surgeries are done on newborn infants with ambiguous genitalia in order that they can be more easily labeled as male or female. Iain Morland in the article *What Can Queer Theory Do for Intersex* emphasizes that most doctors evaluate the appropriateness of the surgical removal of genital tissue based on heterosexist norms. The concern is that individuals cannot "succeed" with ambiguous genitalia because they cannot succeed at heterosexual intercourse. Moreover, many studies that claim that such surgery does improve individuals' lives use the number of surgically "normalized" intersex individuals in heterosexual marriage as the main criteria.[47] Future hormone therapies and surgeries are often required to maintain the sex characteristics as the child enters puberty. Morland, and other queer theorists, offer other aspects of health to be considered, including holistic health, bodily integrity, and the ability to experience sexual pleasure. The main concept they ask the medical community to consider is the possibility of an intersex body as a healthy body.

Third, queer theorists demand an investigation into medical practices as they apply to those who psychologically transgress gender categories. Relatively recently homosexuality was considered a pathology by many physicians. Still today, individuals who are labeled as transgendered are considered to have a pathology. Queer theorists are divided on whether this labeling is helpful or harmful to individuals. In order to bring these individuals to health, physicians can prescribe, and health insurance policies will honor, surgeries or hormone therapies that allow these individuals to construct their bodies in ways that bring them greater psychological well being. Some queer theorists argue that pathologizing the desire to transgress one's sex is mistaking the constructed nature of sex. Other queer theorists argue that health for individuals includes their psychological wellbeing. They assert that transsexuals require hormone therapies and surgeries for their wellbeing in the same way that many post-menopausal women require estrogen therapy or mastectomy survivors require implants. Queer theorists do agree that all sex and gender norms are constructed. They insist that the arguments for or against surgery and treatments cannot be based on what is natural but instead on what is most life giving. Respect for the individual's autonomy is a key part of deciding which treatment is most life giving.

The Theory of Gender Fluidity and Women's Sports

The constructed norm for female health, also, plays a role in the discussion about the female athlete. The cultural ideal of the feminine woman, even in the twenty-first century, runs contrary to the cultural ideal of the athlete. Femininity is still linked to smallness, gentleness, softness, and fragility. In terms of the cultural heterosexual matrix, the feminine is defined as that

47. Morland, "What Can Queer Theory Do for Intersex?" 289–306.

which is conquered, penetrated, or harmed.[48] In contrast athletic ideals remain those of the Greek Olympians: greatness, strength, agility, speed, and victory. By definition, then, the ideal female cannot be the ideal athlete. However, feminists have helped change the culture of sports and femininity in the twentieth and twenty-first centuries. Girls and women participate in sport at many levels in Western society. Yet, many of the cultural attitudes about sex and sport still remain contradictory. Queer theorists call readers to consider how language and culture shape the ideals of womanhood and sport in contemporary society and to imagine how new constructs might help individuals better flourish.

First, the way language is used by and about females and athletes is in itself telling. For example, many of the most frequent metaphors for victory in sport are made in terms of defining the loser as a woman or female body part who has been conquered sexually.[49] These metaphors and epithets construct the heterosexual relationship in terms of dominance and submission and enforce the stereotypes about the male as the ideal athlete and victor. In addition, women athletes in the past century have been routinely mocked in the media as "butch," "mannish," and "muscle molls."[50] On one hand, there has been a shift in thinking about the possibility of female athletes and a shift in opportunity for female athletes. On the other hand, the claim may still be made that the female athlete is *queer* by definition. She does not fit perfectly either the category of woman or of athlete. Thus, by her participation in sport, she transgresses the boundaries society expects of her.

One of the main premises of queer theorists is Ludwig Wittgenstein's adage that one's language defines one's world. Thus, the language examples above do more than simply suggest an unresolved tension that continues to limit girls and women interested in sport. These categories of "female" and "sport" inform sport policies and medical practices concerning female athletes. For example, many female athletes have protested what they see as *paternalism* in athletic regulations that are made to keep female athletes safe and separated from competition from men.[51] Examples include separating female and male athletes in competitions, forbidding females to participate

48. See for example, Weaving, "Unraveling the Ideological Concept," 83–93. Also see Schneider, "'Woman' in the Sport Context," 40–54.

49. For an in-depth discussion on this topic, see Weaving, "Unraveling the Ideological Concept."

50. See Cahn, "Muscle Moll," 147–59.

51. For a discussion on paternalistic rulings in athletics for women, see Schneider, "'Woman' in the Sport Context."

in certain sports that are considered too dangerous, and making new rules for female versions of sports in order to prevent aggressive contact. While some people advocate strongly for same gender sports, others point out that certain sports, for example skeet shooting, became separated by gender only after women started surpassing men at the Olympic level.[52] Of course the biological structure of some women's bodies have both different needs and talents than some men's bodies have. Yet the bodies of many contemporary athletes reveal that the biological talents, strengths, and weaknesses of individuals often do not follow traditionally defined sex stereotypes. This means that some women's bodies are more suited to versions of sport typically defined as male, and some men's bodies are more suited to versions of sport typically defined as female. And, of course, there are many bodies that are difficult to categorize as male or female. Moreover, rules that encourage aggressive physical contact in the male version of a sport and penalize similar contact in the female version of the sport are not based on biological differences but presumed cultural differences between the genders. This can be seen in the differing rules concerning checking in men and women's lacrosse and ice hockey, for example.

Separate rules for men and women athletes are especially problematic when one considers the difficulty there is in clearly defining which athletes are female. This is seen in the Olympic committee's struggle to define who qualifies as female for competition. The Olympic committee's definition of the female body has changed markedly over the past century. When women's events first became part of the Olympic games, participants simply named their designated sex to the committee when applying for competition. The femaleness of the body was determined by the athlete herself.[53] However, in response to allegations of cheating, the Olympic committee began to require a genital exam for females who wished to compete. This new procedure outraged some participants who noted that those registered as male participants were not required to submit to an intimate exam. In

52. See Burke, "Could a 'Woman' Win a Gold Medal," 129–41. For example, Burke writes, "It is when female sporting performance reveals the overlap between genders, that men most ferociously invoke this practice of segregation. For example, the sport of skeet shooting was integrated at the Olympics until 1992 when a Chinese woman, Shan Zang, did so well that she won the gold medal and tied the world record. The IOC responded by segregating the event. . . . Segregation serves to protect the male gender from the recognition that there is an overlap between male and female performance" (ibid., 130).

53. See Dreger, *Hermaphrodites*, 7.

addition, the definition of a female body as that which possesses female genitalia was soon seen as inadequate. The diversity of genital formation made the results of the exam far less clear than the originators had presumed they would be. In 1968, the Olympic committee changed the definition of the female body to include having two X chromosomes. But the new genetic testing found that the results often added to the confusion. This was because athletes, who were clearly phenotypically female, sometimes discovered during the testing that they were genetically XY and no longer defined as women as they had been before 1968.[54] Most recently, in 2012, a hormone test was added. Again, rather than clarifying a murky issue, the new test resulted in a new set of complications. Some athletes were suddenly disqualified for not being women. These athletes, who are genetically and genitally female, were surprised to find themselves assigned as intersex because of a new definition that females who have certain levels of naturally produced testosterone are now no longer defined as females.

The changing definition of the female body also has consequences for the definition of the healthy female body that is at times at odds with the healthy athletic body. For example, in 2012, the International Olympic Committee defended its position on disqualifying *hyperandrogenic* females as females by stating that females with *hyperandrogenism* have a pathological condition that "virilizes" the woman. The committee asserted, "Androgenic hormones have performance-enhancing effects, particularly on strength, power and speed, which may provide a competitive advantage in sports."[55] In other words, the Olympic committee defined those with a competitive advantage in sports as being *pathological* and *not female*. This enforces a cultural ideal that women who are stronger, more powerful, and faster than average women are not really women, at least not really healthy women. The common slur that an athletic woman is "mannish" is now given scientific legitimacy. And past critics of successful female athletes are now being vindicated for their accusations that such women are unnatural in their talents.

But the fact remains that the new, narrower definitions of the female body are clearly created constructs. Indeed, they are constructs that are so new they will feel radically arbitrary and unfamiliar to the majority of the public. Individuals who are genetically female with female genitalia and who are capable of pregnancy and childbirth are being considered, for the

54. See ibid.
55. See International Olympic Committee, *Regulations on Female Hyperandrogenism*.

first time in Western medicine, as *not female*. It has not gone without note that the Olympic committee's redefinition of female has occurred after a century of women athletes gradually narrowing the gap between elite female and male performance at the Olympics.

The complications concerning the regulation of the female athlete's hormonal balances began because of the Olympic committee's anti-doping policy which sought to prevent women and men from taking steroids and testosterone supplements to boost their performance. When the committee expelled some women athletes who were doping they were forced to consider their policy for women who naturally produced high levels of testosterone. However, male athletes are not disqualified if their bodies produce more testosterone than the average male. Moreover, women athletes are not disqualified for taking estrogen supplements. In fact, female athletes who do not menstruate are encouraged to take female hormone therapy. Whether or not this therapy increases the woman's health depends on the definition of women's health that is in vogue. Also, hyperandrogenic women are allowed to use surgery or hormone therapy in order to qualify as female. These issues demonstrate that the very notions of "natural" and "doped" are cultural constructs.[56]

The area of female athletics is an interesting one for queer theory. All of the women thinkers highlighted in this book, regardless of their theory of gender, have encouraged women to be physically active. Indeed, one of the strongest arguments for girls' and women's sports came and continues to come from gender essentialist feminists. These essentialists argue that the female body has an essentially different structure than the male body; but this essential difference does not make the female incapable of sport. Rather, in order to develop her physical talents and maintain her bodily health, the female athlete needs different but equal opportunity in athletics. This is an argument that liberal feminists and existentialist feminists have embraced in order to promote athletics for girls and women. Yet queer theorists question sex essentialism and this argument. While it is obvious that different bodies have different strengths and needs, queer theorists deny that these differences easily defined sex and gender lines. In fact, they claim that the definitions of the sexes do not always promote sporting regulations that help all individuals. Queer theorists claim that

---

56. Rebecca Ann Lock explains, "To protect one's femaleness from the 'man making' effects of steroids is also to protect and recreate the coherent relationship between the anatomics of the body and heterosexuality." Lock, "Doping Ban," 117.

female athletes challenge the boundaries set by language, culture, medical science, and sport regulations. These challenges inspire the rest of society to continue to question the way the constructs of sex and gender unfairly imprison individuals. These challenges also can inspire new policies that will allow more individuals to flourish.

Gender Fluidity and Social Policy

There are a myriad of social issues that affect those who do not fit neatly in the gender binary. The debate over the legality of gay marriage is just one example. Those who believe that marriage is a good for individuals and for society as a whole argue that prohibitions against marriage for those who do not fit the gender binary harm the well-being of individuals and society generally. Those whose sexuality is not heterosexual in orientation can only participate in committed, socially sanctioned, monogamous relationship and enjoy the psychological, emotional, and legal benefits of such relationship if there is marriage equality. Those whose biological sex and/or gender does not fit the gender binary are also unable to participate in marriage without the protections of marriage equality legislation. Heterosexist legislation completely bans the hermaphrodite from marriage. Thus, such legislation has serious consequences for many individuals and for the society in which they live. Connected to the issue of marriage equality are the rights of parents who fall outside of the gender binary. Legislation that prevents such individuals from adopting children or having custody of their biological children is legislation that causes harm to children and families. Queer theorists insist that since all gender roles are culturally constructed, laws that limit the rights of some individuals to parent or to marry based on their sex, gender, or sexuality, are ultimately arbitrary laws. Yet, these laws proclaim to society that certain types of people do not have the fundamental rights to relationship, friendship, and family that are considered in Western society as a key part of human life. These laws dehumanize people who do not fit in the cultural constructs of the heterosexual matrix. Such dehumanization leads to legitimizing other types of bullying and discrimination against those outside the gender binary.

Problems with Queer Theory

Most of the critiques of queer theory concern its *poststructuralism*, its denial of essences, norms, or structures that form reality. Some critics focus on the queer claim that sex is an artificial construct created by language and culture. These critics consider this claim to be an academic theory contrary to the everyday experience of most people. Also, these critics assert that queer theory ignores the reality of bodies and natural law. Other feminist commentators critique queer theorists for not focusing on universal human nature, a focus that might lead to the annihilation of the concept of gender completely. Still other activists criticize queer theory's refusal to assert a ground for ethics and its subsequent tendency towards quietism or sophistry.

First, queer theory is considered by some to be a theory understood and embraced only by a narrow group of elite academics, who ignore the experience of ordinary people. The philosopher Martha Nussbaum lambasted Butler's writing style as being a major part of this problem. "Her written style, however, is ponderous and obscure. It is dense with allusions to other theorists, drawn from a wide range of different theoretical traditions. . . . The ideas of these thinkers are never described in enough details to include the uninitiated."[57] This might seem like an attack on form rather than actual content. But the criticism is really about Butler's philosophical view that theory reigns. Nussbaum criticizes Butler's ideas by critiquing her writing style, for Butler's writing style is demanded by her view that she is but a small part of the dialectic of ideas. She insists on explaining her ideas in the context of the other thinkers in that dialectic. She will not simply write what she thinks on a given topic, because she insists that what she thinks has been determined by what others thought before her. Allusions to Michel Foucault, Jacques Lacan, and Monique Wittig are, thus, par for the course. This intellectual honesty makes her all but inaccessible to anyone outside the academy. Indeed, even many academics find her inaccessible, as Nussbaum asserts.

Queer theory is also considered inaccessible to those outside of the academy because of its radical scientific anti-realism. Outside the postmodern academy, most people are scientific realists who believe that the world scientists describe is the actual world. While gender existentialists are sometimes criticized for underestimating the role of nature in creating

---

57. Nussbaum, "Professor of Parody," 38.

gender, queer theorists are lambasted often for not accepting any role of nature in sex or gender. Critics suggest that queer theorists at the very least must account for the common sense experience people have that their bodies are materially real objects that give rise to their desires, behaviors, and ideas. While Hegelian idealism might appeal to some in the academy, most critics claim that queer theory must make a different case in order to appeal to mainstream society.

Ignoring the body leads to ignoring the real importance of sex and gender, according to some critics. These challengers suggest that queer thinkers ignore the importance of women working together to gain equality in the workplace, to pass laws against sexual harassment, and to support affordable health care for women's issues. Margaret Cruikshank, who labels herself "a 70s feminist" said that as a lesbian "survival after coming-out required a group identity. Lesbianism could well appear to be the central fact of one's existence when embracing it was dangerous."[58] She asserted that accepting a woman who loves women requires an acceptance that sex and sexual preference are real and natural. Cruikshank agrees that some theorists overestimated the role of nature and unfairly demanded certain feminine behavior as the norm. "Gender explains far more, however, than queer theorists seem ready to acknowledge,"[59] she challenged.

Another criticism of queer theory is that queer theory makes too much of sex and gender. For example, Butler suggests that the very notion of a self requires attaching that self to a sex, which is why those marginalized by the sex binary suffer so deeply.[60] This view seems wrong to those feminists who still align with first wave feminism. Some critics who agree with queer theory's view that sex is a construct think that the simple solution is for society to worry less about sex and gender. Rather than troubling the boundaries between male and female, such feminists say that society is not beholden to these constructions. Society can and should become gender neutral.

Yet, there are other feminists who refute the idea that all norms and regulations come from culture and language. These thinkers critique queer theory for ignoring norms and standards that come from nature, reason, or the Divine. They suggest that queer theorists who insist that there are no knowable guidelines for goodness or health exhibit a kind of intellectual

---

58. Cruikshank, "Through the Looking Glass," 155.

59. Ibid.

60. Butler, *Bodies that Matter,* 3.

laziness that lends itself to quietism or sophistry. In other words, queer theory leads to a tolerant acceptance of anything. In contrast, Nussbaum insists that all thinkers need "a normative theory of social justice and human dignity. It is one thing to say that we should be humble. . . . It is quite another thing to say that we don't need any norms at all."[61] Without such norms, Nussbaum worries that any speech act must be considered philosophically valuable.[62] Nussbaum believes that queer theory refuses to make an argument for which behaviors are good and which are to be avoided. Cruikshank agrees and suggests that "Queer Theory appears to romanticize rule breaking,"[63] and that "Queer Theory may align itself unwittingly with consumer culture."[64] Cruikshank wonders how a queer theorist can argue against child sexual abuse, child pornography, or pornography that sexualizes violence against women if queer theorists do not assert some values that transcend culture. Cruikshank and Nussbaum believe that good theory must argue against acts and speech that violate the autonomy and rights of individuals by invoking rationally and naturally endowed concepts of universal values and inalienable rights.

Queer theory, while popular in certain academic circles and certain popular venues, is the most controversial of the theories presented in this book. Arguments that queer theory is too academic and too anti-materialist abound. Many feminists believe that queer theory's lack of a firm ground for values and regulations makes it a theory that can destroy old ideas that are no longer adequate but cannot create or discover a new or better architecture for feminism.

Conclusions

Despite queer theory being introduced in some of the most difficult philosophical prose in the American academy, it has entered public discourse with a remarkable vitality. The work of Judith Butler and Donna Haraway

---

61. Nussbaum, "Professor of Parody," 42.

62. Ibid. "Others, less fond of liberty, might engage in the subversive performances of making fun of feminist remarks in class, or ripping down the posters of the lesbian and gay law students' association. These things happen. They are parodic and subversive. Why, then, aren't they daring and good? Well, there are good answers to those questions, but you won't find them in Foucault, or in Butler."

63. Cruikshank, "Through the Looking Glass," 156.

64. Ibid., 154.

has been groundbreaking in terms of gender studies and identity politics generally. Their work provides a radical Copernican-like revolution in thought that forbids looking at the world through old lenses. Readers who encounter queer theory, whether in academic texts or on Internet blogs, find the boundaries they once saw as fixed become fluid and permeable. Such readers see themselves and their own identities in a new light. Such readers recognize their neighbors, sometimes seeing them for the first time, as human beings marginalized by a discourse that refuses to acknowledge them. This new vision is granted by the troubling of boundaries by queer theory. For most readers of queer theory, even for those critical of it, the heterosexual matrix is dead. Even if the requiem for the sex binary is still being sung in churches, schools, and society, it no longer has the same power as it once had. And while some academics and lay people alike worry about the void left by the death of gendered values, others applaud the increase in tolerance, acceptance, and even love for those who were once marginalized by those values.

Queer theory is young. The next step is not yet decided. There are so many different opinions on which step to take next that queer theorists can scarcely be grouped together. There are theorists who wish to advocate for those values once called masculine or feminine as values open to all to choose. There are others who wish to advocate for an end to all gender distinction. Still others advocate a position of radical tolerance, to let each individual be as each chooses without a search for norms or values. Finally, there are those who insist that good theorists must construct a viable theory of social justice in order to promote human flourishing while acknowledging that all such theory is only theory. These discussions and debates keep queer theory lively and engaged.

5

Conclusions

The Future of Feminist Activism
and the Quandary of Gender

To be truly visionary we have to root our imagination in our concrete
reality while simultaneously imagining possibilities beyond that reality.

—BELL HOOKS[1]

The object of this book has been to encourage readers to think deeply
about the question: What does it mean to be a woman? This question
must be the starting point for conversations about the politics and ethics
of sexual difference. In order to aid in this process, the book has presented
the systematic thought of several women philosophers throughout Western
intellectual history. While the theories of these women are varied, complex,
and subtle in their differences, this book organized these into four basic
systems of thinking about gender: *gender essentialism*, *gender neutrality*,
gender existentialism, and *gender fluidity*. Each theory has been presented in
its own chapter as a historical idea and as a contemporary mode of thought.
Each chapter has described how the specific theory fits with obvious empirical data and common lived experience. Furthermore, each chapter has
described how the theory grounded specific forms of feminist activism. But
each chapter also has included a list of ways that the specific theory falls

1. hooks, *Feminism Is for Everybody*, 110.

short. Thus, at the conclusion it seems that all the theories are simultaneously obviously true and obviously inadequate. While each theory has made critically important points, each theory has significant weaknesses. Clearly, more thinking must be done. This concluding chapter explains why these theories need to be engaged continually in conversation with each other and with new theories that arise. But also this conclusion will discuss how this continued conversation is possible. Readers ought and can live with the quandary of gender while continuing the conversation. Moreover this is essential for the future of further feminist activism. Continuing and deepening the conversation about the nature of woman is important philosophically so that new and deeper understanding of the meaning of woman can be explored. This is important socially and politically in order to develop new social policies that will empower all individuals to flourish as human beings.

The Merits of Dialectical Thinking about Gender

At the end of each course that I teach, students usually ask what I really think. The last day of "Women Philosophers" is no exception. I am often asked about my own answer concerning the nature of women. The students assume that while I am clearly committed to presenting more than one viewpoint I must have a personal and systematic answer about gender that guides my thinking and my acting. But, when it comes to gender theory, I strongly believe that the answer cannot be a simple or single response. Rather, the diverse theses on gender must be held dialectically, in continued conversation. To deny any of these four systems would be to deny important claims that are clearly empirically and ethically true. Yet, the systems cannot be fully integrated, for their claims at specific points are contradictory. The systems must be held together in the form of continued conversation and social/political activity as the merits of each are recognized. I believe that continuing the dialectic is an important part of feminist activism. Briefly, this section will outline the merits of each gender theory so far presented and the type of activism that each theory inspires.

The Merits of Gender Essentialism

Gender essentialism states that there is a definitive female nature, distinct from the masculine. Most gender essentialists argue that the differences between the female and male natures are rooted in biological differences. Most gender essentialists believe that the body of the individual profoundly affects the individual's way of thinking, acting, and experiencing in the world. Of course, there are some gender essentialists who argue that the mind is gendered independently of the body and who advocate specifically for recognizing the essential differences between male and female minds. Nevertheless, all feminist gender essentialists advocate that both masculine and feminine ways of being should be nourished and valued in society. Specifically, they exalt the value of feminine bodies and of feminine natures as gentle, warm, nurturers in a world whose contemporary Western culture often promotes a single-minded focus on power and strength rather than on a holistic practice of cooperation.

Sociologists have found that gender essentialism is the most common understanding of gender held by individuals in Western culture. Indeed, many people find that this theory is the most sensible of the four theories because it usually acknowledges biological differences. Many who support gender essentialism will stress the importance of acknowledging the role of the physical body in the way an individual thinks, moves, and acts in the world. For example, a thirteen-year-old girl may find herself surprisingly incapacitated by cramps and bleeding, after being told for years in health class that menstruation would not impact the way she studies or plays sports. As another example, Mary Wollstonecraft insisted on the ability of her mind to overcome feminine weakness after childbirth; yet she died from complications of childbirth. Most gender essentialists say that proclaiming the importance of the body and biological sex is necessary in accepting the basic facts of experience.

More importantly, gender essentialists claim that acknowledging the role of sex and gender is the best way to truly advocate for women scientifically, theologically, and politically. Women have specific needs that require attention if women are to have true equality in society. Importantly, all feminist gender essentialists claim that advocating for women requires acknowledging the value and importance of the uniquely feminine way of being. Feminist gender essentialists proclaim that the diversity of male and female physical bodies and the diversity of masculine and feminine characters are crucial to the wellbeing of both society and the planet. They advocate the need for gender specific health care, single sex educational opportunities, and same gender sports in order to nourish both the bodies and the cultural ethos of women. They advocate for affirmative actions policies and legal protections that increase women's involvement in leadership roles in order that feminine ways of thinking, leading, and acting can be used to transform the world.

The Merits of Gender Neutrality

The theory of gender neutrality states that each human being is an individual with natural rights and responsibilities regardless of biological sex. Those who advocate for gender neutrality proclaim that despite biological differences in sex, men and women share a universal intellectual and spiritual nature: the mind has no sex. Moreover, they claim that there are not masculine and feminine virtues, but only universal human virtues. With access to equal education and social opportunity both men and women can and should strive for strength, wisdom, modesty, compassion, and self-reliance.

Historians have found that a theory of gender neutrality has grounded the most recent political movements for women's rights. Supporters suggest the view of gender neutrality most adequately explains the contradiction between what a culture claims is biologically feminine and what is true of actual individual women. For example, Sojourner Truth's famous *Ain't I a Woman* speech demonstrated that certain gendered characteristics, such as weakness, emotional instability, and dependence, are clearly not connected to biological differences in sex. Today medical evidence demonstrates that to some degree the pain of menstrual cramps, morning sickness, labor, and childbirth are culturally constructed. Cultural expectation of weakness, lack of exercise, and restrictive clothing such as eighteenth-century corsets and twenty-first-century skinny jeans all contribute to such pains and are products of culture not biology. Further, evidence from social history demonstrates that many so-called feminine limitations have cultural causes rather than natural physical causes. Indeed, evidence of educational outcomes in the twenty-first century shows that girls outperform boys in many areas, such as written expression and mathematical computation, where they were once considered naturally inferior.[2] Data from the history of Olympic records demonstrates that in terms of increasing physical speed and agility, women elite athletes have made substantially more progress than men in the last century.[3] Thus, advocates of gender neutrality claim

2. See, for example, Fogg, "Education Is Leaving Boys Behind."
3. For example, see Watman, "Evolution of Olympic Women's Athletics." For more

that acknowledging how little biological sex affects individuals is necessary in accepting the basic facts of history and contemporary experience.

Moreover, advocates of gender neutrality claim that women will be best served if they are considered as human individuals regardless of gender. Indeed, they argue that advocating for women is best done by ignoring culturally defined gender categories. They advocate the need for co-educational opportunities, equal access to economic and political power, and full equality of all individuals before the law in order to nourish the full potentials of the minds and bodies of all people. They strive politically for an equal rights amendment, petition for an equal pay for equal work act, and argue to lift paternalistic regulations in the military and in sports.

The Merits of Gender Existentialism

Gender existentialism states that gender is a cultural construction that deeply affects the lives, experiences, and actions of gendered individuals. Gender is culturally caused; it is not divinely mandated nor biologically destined. But gender is a real influence at work in an individual's identity, according to gender existentialists. While children are born biologically sexed, they are not yet gendered. Only through education, socialization, and media propaganda are children molded into gendered people. But gender roles foster neither authentic individual freedom nor true equality among persons. Feminist gender existentialists argue for changes in culture in order to help individuals discover a more authentic way to choose to flourish.

Sociologists and psychologists have discovered that cultural constructions of gender do affect an individual's sense of identity. The ways individuals think and act are radically influenced by advertising, literature, film, and media portrayals of gender. This same data demonstrates that legal equality does not correlate with actual gender equality. For example, while the vast majority of occupations are now legally open to both men and women, there are not equal numbers of men and women in all fields. Specifically, physics, engineering, and philosophy are fields where more than two thirds of professionals are male although the number of boys and girls interested and academically successful in these disciplines has been equal in recent

---

examples, the history of Olympic records can be found at http://www.iaaf.org/news/ report.

years.[4] Gender existentialists say that such data reveals that boys and girls are not naturally predisposed to certain disciplines but are culturally habituated to adopting certain gender roles. Gender existentialists also point to data that shows the way race, culture, and socio-economic class play into gender stereotyping.[5] Such data shows that most gender roles are purely cultural but have strong holds on the psyches of individuals.

Feminist gender existentialists claim that gender cannot be ignored in the quest for equality. They advocate for recognizing the affects of gender on the psyches of children and adults. For example, employers who are trying to be gender neutral in their hiring and promotion strategies ought to consider the way women are socialized to present themselves as obedient, even though they may in fact be doing creative leadership. Being aware of the affects of gendered behavior and gender bias can help leaders create better systems that promote real equality. Of course, gender existentialists also advocate for changes in education, marketing, media, and political policy that will decrease gender typing in the first place. These activists argue that gender roles most often force girls to truncate their natural talents, aspirations, and freedom to choose to become themselves authentically.

The Merits of Gender Fluidity

The theory of gender fluidity states that biological sex categories are constructs of human culture that serve to reinforce culturally accepted gender roles. Individuals are cultured into specific gender and sex roles as soon as they are classified as a specific biological sex. However, individuals perform their gender throughout their lives, sometimes in ways that correspond to cultural expectations and sometimes in ways that reject these expectations. The performance of gender includes both physical and non-physical performance. In this sense, both the sex and the gender of an individual are fluid, changing with the individual's performance and society's interpretation of that performance. Queer theorists argue that society, in accepting that sex and gender are cultural constructs rather than fixed scientific or metaphysical essences, ought to accept that all gender roles are fluid. Feminist queer theorists advocate that society ought to create structures that

4. See, for example, Huhman, "STEM Fields and the Gender Gap," and Paxton, "Quantifying the Gender Gap."

5. For a fuller discussion on the role of race and class in gender role creation, please see chapter 3 of this book.

seek to help all people flourish in lives that are experienced as livable and meaningful.

Scientific evidence concerning biological sex and sociological evidence concerning gender reveal that queer theorists are right to conclude that the current sex and gender binary are not empirically adequate. For example, as many as 1 in 100 people do not have bodies that correlate with the standard classifications of the biological male or female.[6] Moreover, as many as five to ten percent of women have an abundance of naturally produced testosterone caused by a condition called hyperandrogenism, a term that literally means "overly male."[7] Recently the Olympic committee has ruled that this condition disqualifies an individual from participating as a female in the Olympics. Such individuals may only compete at the Olympic level as men.[8] Queer theorists argue such facts demonstrate that the taxonomy of biological sex is clearly not essentially defined. Moreover, they claim that the classification of biological sex stems from culturally held notions about gender that continually change. For example, the Olympic ruling that disqualified hyperandrogenic individuals as women noted that their decision hinged on the "virilization" that testosterone caused, specifically as it relates to strength, speed, and agility in an athlete. In addition, queer theorists note that there has been substantial sociological and psychological evidence for centuries that gendered fashion, behavior, and modes of thinking are fluid rather than essentially fixed. Historical evidence of the existence of transvestitism, homosexuality, and trans-sexuality is ample. Also ample is the evidence of the fluidity of gender norms in terms of fashion and behavior.

Queer theorists argue for an acknowledgement of the inadequacy of the gender binary as a classification system in medicine, in science, in psychology, and in philosophy. Furthermore, in order to account for and advocate for all those individuals who are left outside the traditional gender binary, feminist queer theorists argue for an acceptance of gender diversity and gender fluidity through legal protections as well as through increased cultural awareness and greater acceptance of all human individuals.

6. Dreger, "Hermaphrodites," 42–45.

7. See Carmina, "Ovarian and Adrenal Hyperandrogenism."

8. International Olympic Committee, "IOC Regulations on Female Hyperandrogenism."

The Quandary of Gender Theory

All four of these theories make important points that are supported by empirical evidence. All four of these theories have been used and are currently being used by activists who seek to support the flourishing of all individuals in society. But in many places these theories contradict one another. Gender essentialists and queer theorists both accept and advocate for acknowledging gender diversity. However, feminists who come from traditions of gender neutrality or gender existentialism deny real gender difference as significant or valuable. Both philosophically and politically these groups often find themselves at odds with each other. Yet both seem to be saying something right.

There is another deep philosophical and political divide at play in the quandary as well. The first three theories advocate for the recognition of the reality of biological sex. Yet, the fourth theory claims that biological sex is a fluid construct. This theoretical divide means that queer theorists question whether terms and phrases such as "feminism," "womanism," "justice for women," or "women's studies" are accurate or helpful in seeking a more just society. Perhaps, these terms simply reinforce false stereotypes that prevent real justice. Indeed, queer theory calls into question the very title of this book—*Thinking Woman*—and its method of looking at exclusively women philosophers. Queer theory asks if the category of woman is a necessary or legitimate category. On the one hand, clearly the answer must be negative. Such categorization seems socially uncaring to many who are excluded from the gender binary. Moreover, the categorization seems scientifically untenable given the evidence that denies any normative definition of woman exists in nature or in culture. On the other hand, surely there is something deeply meaningful about the concept of woman. When one reads or hears the word "woman," one has a picture of the referent to the word. The word is not nonsense. Indeed, the concept has been historically useful and appears to continue to be necessary in discussing medicine, science, and policymaking.

Thus, the quandary of gender remains. Feminists and womanists in the contemporary age owe much to the women highlighted in this book. And they owe much to the many other thinkers not presented in this book who have done serious philosophical work on this question. But, there is still much work to be done. In order to continue the philosophical conversation about gender it is necessary to consider the roots of the major sources of disagreement and the fruits of the major precepts of agreement in order that gender theory may continue to thrive intellectually and politically.

Moving Forward in the Dialectic

In order to move forward in creating a society that helps all individual flourish, there must be an examination of some of the central unresolved philosophical issues that are at play in these gender theories. Indeed, part of the reason why the question of gender cannot be systematically answered is because of two underlying philosophical issues that cannot be answered sufficiently at this point. The first concerns the identity of a person, specifically whether the person is most accurately defined in terms of her physical nature or in terms of her intellectual nature. This is called the mind/body problem. The second concerns the classification of a person, specifically whether individuals naturally belong to classifications or whether classifications are human constructions. This issue of taxonomy involves the debate between *realism* and *nominalism*.

A Question of Identity: The Mind/Body Problem

Whether or not biological sex is an essential part of the individual hinges on the relationship between the mind and body in an individual. The philosophical views of each theorist concerning the mind and the body were discussed in detail in each chapter. Because these theorists' views of the relationship of the mind and body are related to their views about sex and gender, a brief analysis of the ways these theories about the mind and body intersect is helpful.

Historically, many gender essentialists, such as Hildegard of Bingen and Edith Stein, have been *hylomorphists*, who asserted that the soul is the form of the body. *Hylomorphists* maintain that a difference in the structure of the body is due to a difference in the structure of the soul. The shape, muscle tone, biological function, and chemical make-up of a female body are affected by the female soul that forms that body. Some contemporary gender essentialists are materialists who believe that the soul or mind is composed of the same physical substance as the body. Focusing on the brain, rather than the soul or mind, materialists would expect sexual difference to affect the character of an individual to the same degree that sexual difference affects the brain; although neuroscience has not come to a consensus on the degree that sexual difference affects the brain.

In contrast, those early modern and Enlightenment feminists who held the theory of gender neutrality proposed a dualism of mind and body. Christine de Pizan, Mary Astell, and Mary Wollstonecraft proposed that the mind has no sex. They, also, suggested that the mind is a separate substance from the body, although certainly intimately related to that body. While the body is sexed, the mind is not. Indeed, it is the job of the mind to regulate the data given by the body rationally. This view faces the most criticism from contemporary philosophers and scientists who cite the lack of evidence supporting the theory that the body and soul are separate substances. However, this view of the mind as an independent and autonomous substance that controls the body is still a dominant view in Western culture.

Finally, from a third point of view, gender existentialists present evidence of the radical ways the mind affects the body. Rather than considering the effects of the body's chemistry on the mind, these philosophers suggest the need to consider how culture informs the mind's way of thinking about the body. This view, a form of *idealism*, is exaggerated by queer theorists who argue that the body is only known as a projection of the mind. Judith Butler, for example, articulates the ways that the mind sculpts and fashions a body that mirrors the image of the body in the mind. Butler also makes the more radical point that the mind is what defines the limits of the self's body, determining what is self and what is other. In the most fundamental sense, the mind projects the very image of the body that the mind claims to see. This is evident of course in dreams, but Butler maintains this is true in all human experiences of the body.

These differences in understanding the role of the mind for the body and the body for the mind have obvious implications for theorists who are discussing the way gender relates to sex as well as the way both sex and gender relate to the individual's identity. Yet, neither contemporary philosophy nor science is definitive on the subject of the mind/body problem. On one hand, materialists as diverse as Daniel Dennett and Richard Dawkins have written books that claim to prove that all mental and psychological characteristics can be reduced to physical factors such as brain chemistry or DNA.[9] On the other hand, idealists such as Judith Butler and Donna Haraway ably argue that the empirical data collected by these materialists

9. See Dennet, *Consciousness Explained*; Dawkins, *Selfish Gene*.

are collected and categorized by minds. They insist on recognizing that the observing, (and biased) mind of the scientist is prior to the data he collects.

Interestingly, there is a great deal of new research in neuroscience and psychology that further confuses the issue. For example, Richard Hanson, an advocate of mindfulness, and Norman Doidge, an advocate of positive thinking, have both written books recently that others have suggested actually propose dualism. Their works describe evidence that mental ideas and attitudes affect physical neural tissues.[10] Their works present data that demonstrate that changes in ideas caused by meditation or talk therapy change the physical neural structure of the brain more profoundly than chemical intervention. Their research claims there are higher rates of healing in the body through mindfulness or positive thinking than physical medication. Importantly, they also admit that some people do have better results with medication than meditation.

The mind/body problem is truly a philosophical problem in our contemporary age. Perhaps, a way forward would be considering the possibility of a mind-body duality. As a metaphor, the reader might consider the wave-particle duality of a photon. Physicists have come to accept that the photon, for example, is both a wave and a particle. This paradoxical dual nature is also accepted for electrons. In a similar way, an individual might consider that the individual's mind has a dual nature, both material and psychic. This view of the mind and body as a duality requires further research and analysis. However, it might be a path forward for philosophers and gender theorists who wish to continue the conversation while accepting both the body's impact on mental attitudes and the mind's impact on the nature of the body.

Truly, researchers do not yet understand the human individual or the mechanisms by which identity is formed from physical, cultural, or autonomous causes. However, continuing the conversation about the role of sex and gender requires continuing the conversation about the relationship between the mind and the body.

A Question of Taxonomy: Nominalism Versus Realism

A second key philosophical issue in the dialogue about gender concerns whether the categories of male and female are fixed transcendent categories, naturally evolving categories, or fluid human constructs. Indeed, the

---

10. See Hanson and Mendius, *Buddha's Brain*; Doidge, *Brain That Changes Itself.*

names of the theories themselves suggest how fundamental the philosophical standpoint is concerning the taxonomy of gender. These philosophical views were discussed in each chapter as they related to the theory of gender at hand. Putting these theories of taxonomy together is critical to moving forward in gender theory.

First, gender essentialists believe that the categories of sex and gender are real and discoverable by the human mind. This is a position of philosophical *realism*. Briefly, *realists* claim that the categories by which scientists and philosophers classify things are real categories. By using empiricism and logic human minds can discover universal essences that allow them to correctly categorize individuals. Gender essentialists believe that the categories of male and female are fixed essences that can be observed in nature. Some gender essentialists, such as Hildegard and Edith Stein, believe these essences to be created by the Divine. Other gender essentialists suggest that sex and gender diversity are evolutionary traits. Thoughtful gender essentialists from Hildegard to Stein to Evelyn Fox Keller admit that gender is more complex than the simple cultural gender binary but maintain that there are real categories of male and female that can be discovered.

Second, both gender existentialists and those who advocate for gender neutrality claim that the categories of masculine and feminine gender are human constructs while maintaining that the biological sex categories of male and female are real structures in nature. Both these types of theorists argue that what appears to be a fixed category of gender is a culturally constructed type that can be observed as changing from culture to culture and individual to individual. However, these theorists maintain that the basic structures of biological sex are real scientific categories.

Third, the advocates of gender fluidity proclaim that all categories including those of gender and sex are human constructs. This position of radical *nominalism* asserts that human minds create categories in order to make sense of their world. In this view, the words male and female are simply words used to create categories. The categories only exist as mental constructs that conscious beings use.

The debate between *realism* and *nominalism* is a debate that has long been waged in Western philosophy and science. Scientists debate whether they are creating theories and categories by which humans explain the world or whether they are discovering real laws and essences that exist independently from human minds. In gender theory the issue relates to whether or not male and female are human words, existing only nominally, or whether they are transcendent or natural essences with a real existence. Similar debates are occurring about the constructs of race and ethnicity. There is not consensus among philosophers or scientists on this issue. However, in order to think more clearly about the role of sex and gender we must continue to think deeply about this broader philosophical issue.

The philosophical issue of taxonomy underlies many of the debates in gender theory and in gender politics. For example, feminist activism grounded in gender neutrality has a specific goal contrary to that of the feminist activism of gender essentialists. Shulamith Firestone famously said, "The end goal of feminist revolution . . . . [is] not just the elimination of male privilege but of the sex distinction itself; genital differences between human beings would no longer matter culturally."[11] Yet, gender essentialist activists speak of the feminist revolution as the creation of a political order that embraces sex and gender diversity. As Charlotte Witt claims, "All the people I spoke with thought that they would not be the same person if they were a different gender; the world, it seems, is filled with gender essentialists."[12] In order to best advocate for women and all people, bringing these feminists together in conversation is important. Because the difference in their agendas is rooted in their differing metaphysics, discussing these root questions is crucial to continuing the dialogue in a fruitful way.

Common Ground

While discovering these root issues demonstrates how difficult the dialogue must be, this dialogue is possible because there is marked common ground in these theories. Despite differences in philosophical worldview there are common precepts among all the women philosophers discussed in this book. These thinkers, as diverse as Hildegard of Bingen and Judith Butler, share a common set of *axioms* that guide their philosophical thinking and debate. *Axioms*, by definition, are statements that are the grounds for further discussion and inquiry. *Axioms*, by definition, are not grounded in empirical data or rational proof but are the starting points for evaluating observations and arguments. Some of these women declare that these axioms are part of their theological faith, and others claim they are self-evident. It is important to note that Simone de Beauvoir, Judith Butler, and

11. Quoted in Evans, *Feminist Theory Today*, 67.
12. Witt, *Metaphysics of Gender*, xi.

Donna Haraway hold these precepts to be axiomatic even as atheists who also deny the universality of moral sentiment and reason.

Every Human Being Has Equal Value

Despite the appearance or reality of sexual difference, all human beings have equal worth and dignity. For those writing in the Judeo-Christian tradition this value is considered God-given. For those moderns who have taken this axiom to lie outside as well as inside of the Judeo-Christian tradition, this value is considered to be inherent in being human. For the postmoderns, this precept is simply axiomatic, left ungrounded. For all the thinkers in this book, this statement of value is a vital precept of ethics. All humans ought respect the dignity of other persons and their right to live a flourishing life. This ethical premise grounds all the thinking women activists highlighted in this book as they advocate for social structures that they hope will help all people flourish. Of course, there remain disagreements on which policies best promote such flourishing. These disagreements are inevitable given the differences in gender theories that advocate for policies that foster diversity or universality respectively. But further discussion can continue fruitfully if it is grounded on this common premise that human flourishing for all people is the good that is sought.

Dialogue Is Possible

Despite the appearance or reality of sexual difference, human conversation can be productive. Those writing in the Judeo-Christian tradition have a common faith in a Scripture that asserts the possibility of transcendent truths being articulated in human language. Both amongst the builders of the tower of Babel and amongst the disciples at Pentecost, the power of human communication is obvious and considerable. Hildegard and Stein both used theology to explain that communication and empathy is possible through excellent preaching, quality education, and continued conversation. For the modern thinkers, the universal nature of reason and moral sentiment were considered the foundation of the democratic hope that dialogue between diverse groups can lead to unity and positive political and social action. For the postmoderns who assert that language and theory create reality, the dialogue that creates new theory is the only path to a society that better serves human beings. All these theorists believe in the power of discourse. Keeping the four theories of gender in conversation with each other will not immediately solve the quandary of gender, but it will allow thinkers to live with the quandary while working together to improve society.

Living with Quandary

Continuing the discussion is both possible and necessary for further activism. In this last section of the book, the practical implications for what it means to continue the dialogue will be considered in four areas: Science and Healthcare, Theology, Politics, and Philosophy.

Science and Health Care

Sex and gender are critical areas of study in science and medicine. Virginia Miller and Evelyn Fox Keller among others have made a strong gender essentialist argument for the necessity of considering both sex and gender in science and medicine. Keller argues that women bring a unique and broadening perspective to the sciences. In part this is due to the way women are cultured to use science for understanding rather than domination. It is also due in part to women's natural interest in studying female bodies. Since more women have come into the sciences, there have been marked changes in the design of scientific experiments and in the scope of scientific inquiry. Yet, Miller has adequately demonstrated that the previous lack of consideration of biological sex has harmed women's health care. Clearly the genetic structure and the hormonal balance of women's bodies must be taken into consideration when new treatments are being developed and tested. In addition, Miller thoughtfully articulates the need for physicians to consider how cultural understandings of gender and the gendered experience of patients and research subjects affects treatment.

However, intersex and queer theorists insist that science can no longer ignore the necessity to widen medical research beyond that of male and female subjects. Because of the diversity of human bodies and human psyches, doctors and scientists need to consider each individual when treating patients. Discussing how to structure research in order to get the best data that will improve health care for the most people requires a constant discussion between scientists and health care professionals about sex and gender in their patients.

Such discussion is especially complicated for those scientists and medical professionals who deal with understanding issues that involve the mind/body problem. Those who treat individuals who classify themselves as transsexual, transvestite, or transgender must continue to think deeply about the role of gender in psychological and physical health. Whether the professional considers gender to be culturally, chemically, neurologically, or spiritually constructed will affect how that professional treats the patient both in terms of physical health care and in terms of psychological health care.

But while scientists and medical professionals are thinking deeply and continuing the conversation, they cannot ethically wait to act. Questions of healthcare are immediate. Yet, health care decisions cannot be simply left to individual or even cultural whim. Scientists and health professionals must continue to act according to their discipline's current concept of health and wellness while thinking deeply and broadly about these issues. For the most part, professional organizations are doing just this. For example, The American Academy of Pediatrics has made a stand that doctors should not remove children's healthy genital tissue merely to appease the culture of the parents. Thus, the AAP has a stance against female genital mutilation, even if requested by family members.[13] Similarly, the AAP no longer advocates for the immediate surgical removal of micro-penises in healthy infants or for other forms of surgical alteration of healthy genitals in order to make children appear to fit in the sex binary.[14] However, as children mature into adults, medical professionals consider mental health as well as physical health. With relatively new surgical procedures that allow individuals to transform their bodies, the American Medical Association considers surgically altering the genitals as one form of legitimate therapy to help some individuals live more well lives.[15] Researchers and medical practitioners are right to act in accordance with the definitions of health that are most current. But medical professionals must also continue to discuss these issues, philosophically as well as medically, as they create the guidelines that help them strive for compassionate health care.

13. See for example, Louden, "AAP Retracts Controversial Policy."

14. For the previous recommendation, see Committee on Genetics, "Evaluation of the Newborn," 138–42. For the more current recommendation, see Lee et al., "Consensus Statement." Also see Karkazis, "Ethics for the Pediatrician."

15. The American Medical Association put the following article online for its members: Coleman et al., "Standards of Care."

In Theology, Religion, and Ecclesiology

Gender is a critical issue in both the theory and the practice of theology. For the church, mosque, and synagogue, this is far from an academic issue. Religious communities have been built and torn apart by issues of gender. Religious communities have divided over support or condemnation of gendered political issues such as women's rights to vote, own property, and divorce their husband for physical abuse. Denominations have divided over ecclesiological issues involving women's ordination and church blessings of same-sex unions. At stake is rarely the commitment to or renunciation of a sacred text or creed as all members of a religious community often share the same commitments. Rather it is different understandings of gender that often underlie the different positions taken. A deep look at these differing theories and a commitment to continue the dialogue can help religious communities continue the discussion while remaining intact.

Gender essentialism, with its assertion that gender is a real part of the identity of the individual, lends itself to religious rules that differentiate between gendered people. For example, Hildegard of Bingen argued that women's bodies required different regulations for Lenten fasting than men's. Edith Stein argued for single sex education in Roman Catholic schools in order to best nurture feminine natures and encourage feminine virtues. Mary Daly argued that single sex women's communities were necessary for fostering women's religious life and attitudes towards the Divine. Many feminist gender essentialists advocate for equal power for women in the religious hierarchy and for inclusive language in liturgies that lift up both feminine and masculine ways of being. Their arguments hinge on the necessity of recognizing the equal value of the feminine in creation and in the divine. On another issue, gender essentialists have made most of the religious arguments for and against gay marriage. Those opposed to gay marriage have claimed that marriage is ordained as a unity of individuals of two complimentary genders that harmonize together. Those promoting gay marriage have claimed that marriage is ordained as a blessing of monogamous relationship. Because some individuals are naturally drawn to individuals of their same sex and gender, same-sex monogamous relationships should have the same status as heterosexual relationships. Both these views assume that sex and gender are real properties of persons.

In contrast, those who advocate gender neutrality or gender existentialism often have denounced rules that divide men and women in worship and in religious regulations. In a vast majority of Western religious communities a theory of gender neutrality was used to advocate for new rules concerning marriage, especially in regard to equal rights of husbands and wives to individual bodily security and autonomy. In many denominations a theory of gender neutrality that claims that gender is not an essential part of a person's identity has led to the ordination of women as clergy. In some denominations a view that the terms "feminine" and "masculine" are cultural constructs has led to neutering the language used for the Transcendent who is beyond gender. New arguments for blessing same-sex marriages rest on the idea of marriage as a blessing of two souls coming together, thus neutralizing the concentration on the sex of the individuals. Counterarguments assert that marriage is solely for the physical reproduction of children, thus making marriage heterosexual by definition.

As a third point of view, those who advocate for a queer theory of gender seek acceptance of gender diversity. A queer view of gender has led some religious people to use language that encourages thoughtful deconstruction of the ideas of masculine and feminine in order to lift up the terms in ways that are most in line with the principles of human dignity implicit in the Torah, Gospels, and Koran. Generally queer theory requires people to consider the ways that gender roles prevent some individuals from living a full authentic human life. For example, gender roles can prevent individuals from following an authentic call to the clergy or to marriage. Queer theorists ask that congregations consider ways to be more inclusive to all congregants.

Differences in gender theory, therefore, can make conversation difficult concerning a number of issues from inclusive language in liturgy to rules that guide marriage and ordination. However rooting the conversation in the commitment to recognizing human value as a gift of the divine can give such discussions common ground. Indeed, recognizing that some divisions are due to gender theory is in itself a recognition that can spur better conversation as religious communities seek to help their members flourish spiritually.

In Education, Society, and Politics

Feminism literally means a stance that supports women. Feminist activism is simply activism that works to support women. Feminists stand united in their position that women are valuable members of society. Feminists decry policies that devalue women, silence feminine voices, or restrict feminine bodies. In some areas feminists seem united, but in others differences in gender theories divide feminists on which policies are best for women.

Unity is particularly strong in feminist efforts to raise awareness about the effects of domestic violence, sexual assault and rape for individual women and for society generally. Such abuse not only affects the bodies, but also the minds of girls and women. The psychological effects of abuse often have long term repercussions that limit individual women's sense of self-worth and ability to speak and lead in society. Thus, many feminists advocate criminalizing domestic abuse and sexual assault, and many feminists denounce using sexual assault and rape as strategies of war.

However, despite such points of unity, inner-feminist debate is perhaps nowhere so fierce as in the political and social realm. While feminists agree about the need to help all people flourish, consensus on which policies best help women is often difficult to reach. Gender essentialists expect women to have distinct needs and specific talents and attitudes. Feminists with this theory are more likely to argue for policies that offer specific protections for girls and women in order to help them thrive. Gender essentialists are also likely to expect female leaders to provide a certain type of leadership that lifts up specifically feminine virtues such as compassion and non-violence. Yet, feminists who come with a theory of gender neutrality are more likely to object to any policies that cannot be universally applied to all individuals regardless of sex and gender. These theorists will expect women to be the same kind of leaders as men, diverse in political stance. In contrast, gender existentialists will find themselves fighting against both points of view. They will argue against gender essentialists who advocate feminine virtues while objecting to those who claim simple legal equality for women is adequate. Finally, queer theorists will seek to support those who are outside the gender binary as well as those inside of it, asking about protections for those who are transgendered or transsexual.

Specific policies are places for battles between the different theorists. Some advocate for single sex education in order to nurture feminine values or in order to help girls specifically resist unhealthy cultural expectations. Others insist on the importance of co-education to ensure equality in the classroom and a commitment to universal human values. Some queer theorists have advocated that women's institutions admit intersex, transsexual, and transgendered individuals while remaining women's institutions. Feminists disagree on other issues as well including policies regulating birth control, abortion, child custody, divorce, family and medical leave, and women in the military. Clearly there is more than one way to be a feminist. However, active conversation about gender theory can help feminists both remember their fundamental unity as well as clarify the points of disagreement. This can help deepen and widen the dialogue on social and political issues in order to ground ever more fruitful discussion about the future of activism.

In Philosophy

Women make up less than 20 percent of the number of professional academic philosophers. As lean as that number is, far fewer women wrote and published in philosophy before the late twentieth century. But this fact ought not obscure the truth that there have always been women doing philosophy. Many of these women wrote philosophically about the nature of womanhood. There is a canon of women philosophers thinking about women's issues. This book's goal was to bring this canon to light in an accessible platform for the sake of further feminist activism. This book asserts that philosophy is a discipline that can house, foster, and nourish gender studies and feminist activism.

This book is a work of philosophy that strives to do just this. Different theories of gender have been examined and questioned in order that the reader might continue to wrestle with the issues at hand in a deeper and more meaningful way. In the end, this book's contribution to the field of gender studies is simply the acknowledgement that gender theory in the early twenty first century is in a *philosophical* quandary. If there is a correct and rigid taxonomy for sex and gender, clearly society and science have not yet discovered it. Yet, gender is still a category without which society simply cannot do. Philosophers ought not simply adopt a position of moderate skepticism but must actively engage in the discussion. Further, as members of society, philosophers must recognize that their discussions can inform policies that aim at helping all individuals flourish. Also, feminist activists must recognize the need for continued intellectual conversation about gender as part of its agenda. This conversation must include contemplation about the issues of the mind/body problem and about taxonomy. Such contemplation will allow for increased activism for policies that allow more authentic and more autonomous living for individuals in society.

Living with the quandary of gender means a continued role for philosophers, whether academic professionals or diverse lay thinkers. Everyone interested in activism to end oppression of all people can and must participate in thoughtful discussions about gender in order to advocate for policies, social structures, and modes of thought that will help all people flourish.

Bibliography

Allen, S. Prudence. *The Concept of Woman*. Grand Rapids: Eerdmans, 1985.

Altmann, Barbara, and Deborah McGrady. *Christine de Pizan as a Defender of Woman*. New York: Routledge, 2003.

Andolsen, Barbara Hilkert, et al. *Women's Consciousness, Women's Conscience: A Reader in Feminist Ethics*. Minneapolis, MN: Winston, 1985.

Anzaldúa, Gloria. *Borderlands/La Frontera: The New Mestiza*. San Francisco: Spinsters/ Aunt Lute, 1987.

Aristotle. *Metaphysics*. Translated by W. D. Ross. Oxford: Clarendon, 1924.

Astell, Mary. *The Christian Religion as Profess'd by a Daughter of the Church*. Edited by Jacqueline Broad. The Other Voice in Early Modern Europe. The Toronto Series 24. Toronto: CRRS, 2013.

———. *A Serious Proposal to the Ladies: Part I and II*. Edited by Patricia Springboard. Peterborough, ON: Broadview, 2002.

———. *Some Reflections Upon Marriage*. Edited by Sharon L. Jansen. Steilacoom, WA: Salters Point, 2014.

Augustine. *Confessions*. Edited by J. J. O'Donnell. Oxford: Clarendon, 1992.

Bair, Deirdre. *Simone de Beauvoir: A Biography*. New York: Summit, 1990.

Beauvoir, Simone de. *America Day by Day*. Translated by Patrick Dudley. London: Duckworth: 1952.

———. *Second Sex*. Translated by H. M. Parshley. New York: Vintage, 1989.

———. *She Came to Stay*. Translated by Yvonne Moyse and Roger Senhouse. London: Flamingo, 1984.

Behr-Sigel, Elisabeth. *The Ministry of Women in the Church*. Translated by Steven Bigham. Redondo Beach, CA: Oakwood, 1991.

Benhabib, Seyla, et al. *Contentions: A Philosophical Exchange*. New York: Routledge, 1995.

Benston, Margaret. "The Political Economy of Women's Liberation." *Monthly Review* 21.4 (1969) 13–25.

Bernard, Jacqueline. *Journey Toward Freedom: The Story of Sojourner Truth*. New York: Norton, 1967.

Birk, Bonnie. *Christine de Pizan and Biblical Wisdom: A Feminist Theological Point of View*. Milwaukee, WI: Marquette University Press, 2005.

Borden, Sarah. *Edith Stein*. New York: Continuum, 2003.

———. "Edith Stein's Understanding of Woman." *International Philosophical Quarterly* 46 (2006) 171–90.

Botting, Eileen Hunt. *Family Feuds: Wollstonecraft, Burke, and Rousseau on the Transformation of the Family*. Albany, NY: State University of New York Press, 2006.

Brake, Elizabeth. "Rawls and Feminism: What Should Feminists Make of Liberal Neutrality?" *Journal of Oral Philosophy: An International Journal of Moral, Political and Legal Philosophy* 1 (2004) 293–309.

Brandli, Mara. "Radicalizing Feminist Theory with Marx and Buddha." *Dialogue* 54 (2011) 42–47.

Burke, Michael. "Could a 'Woman' Win a Gold Medal in the 'Men's' One Hundred Meters? Female Sport, Drugs and the Transgressive Cyborg Body." In *Philosophical Perspectives on Gender in Sport*, edited by Paul Davis and Charlene Weaving, 129–41. New York: Routledge, 2010.

Butler, Judith. *Bodies That Matter: On the Discursive Limits of "Sex"*. New York: Routledge, 1993.

———. *Gender Trouble: Feminism and the Subversion of Identity*. New York: Routledge, 1999.

———. "How Can I Deny That These Hands and This Body Are Mine?" *Qui Parle* 11 (1997) 1–20.

———. *Undoing Gender*. New York: Routledge, 2004.

Cahn, Susan K. "From the 'Muscle Moll' to the 'Butch' Ballplayer: Mannishness, Lesbianism, and Homophobia in U.S. Women's Sports." In *Philosophical Perspectives on Gender in Sport and Physical Activity*, edited by Paul Davis and Charlene Weaving, 147–59. New York: Routledge, 2010.

Calhoun, Cheshire. "Justice, Care, Gender Bias." *The Journal of Philosophy* 85 (1988) 451–63.

Card, Claudia. *The Cambridge Companion to Simone de Beauvoir*. Cambridge: Cambridge University Press, 2003.

Carmina, E. "Ovarian and Adrenal Hyperandrogenism." *Annals of the New York Academy of Science* 1092 (2006) 130–37.

Carol, Rebecca, et al. *Alice Paul Biography*. http:/www.alicepaul/org.

Chamberlain, Marcia Kathleen. "Hildegard of Bingen's Causes and Cures: A Radical Feminist Response to the Doctor-Cook Binary." In *Hildegard of Bingen: A Book of Essays*, edited by Maud Burnett McInerney, 53–73. New York: Farland, 1998.

Chevalier-Skolnikoff, S. "Homosexual Behavior in a Laboratory Group of Stumptail Monkeys (*Macaca arctoides*): Forms, Contexts, and Possible Social Functions." *Archives of Sexual Behavior* 5 (1976) 511–27.

———. "Male-Female, Female-Female, and Male-Male Sexual Behavior in the Stumptail Monkey, with Special Attention to the Female Orgasm." *Archives of Sexual Behavior* 3 (1974) 95–116.

Christine de Pizan. *The Book of the City of Ladies*. Translated by Rosalind Brown-Grant. New York: Penguin Classics, 1999.

———. *The Writings of Christine de Pizan*. Selected and edited by Charity Cannon Willard. New York: Persea, 1994.

Coleman, E., et al. "Standards of Care for the Health of Transsexual Transgender and Gender-Nonconforming People." *International Journal of Transgenderism* 13 (2011) 165–232.

Collins, Patricia Hill. *Black Feminist Thought: Knowledge, Consciousness, and the Politics of Empowerment*. New York: Routledge, 2000.

——. "The Social Construction of Black Feminist Thought." In *Women, Knowledge, and Reality: Explorations in Feminist Philosophy*, edited by Ann Garry and Marilyn Pearsall, 222–48. London: Routledge, 1996.

Committee on Genetics; Section on Endocrinology, Section on Urology. "Evaluation of the Newborn with Developmental Anomalies of the External Genitalia." *Pediatrics* 106 (2000) 138–42.

Cox, Brian, and Jeff Forshaw. *The Quantum Universe*. Philadelphia: Da Capo, 2011.

Critchlow, V., et al. "Sex Difference in Resting Pituitary-Adrenal Function of the Rat." *American Journal of Physiology* 205 (1963) 807–15. http://ajplegacy.physiology.org/content/205/5/807.short.

Crocker, Hannah Mather. *Reminiscences and Traditions of Boston*. Edited by Eileen Hunt Botting and Sarah L. Houser. Boston: American Ancestors, 2011.

Cruikshank, Margaret. "Through the Looking Glass: A 70's Lesbian Feminist Considers Queer Theory." *Journal of Lesbian Studies* 11 (2007) 153–57.

Daly, Mary. *Beyond God the Father*. Boston: Beacon, 1973.

Davis, Angela Y. *The Angela Y. Davis Reader*. Edited by Joy James. Malden, MA: Blackwell, 1998.

——. *Are Prisons Obsolete?* New York: Random House, 2003.

——. *The Autobiography of Angela Davis*. New York: Random House, 1974.

——. *Blues Legacies and Black Feminism*. New York: Random House, 1998.

——. *Women, Culture & Politics*. New York: Random House, 1984.

——. *Women, Race & Class*. New York: Random House, 1983.

Davis, Paul, and Charlene Weaving, eds. *Philosophical Perspectives on Gender in Sport and Physical Activity*. New York: Routledge, 2010.

Dawkins, Richard. *The Selfish Gene*. Oxford: Oxford University Press, 1976.

Deleuze, Gilles, and Felix Guattari. *Qu'est-ce que la philosophie?* Paris: Minuit, 1991.

Dennett, Daniel. *Consciousness Explained*. Boston: Little, Brown, 1991.

Doidge, Norman. *The Brain That Changes Itself: Stories of Personal Triumph from the Frontiers of Brain Science*. New York: Penguin, 2007.

Dreger, Alice Domurat. *Hermaphrodites and the Medical Invention of Sex*. Cambridge, MA: Harvard University Press, 1998.

Farrington, B. "*Temporis Partus Masculus*: An Untranslated Writing of Francis Bacon." *Centaurus* 1 (1951) 193–205.

Fierro, Nancy. *Hildegard of Bingen and Her Vision of the Feminine*. Kansas City: Sheed & Ward, 1994.

Fischer, Marilyn. "Feminism and the Art of Interpretation: Or, Reading the First Wave to Think about the Second and Third Waves." *The American Philosophical Association Newsletter* 5 (2005) 3–6.

Flanagan, Sabina. *Hildegard of Bingen: A Visionary Life*. London: Routledge, 1989.

Fogg, Ally. "Education Is Leaving Boys Behind." *The Guardian*. December 13, 2012. http://www.theguardian.com/commentisfree/2012/dec/13/education-leaving-boys-behind.

Franco, Veronica. *Poems and Selected Letters*. Edited and translated by Ann Rosalind Jones and Margaret F. Rosenthal. Chicago: University of Chicago Press, 1998.

Friedan, Betty. *The Feminine Mystique*. New York: Norton, 1963.

Fullbrook, Edward, and Kate Fullbrook. *Simone de Beauvior: A Critical Introduction*. Cambridge: Polity, 1998.

Garber, Rebecca L. "Where Is the Body? Images of Eve and Mary in the *Scivias.*" In *Hildegard of Bingen: A Book of Essays*, edited by Maud Burnett McInerney, 103–32. New York: Farland, 1998.

Garcia, Vanessa. "Why I Won't Lean In." *Huffington Post*. July 19, 2013. http://www. huffingtonpost.com/vanessa-garcia/why-i-won't-lean-in-b-3586527.html.

Garry, Ann, and Marilyn Pearsall. *Women, Knowledge, and Reality: Explorations in Feminist Philosophy.* London: Routledge, 1996.

Gelman, Susan, et al. *Mother-Child Conversations about Gender: Understanding the Acquisition of Essentialist Belief.* Monographs of the Society for Research in Child Development; serial no. 275, 69:1. Boston: Blackwell, 2004.

George, Margaret. *One Woman's "Situation": A Study of Mary Wollstonecraft.* Urbana, IL: University of Illinois Press, 1970.

Gilbert, Olive. *Sojourner Truth: Narrative and Book of Life.* Chicago: Johnson, 1970.

Gilligan, Carol. *In a Different Voice: Psychological Theory and Women's Development.* 1850. Reprint. Cambridge, MA: Harvard University Press, 1982.

Godwin, William. *Memoirs and Posthumous Works of Mary Wollstonecraft.* 1798. Reprint. New York: Haskell House, 1969.

Gray, Emma. "Gymboree Onesies: 'Smart Like Dad' for Boys, 'Pretty like Mommy' for Girls." *The Huffington Post.* November 16, 2011. http://www.huffingtonpost.com/2011/11/16/gymboree-onesies_n_1098435.html.

Halim, Mary Ling, and Diane Ruble. "Gender Identity and Stereotyping in Early and Middle Childhood." In *Handbook of Gender Research in Psychology: Gender Ressearch in General and Experimental Psychology*, edited by Joan C. Chrisler and Donald. R McCreary. New York: Springer, 2010.

Hanson, Richard, and Richard Mendius. *The Buddha's Brain.* Oakland: New Harbinger, 2009.

Haraway, Donna. *The Haraway Reader.* New York: Routledge, 2004.

———. *Modest_Witness@Second_Millennium. FemaleMan_Meets_OncoMouse: Feminism and Technoscience.* New York: Routledge, 1997.

———. *Primate Visions: Gender, Race, and Nature in the World of Modern Science.* New York: Routledge, 1989.

———. *Simians, Cyborgs and Women: The Reinvention of Nature.* New York: Routledge, 1991.

Harlow, Harry, and Clara Mears. *The Human Model: Primate Perspectives.* New York: Wiley, 1979.

Heidegger, Martin. *What Is Philosophy?* Translated by Jean T. Wilde and William Kluback. New York: Rowman and Littlefield, 1956.

Heisenberg, Werner. "Über quantentheoretische Umdeutung kinematischer und mechanischer Beziehungen." *Zeitschrift für Physik* 33 (1925) 879–93.

Hildegard of Bingen. *Book of Divine Works (with Letters and Songs).* Edited by Matthew Fox. Translated by Robert Cunningham (*Divine Works*), Jerry Dybdal (*Songs*), and Ron Miller (*Letters*). Santa Fe: Inner Traditions/Bear, 1987.

———. *The Letters of Hildegard of Bingen.* Translated by Joseph L. Baird and Radd K. Ehrman. 3 vols. Oxford: Oxford University Press, 2004.

———. *On Natural Philosophy and Medicine: Selections from Cause et Cure.* Translated by Margret Berger. Cambridge: D. S. Brewer, 1999.

———. *Scivias.* Translated by Bruce Hozeski. Santa Fe: Bear, 1986.

———. *Secrets of God: Writings of Hildegard of Bingen*. Translated and selected by Sabina Flanagan. Boston: Shambhala, 1996.

Hinlicky Wilson, Sarah. *Woman, Women, and the Priesthood in the Trinitarian Theology of Elisabeth Behr-Sigel*. New York: Bloomsbury, 2013.

Hole, Judith, and Ellen Levine. *Rebirth of Feminism*. New York: Quadrangle, 1971.

hooks, bell. *Ain't I a Woman: Black Women and Feminism*. Cambridge, MA: South End, 1981.

———. *Communion: The Female Search for Love*. New York: HarperCollins, 2002.

———. "Dig Deep: Beyond *Lean In*." *The Feminist Wire*. October 28, 2013. thefeministwire.com2013/10/17973.

———. *Feminism Is for Everybody: Passionate Politics*. Cambridge, MA: South End, 2000.

———. *Feminist Theory from Margin to Center*. Cambridge, MA: South End, 1984, 2000.

———. *Teaching Community: A Pedagogy of Hope*. New York: Routledge, 2003.

hooks, bell, and Cornell West. *Breaking Bread: Insurgent Black Intellectual Life*. Boston: South End, 1991.

Huhman, Heather R. "STEM Fields and the Gender Gap: Where Are the Women?" *Forbes*, June 20, 2012. http://www.forbes.com/sites/work-in-progress/2012/06/20/stem-fields-and-the-gender-gap-where-are-the-women/.

Humm, Maggie. *The Dictionary of Feminist Theory*. Columbus, OH: Ohio State University Press, 1990.

Institute of Medicine (US), Committee on Understand the Biology of Sex and Gender Differences. *Exploring the Biological Contributions to Human Health: Does Sex Matter?* Edited by T. M. Wizemann and M. L. Pardue. Washington, DC: National Academy, 2001.

International Olympic Committee. "IOC Regulations on Female Hyperandrogenism." www.olympics.org/Documents/Commissions_PDFfiles/Medical_commission/2012-06-22-IOC-Regulations-on-Female-Hyperandrogenism-eng.pdf.

Irigaray, Luce. *An Ethics of Sexual Difference*. Translated by Carolyn Burke and Gillian C. Gill. Ithaca: Cornell University Press, 1993. Originally published in Luce Irigaray, *Ethique de la Difference Sexeulle* (Paris: Les Editions de Minuit, 1984).

Karkazis, Katrina. "Ethics for the Pediatrician: Disorders of Sex Development: Optimizing Care." *Pediatrics in Review: An Official Journal of the American Academy of Pediatrics* 31 (2010) e82–e85. http://pedsinreview.aappublications.org/content/31/11/e82.full.pdf+html.

Keller, Evelyn Fox. "Feminism and Science." In *Philosophy of Science*, edited by Richard Boyd et al., 279–88. Cambridge, MA: MIT, 1993.

———. *Reflections on Gender and Science*. New Haven: Yale University Press, 1985.

Keller, Evelyn Fox, and Helen E. Longino, eds. *Feminism & Science*. Oxford Readings in Feminism. Oxford: Oxford University Press, 1996.

Kelly, Gary. *Revolutionary Feminism: The Mind and Career of Mary Wollstonecraft*. New York: St. Martin's, 1996.

Kinsey, A. C., et al. *Sexual Behavior in the Human Female*. Philadelphia: W. B. Saunders, 1953.

Klapisch-Zuber, Christiane, ed. *Silences of the Middle Ages*. Vol. 2 of *A History of Women in the West*. Cambridge, MA: Belknap, 1992.

Kotef, Hagar. "On Abstractness: First Wave Liberal Feminism and the Construction of the Abstract Woman." *Feminist Studies* 35 (2009) 495–522.

Kristeva, Julia. *The Kristeva Reader*. Edited by Toril Moi. New York: Columbia University Press, 1986.

———. "The Reinvention of the Couple." Translated by Jean Burrell. *Diogenes* 216 (2007) 29–45.

Kuhn, Thomas S. *The Structure of Scientific Revolutions*. Chicago: University of Chicago Press, 1962.

Lee, P. A., et al. "Consensus Statement on Management of Intersex Disorders." *Pediatrics* 118 (2006) e488–e500. http://pediatrics.aappublications.org/content/118/2/e488.full.pdf+html.

Lerner, Gerder. *The Grimke Sisters of South Carolina*. Chapel Hill: The University of North Carolina Press, 1967.

Lock, Rebecca Ann. "The Doping Ban: Compulsory Heterosexuality and Lesbophobia." In *Philosophical Perspectives on Gender in Sport*, edited by Paul Davis and Charlene Weaving, 112–28. New York: Routledge, 2010.

Lloyd, Elisabeth A. "Pre-Theoretical Assumptions in Evolutionary Explanations of Female Sexuality." *Philosophical Studies* 69 (1993) 139–53.

Louden, Kathleen. "AAP Retracts Controversial Policy on Female Genital Cutting." *Medscape*, June 2, 2010. https://coursewebs.law.columbia.edu/coursewebs/cw_14F_LAW_L8152_001.nsf/0f66a77852c3921f852571c100169cb9/6FD7CE46A573A48585257D3F00727C66/$FILE/11.5+AAP+Retracts+Controversial+Policy.pdf?OpenElement.

Lunardini, Christine A. *From Equal Suffrage to Equal Rights: Alice Paul and the National Women's Party 1910–1928*. New York: New York University Press, 1986.

MacKinnon, Catherine. *Are Women Human? And Other International Dialogues*. Cambridge, MA: Harvard University Press, 2007.

Maddocks, Fiona. *Hildegard of Bingen: The Woman of Her Age*. New York: Doubleday, 2001.

Masters, W. H., and V. Johnson. *Human Sexual Response*. Boston: Little, Brown, 1966.

McCallister, Linda Lopez. *Hypatia's Daughters: Fifteen Hundred Years of Women Philosophers*. Bloomington, IN: Indiana University Press, 1996.

McClendon, John H., III. "Angela Davis: Marxist Philosophy, Patricia Hill Collins, and the Matter of Black Feminist Thought." *APA Newsletter* 10 (2010) 2–9.

McInerney, Maud Burnett, ed. *Hildegard of Bingen: A Book of Essays*. New York: Farland, 1998

———. "Like a Virgin: The Problem of Male Virginity in the *Symphonia*." In *Hildegard of Bingen: A Book of Essays*, edited by Maud Burnett McInerney, 133–54. New York: Farland, 1998.

Mews, Constant J. "Heloise and Hildegard: Re-visioning Religious Life in the Twelfth Century." *Tjurunga* 44 (1993) 20–29.

———. "Hildegard and the Schools." In *Hildegard of Bingen: The Context of Her Thought and Art*, edited by Charles Burnett and Peter Dronke, 89–110. London: Warburg Institute, 1995.

Miles, Judy. "Empathy and the Other in Edith Stein and Simone de Beauvoir." *Simone de Beauvoir Studies* 10 (1993) 181–85.

Miller, Virginia. "Sex-Based Physiology Prior to Political Correctness." *American Journal of Physiology: Endocrinology and Metabolism* 52 (2005) 359–60.

Miller, Virginia, et al. "Embedding Concepts of Sex and Gender Health Differences into Medical Curricula." *Journal of Women's Health* 22 (2013) 194–202.

———. "Physiology's Impact: Stop Ignoring the Obvious—Sex Matters!" *Physiology* 29 (2014) 4–5.

Mohanty, Chandra Talpade. *Feminism without Borders: Decolonizing Theory, Practicing Solidarity.* Durham: Duke University Press, 2003.

Morin, Gertrude. "Edith Stein's Appreciation of the Feminine Function." *Journal of Evolutionary Psychology* 17 (1996) 188–94.

Morland, Iain. "What Can Queer Theory Do for Intersex?" *GLQ: A Journal of Lesbian & Gay Studies* 15 (2009) 285–312.

Morris, D. *The Naked Ape: A Zoologist's Study of the Human Animal.* London: Cape, 1967.

Neyer, Maria Amata. *Edith Stein: Her Life in Photos and Documents.* Translated by Waltraut Stein. Washington, DC: ICS, 1999.

Noddings, Nel. *Caring: A Feminist Approach to Ethics.* Berkley: University of California Press, 1984.

Nussbaum, Martha. *Not for Profit: Why Democracy Needs the Humanities.* Princeton: Princeton University Press, 2010.

———. "The Professor of Parody: The Hip Defeatism of Judith Butler." *New Rebublic.* February 22, 1999, 37-45.

Oben, Freda Mary. *Edith Stein: Scholar, Feminist, Saint.* New York: Alba House, 1988.

Ortega y Gasset, José. *What Is Philosophy?* Translated by Mildred Adams. New York: Norton, 1960.

Parekh, Ameeta, et al. "Adverse Effects in Women: Implications for Drug Development and Regulatory Policies." *Expert Review of Clinical Pharmacology* 4 (2011) 453–66.

Paxton, Molly. "Quantifying the Gender Gap: An Empirical Study of the Underrepresentation of Women in Philosophy." *Hypatia* 27 (2012) 949–57.

Perry, Ruth. *The Celebrated Mary Astell: An Early English Feminist.* Chicago: University of Chicago Press, 1986.

Peterson, Christopher. "The Return of the Body: Judith Butler's Dialectical Corporealism." *Discourse* 28 (2006) 153–77.

Plato. "Apology." *Five Dialogues.* Translated by G. M. A. Grube. Indianapolis: Hackett, 1981.

Rand, Ayn. *The Virtue of Selfishness: A New Concept of Egoism.* New York: Signet Classics, 1964.

Roden, Frederick S. "Two 'Sisters in Wisdom': Hildegard of Bingen, Christina Rossetti, and Feminist Theory." In *Hildegard of Bingen: A Book of Essays,* Maud Burnett McInerney, 227–57. New York: Farland, 1998.

Rosenbaum, Mike. "Fastest Mile Times: The Women's Mile World Records." *Track and Field.* http://trackandfield.about.com/od/distanceevent1/p/Fastest-Mile-Times-The-Womens-Mile-World-Records.htm.

Rossi, Alice S., ed. *The Feminist Papers: From Adams to de Beauvoir.* New York: Columbia University Press, 1973.

Rousseau, Jean Jacques. *Emile: or, On Education.* Translated by Allan Bloom. New York: Basic Books, 1979.

Salih, Sara. *Judith Butler.* New York: Routledge, 2002.

Sandberg, Sheryl, with Nell Scovell. *Lean In: Women, Work, and the Will to Lead.* New York: Knopf, 2013.

Sappho. *Poems.* www.sacred-texts.com/cla/sappho/sappho2.htm.

Schneider, Angela J. "On the Definition of 'Woman' in the Sport Context." In *Philosophical Perspectives on Gender in Sport and Physical Activity*, edited by Paul Davis and Charlene Weaving, 40–54. New York: Routledge, 2010.

Shanley, Mary L. "Father's Rights, Mother's Wrongs? Reflections on Unwed Fathers' Rights and Sex Equality." *Hypatia* 10 (1995) 74–103.

Sherr, Lynn. *Failure Is Impossible: Susan B. Anthony in Her Own Words*. New York: Times Books, 1995.

Simons, Margaret A. *Beauvoir and The Second Sex: Feminism, Race, and the Origins of Existentialism*, Lanham, MD: Rowman and Littlefield, 1999.

———. *Feminist Interpretations of Simone de Beauvoir*. University Park, PA: Pennsylvania State University Press, 1995.

Sochen, June, ed. *The New Feminism in Twentieth Century America*. Lexington, MA: D. C. Heath, 1971.

Stanton, Elizabeth Cady and Susan B. Anthony. *Elizabeth Cady Stanton/Susan B. Anthony: Correspondence, Writings, Speeches*. Edited by Ellen Carol DuBois. New York: Schocken, 1981.

Stein, Edith. *Essays on Woman*. Edited by L. Gelber and Romaeus Leuven. Translated by Freda Mary Oben. Collected Works of Edith Stein 2. Washington, DC: ICS, 1996.

———. *Finite and Eternal Being*. Translated by Kurt F. Reinhardt. Collected Works of Edith Stein 9. Washington, DC: ICS, 2002.

———. *Life in a Jewish Family: Her Unfinished Autobiographical Account*. Edited by L. Gelber and Romaeus Leuven. Translated by Josephine Koeppel. Collected Works of Edith Stein 1. Washington, DC: ICS, 1985.

———. *On the Problem of Empathy*. Translated by Waltraut Stein. Collected Works of Edith Stein 3. Washington, DC: ICS, 1989.

———. *Self-Portrait in Letters, 1916–1942*. Translated by Josephine Koeppel. Collected Works of Edith Stein 5. Washington, DC: ICS, 1993.

Steinem, Gloria. *Moving Beyond Words*. New York: Simon and Schuster, 1994.

Tomalin, Claire. *The Life and Death of Mary Wollstonecraft*. New York: Harcourt Brace Jovanovich, 1974.

Tripp, Maggie, ed. *Woman in the Year 2000*. New York: Arbor, 1974.

Truth, Sojourner, and Olive Gilbert. *The Narrative of Sojourner Truth: A Bondswoman of Olden Time*. Edited with notes by Nell Irvin Painter. New York: Penguin, 1998.

Walker, Rebecca. *To Be Real: Telling the Truth and Changing the Face of Feminism*. New York: Anchor, 1998.

Warnke, Georgia. *Debating Sex and Gender*. Fundamentals of Philosophy Series. Oxford: Oxford University Press, 2011.

Washington, Margaret. *Sojourner Truth's America*. Urbana, IL: University of Illinois Press, 2009.

Watman, Mel. "Evolution of Olympic Women's Athletics, 1928 to the Present Day." International Association of Athletics Federations, July 25, 2008. http://www.iaaf.org/news/news/evolution-of-olympic-womens-athletics-1928-to.

Weaving, Charlene. "Unraveling the Ideological Concept of the Female Athlete: A Connection between Sex and Sport." In *Philosophical Perspectives on Gender in Sport and Physical Activity*, edited by Paul Davis and Charlene Weaving, 83–93. New York: Routledge, 2010.

Weinman Lear, Martha. "The Second Feminist Wave." *New York Times Magazine,* March 10, 1968, 24–25, 50–60.

Witt, Charlotte. *The Metaphysics of Gender.* Studies in Feminist Philosophy. Oxford: Oxford University Press, 2011.

Wolf, Naomi. *The Beauty Myth: How Images of Beauty Are Used Against Women.* New York: HarperCollins, 1991.

———. *Fire with Fire: The New Female Power and How It Will Change the 21st Century.* New York: Random House, 1993.

———. *Misconceptions: Truth, Lies, and the Unexpected on the Journey to Motherhood.* New York: Random House, 2001.

Wollstonecraft, Mary. *Letters on Sweden, Norway, and Denmark.* Teddington, UK: Echo Library, 2005.

———. *A Vindication of the Rights of Men.* Edited by Sylvana Tomaselli. Cambridge: Cambridge University Press, 1995.

———. *A Vindication of the Rights of Woman.* Edited by Eileen Hunt Botting. New Haven: Yale University Press, 2014.

Glossary

Analytic Philosophy: A method of doing philosophy that analyzes human language in order to get clear about the nature of reality.

Autonomy: Self-governance; freedom to make rules for one's own life.

Bad Faith: Myths that are believed by an individual to be true; ideas that constrain the individual's ability to live authentically.

Bourgeois: The Marxist term for those people who own the means of production.

Chicana Feminism: A movement of thought and action that celebrates and seeks to support women of Mexican descent.

Communism: A position that supports the abolition of private property in order to create conditions which will support the free development of all people.

Deconstructionism: The philosophical project of questioning and analyzing concepts in order to reduce their unconscious power.

Difference Feminism: The term coined by Carol Gilligan; the stance that feminism should advocate for the unique voice of women.

Empirical Evidence: Evidence that is supported by data that is known through the senses.

Existentialism: A philosophical position that claims that individuals are in a process of becoming what they are.

Epistemology: The study of knowledge and how things are known.

Facticity: The fixed conditions of one's life.

Feminism: A stance that advocates for women.

Feminist Activism: Active engagement in the world in order to create structures and policies that help women thrive.

First Wave Feminism: The era of feminism from 1776-1920; the stance that men and women should have equal legal, political, and economic rights.

Gender: The classification of male or female that includes social, psychological, emotional, and intellectual characteristics.

Gender Binary: The systematic categorization of individuals into two and only two genders, male and female.

Gender Essentialism: The philosophical position that claims that gender is an essential part of an individual's identity.

Gender Neutrality: The philosophical position that claims that gender is not an essential part of an individual's identity.

Gender Existentialism: The philosophical position that claims that individual's are formed by culture into gendered persons.

Gender Fluidity: The philosophical position that claims that both sex and gender are constantly changing categories that are culturally defined.

Gender Complementarity: The philosophical position that the male and female genders are complementary but distinct ways of being in the world.

Hegemony: A systematic way of thinking that acquires cultural force.

Heterosexual Matrix: A systematic way of thinking that enforces heterosexual sexual relationship as the ideal.

Hylomorphism: The philosophical position that states that the mind, or soul, is the form of the body and has no separate existence apart from the body.

Hyperandrogenism: The medical condition in which a female body produces more testosterone than average.

Idealism: The philosophical position that reality is constructed by thought rather than matter.

Intersex: A label for those individuals who do not fall neatly into the sex binary of male or female.

Liberalism: The political stance that all people are created equal with natural rights to life, liberty, and private property.

Liberal Enlightenment Feminism: Feminism built on the Enlightenment principle that reason is the essential attribute of any person and the liberal principle that all people are created equal with natural rights to life, liberty, and private property.

Materialism: The philosophical position that reality is constructed by matter and material forces.

Metaphysics: The philosophical study of that which transcends the material world.

Modern philosophy: Philosophy done in the time period of 1650-1800; philosophy that supposes the supremacy of reason over emotion, of mind over body, and of individual discovery over adherence to ancient authorities.

Noumena: That which exists in and for itself.

Phenomena: That which is observed by a mind.

Phenomenology: A method of doing philosophy that focuses on studying the common experiences of human life rather than metaphysics.

Primogeniture: The legal benefits of being the first-born son.

Proletariat: The Marxist term for the working class; those people who are means of production.

Post-Modern Philosophy: Philosophy that is written after 1800 and refutes certain principles of modern philosophy such as the infallibility of reason.

Quietism: A philosophical position that supports inaction or the status quo.

Second Wave Feminism: A term coined by Margaret Lear for feminism of the 20th century; feminism based on the theory of gender existentialism.

Sex: The classication of male or female based on biological factors.

Socialism: An economic theory that seeks some equalizing of economic power among citizens or some form of community control over certain modes of production.

Suffrage: The right to vote.

Theory of Illumination: The theory, stated by Augustine, that insight is possible because the divine light of God illumines the human mind.

Third Wave Feminism: A label for feminist theory that rejects aspects of second wave feminism.

Womanism: Activism that appreciates the unique way of thinking that characterizes African American women

Name/Subject Index